THE IMPRESSIONISTS

THE IMPRESSIONISTS

Robert Katz and Celestine Dars

Colour
Library
Direct

THE IMPRESSIONISTS

CLD 20430

This edition published in 1997 for
Colour Library Direct
Godalming Business Centre
Woolsack Way, Godalming
Surrey GU7 1XW

First published in 1991
New revised edition published 1994

ISBN 1-85833-744-5

Printed and bound in Spain

CONTENTS

◆

A HISTORY
OF
IMPRESSIONISM

FRANCE AND IMPRESSIONISM

T HE IMPRESSIONISTS DID NOT choose their name – it was foisted upon them in 1874 by a critic hostile to their work. However the name soon stuck and was used to describe a group of artists who never intended to be a unified radical movement, who never set out to shock or be revolutionaries. What they had in common was that they were all in Paris in the early 1860s and quickly got to know each other – some in art schools which they abandoned early on, some in the cafés where they would meet – and realized that they shared a desire to paint the landscape, cityscape, and modern life in new ways. The first Impressionist exhibition took place because none of these artists had achieved any regular success at the official Salon, the major venue for the Paris art market, whose juries were notoriously inconsistent and reactionary.

The first exhibition by this group did little to challenge the all-powerful Salon, but it crystallized critical opinion and pushed the so-called Impressionists into the limelight. They were pilloried by hostile critics and supported by writers such as Baudelaire and Zola who saw in their work an important advancement of art into the modern era. But the Impressionists did not seek to criticize their society; they were largely middle class and politically conservative in an age permanently on the brink of upheaval. They remained true to aesthetic ideas which, with few exceptions, kept them from depicting the grinding poverty caused by rapid industrial expansion, and the sporadic outbursts of war and violence that punctuated the history of their times.

JONGKIND
The Sainte Catherine's
Market at Honfleur
oil on canvas
1865. 42 × 66 cm
(DETAIL)

APRIL 1874: SHOCK OF THE NEW

*The Impressionist eye is, in short, the most advanced eye in
human evolution . . .*

JULES LAFORGUE, 1883

For one month from 15th April 1874 a new exhibition was to be seen at 35 boulevard des Capucines in Paris. Félix Nadar, a well-known photographer, had lent his studio free of charge to a group of artists who had come together as the *Société anonyme des artistes peintres, sculpteurs, graveurs, etc.* (a joint stock company of artists, painters, etc.). The show was open from ten to six during the day and eight to ten at night for an admission price of one franc. Among the twenty-nine artists showing their work were Paul Cézanne, Edgar Degas, Armand Guillaumin, Claude Monet, Berthe Morisot, Camille Pissarro, Pierre-Auguste Renoir, and Alfred Sisley.

The show was rapidly becoming a disaster. The members of the *Société anonyme* who had banded together to stage the show had of course aimed to generate sales as well as a greater awareness of their work with the public. Around 3,500 people visited the exhibition before it closed on 15th May but very few pictures were bought – the work of Degas and Morisot remained unsold, whilst Renoir had to knock down the price of his painting *La Loge* from 500 to 425 francs before he could sell it. In general the public came for the novelty value, to see a *cause célèbre* in the making. Only the critics were triumphant. Writing in the satirical journal *Charivari* on 25th April 1874, Louis Leroy, a minor critic and playwright, composed an acerbic satirical review of the exhibition in the form of a tour around it in the company of an

imaginary landscape painter called Joseph Vincent. Having relentlessly debunked most of the other artists on show, Leroy devoted part of the climax of his satire to a picture by Claude Monet:

A catastrophe seemed to be imminent, and it was reserved for M. Monet to contribute the last straw.

"Ah, there he is!" he cried, in front of No.98. "I recognize him, *papa* Vincent's favourite! What does that canvas depict? Look at the catalogue."

"*Impression, Sunrise.*"

"*Impression* – I was sure of it. I was just telling myself that, since I was impressed, there had to be some impression in it . . . and what freedom, what ease of workmanship! Wallpaper in its embryonic state is more finished than this seascape."

Monet had chosen the title of this picture in some haste for the exhibition catalogue, not wanting to call it a simple "seascape", and in doing so he had unwittingly provided Leroy with the hook-line for his piece. The review appeared under the headline *Exhibition of the Impressionists*. Leroy had coined a name which would be certain to outlive his own.

What were these so-called Impressionists doing that was so unacceptable? Leroy had put his finger on the obvious qualities of one aspect of their work, what henceforth would be called the "Impressionist" use of paint – a

CAMILLE PISSARRO
Self-portrait
1873

method that was as shocking as it was new to its public. Standing in front of Monet's *Boulevard des Capucines*, Leroy's imaginary companion declares:

> "Is that brilliant enough for you now? There's an *impression*, or I don't know what it means. Only be so good as to tell me what those innumerable black tongue-lickings in the lower part of the picture represent?"
>
> "Why, those are people walking along," I replied.

Leroy, of course, could read the painting and see the effect that Monet's brushwork intended to convey, but a tradition of officially-sanctioned, respected and respectable Salon painting – which stressed the suitability of subject, quality and finesse of finish – inevitably meant that the public were looking at Monet's *Boulevard des Capucines* and *Impression, Sunrise*, or Degas' ballerinas, with a conservative, unprepared eye. To many, all that really could be seen from a couple of feet were blotches, strokes and scrapes of compacted pigment, which viewed from a "safe" distance would then coalesce into meaningful shapes. The "Impressionist technique" (in reality each artist was developing his own), allied with a new approach to colour and a new range of subject matter, made the *Société anonyme*'s first exhibition the laughing-stock of Paris. Yet it represented to the world at large a revolution in art that had been gathering since the early 1860s, when Edouard Manet caused a scandal with his *Luncheon on the Grass* (*Déjeuner sur l'herbe*).

In the early 1860s Frédéric Bazille, Monet, Renoir, and Sisley had met in Paris to study at the atelier of the Swiss painter Charles Gleyre, whilst Pissarro had come to know

Monet and Paul Cézanne. The high period of Impressionism was brief; merely a decade later a somewhat diluted form of Impressionism had already been adopted by numerous conventional artists. Its influence, however, has lasted to this day.

The idea of an independent show outside the auspices of the Salon – the annual exhibition of the Académie des Beaux-Arts held in the Louvre's Salon d'Apollon and later in the enormous Palais d'Industrie – was increasingly discussed. Hitherto, the Académie des Beaux-Arts determined almost exclusively the showing of art. Without the sanction of the Salon an artist's work was practically unseen by the bourgeoisie which constituted his (and increasingly her) public. Furthermore, the atelier system of apprenticeship to a teacher who would prepare his students for the Ecole des Beaux-Arts, the teaching arm of the Académie, followed by the winning of one of the school's competitions, was the only way an artist could expect to learn and then progress in a career which depended on the patronage of conservative institutions and patrons. For good or ill, Leroy's insistence on the word "impression" tied together for posterity a group of artists whose aims were frequently at loggerheads, yet who had set out together, rejecting the Salon which had so often rejected them.

What the unimaginative public and critics like Leroy found gross and unpolished, slapdash and meaningless in the work of the Impressionists shown at Nadar's studio was exactly what later generations came to value most in it. Writing in 1883 to introduce a small show by Pissarro, Degas, and Renoir in Berlin, the poet Jules Laforgue (who died three years later at the age of twenty-seven) considered the Impressionists' work in a

EDOUARD MANET
By Fantin-Latour
1867

remarkable essay. What he had to say then evokes the qualities that were to make Impressionism a lasting and vital phenomenon. He pays particular attention to the Impressionists' capturing of the conditions of light, colour, and form as they are transmitted unmediated to the artist's eye at a particular moment in time:

> In a landscape bathed with light, in which entities are modelled as if in coloured *grisaille* [i.e. monochrome painting in greyish colour], the academic painter sees nothing but white light spreading everywhere, whilst the Impressionist sees it bathing everything, not in dead whiteness, but in a thousand conflicting vibrations, in rich prismatic decompositions of colour. Where the academic sees only lines at the edge of things . . . the Impressionist sees real living lines, without geometrical form, built from thousands of irregular touches which, at a distance, give the thing life. Where the academic sees only things set down in regular, separate positions . . . the Impressionist sees perspective established by thousands of imperceptible tones and touches, by the variety of atmospheric states, with each plane not immobile, but shifting . . . The Impressionist sees and renders nature as she is, which is to say solely by means of coloured vibrations. Neither drawing, nor light, nor modelling, nor perspective, nor chiaroscuro: these infantile classifications all resolve in reality into coloured vibrations, and must be obtained on the canvas solely by coloured vibrations.

CLAUDE MONET
By Renoir
1875

ART IN THE SECOND EMPIRE

Stop, monsieur le Président, here is France's shame.
JEAN-LÉON GÉRÔME TO PRÉSIDENT LOUBET, 1900

Pissarro, Manet, Degas, Sisley, Monet, Bazille, and Morisot were all born between 1830 and 1841 into a France whose recent history had been as dramatic and changeable as the era the painters were to live through. France had not had a history of durable regimes; by the end of 1830 the King, Charles X, had abdicated after the July revolution in Paris, to be replaced by the Duke of Orleans, Louis Philippe, who assumed the lieutenant-generalship of France. Louis Philippe devoted himself to the bourgeoisie and the *juste milieu*, but ironically ruled amidst periodic riot and revolt until 1848 when Paris once again erupted in revolution, causing the abdication of Louis Philippe and the birth of the Second Republic. Two of the new republic's first acts were the Proclamation of Universal Suffrage and the Abolition of Slavery. In December 1848 Louis Napoleon, nephew of Napoleon I, was elected President of the Republic. Three years later, after the *coup d'état* of 1851, Louis Napoleon became Emperor Napoleon III. Napoleon III marked the start of his rule with a crack-down on political dissent and a suppression of the press while at the same time regulating the price of bread and encouraging growth in industry and commerce. France had languished behind the rest of Europe as the Industrial Revolution gained momentum, but Napoleon III's reign saw the development of banking institutions – the Crédits Mobilier, Lyonnais, and Agricole – as well as railways and factories. As a patron of the arts, and of painting in particular, Napoleon III and his Arts Minister, Comte de Niewerkerke, were generous in reforming and developing a useful system of patronage, education and officially-commissioned works of art for public buildings.

In 1863 the Salon des Refusés, a massive exhibition of paintings which had been rejected by the Salon and for which Napoleon III bore great responsibility in many ways, marked the beginning of a new era of artistic freedom, even though it was a subtle attempt by the authorities to discredit critics of the official Salon. Not surprisingly, the Emperor's personal taste in painting favoured the academic style with its high finish and erudite classical and biblical subjects, although Romantics like Delacroix had little trouble making very successful careers for themselves under the Second Empire. However, a group of Realists who were more concerned with "common subjects", which had emerged under the vociferous leadership of Gustave Courbet, was anathema to Napoleon III's imperial sensibilities (as indeed were Courbet's socialist politics).

The new art, shortly to be named Impressionism, which succeeded Courbet, took as its subject matter not only nature, but also the prosperous middle class which had begun to make itself felt in the Second Empire.

Edouard Manet's *Music in the Tuileries Gardens* (*Musique dans le Jardin des Tuileries*) of 1862 is regarded as one of the first great paintings of modern urban life, and what it shows is a bustling middle-class crowd of professionals and artists at their leisure. It is representative of a nation, transformed in part by the policies of Napoleon III into an economically competitive state ready to enjoy its new found success and confidence.

To advance his nation further, Napoleon III had embarked on a series of successful wars against Austria, Russia, and China. In 1855 and 1867 the spectacular Expositions Universelles in Paris, rivalling the British Great Exhibition of 1851, announced to the nation and the world that France had arrived. Alas, the vagaries of French history caught up with Napoleon III. In 1870, just as he was attempting a measure of political liberalization, he seriously misjudged the nation's readiness for conflict and engaged in war against Prussia on a point of diplomatic etiquette. (The French were so convinced they could win this war they issued their officers with maps of Germany only!) Hopelessly out-organized, out-manouevred and out-gunned by the very artillery pieces which Krupps had exhibited to great acclaim in the 1867 Paris Exposition, the French armies disintegrated, with the loss of the important eastern province of Alsace-Lorraine. The Prussians invaded Paris in September 1870, and the Second Empire fell soon after.

After the Prussians had paraded through Paris and the new, broadly-republican government had attempted to disarm the National Guard there, the city erupted into revolution resulting in the Commune of 1871. Victor Hugo called it *l'année terrible*, a brief violent revolution which rose against the

EDGAR DEGAS
Self-portrait
c.1855

PIERRE-AUGUSTE RENOIR
Self-portrait
c.1875

government and ended in massacre. In one week 20,000 Parisians were killed as civil war erupted in the streets of what had recently been *la ville lumière*, the dazzling capital of Europe. Scarcely two years before Monet's *Boulevard des Capucines* went on show in 1873, the boulevards of Paris had been stripped of trees cut down for firewood; the animals in the zoos, including the elephants (but not the hippo, which no butcher could afford to buy), as well as the city's racehorses, had been slaughtered for food in the beseiged and starving city. Yet these momentous events touched the work of the Impressionists very little. There is no trace of upheaval in any of the Impressionists' paintings; most fled to avoid the war and only Manet and Degas remained in Paris. The former, who had been an anti-imperialist since the age of sixteen, was the only one amongst the group to record the bloody events of the Commune. But we shall see, the relationship of Manet and Degas with the other Impressionists is a special case in itself.

The Franco-Prussian war and the brief and bloody rise and fall of the Paris Commune formed the conclusion to the Second Empire. During the childhood and adolescence of the Impressionists many changes had swept over France, such as the massive construction of railways throughout the country to rival the systems of both Britain and the German states. Between 1851 and 1859 the French railways had trebled in length, facilitating the further expansion of industry and communications. Importantly for the Impressionists and their precursors who painted in the open air, the growth of the railways made the countryside available to the city-dweller in a way that was to have great consequences. During the Second Empire and well into the

Third Republic, the cities, and Paris in particular, were undergoing fundamental change whilst in rural France the way of life was altered very little – only the occasional industrial chimney is to be seen poking up in the background of the Impressionists' landscapes.

In 1853 Napoleon III had appointed Baron Georges-Eugène Haussmann, Prefect of the Seine, to set about the reconstruction of Paris. This he began with grandiloquent gusto, aiming to transform a city of narrow streets and congested, practically medieval areas – a city with a hopelessly inefficient transport and sanitation infrastructure, a city where the bourgeoisie lived cheek by jowl with the very poorest underclass – into a modern European capital. Haussmann built great sewers after the example of London, but for the removal of rainwater, not, unfortunately, for sewage, and gutted huge sections in the centre of the city to make way for broad boulevards with pavements, avenues of trees and clear sightlines for the military – popular uprisings would thus be easier to control. Haussmann built eighty-five miles of new roads that included the rue de Rivoli and the boulevard Saint-Michel. Along these new roads, modern buildings quickly sprang up, their height and style controlled by the authorities. For more than a decade Paris was a wonderland of new buildings, roads, squares, and other construction projects.

The Impressionists found the transformed city and its *banlieues* (suburbs) an ideal place for a new and modern kind of art, a place which, according to writer Edmond de Goncourt, made one a "stranger . . . to these new boulevards with no turnings, no chance perspectives, implacably straight, which are no longer of Balzac's world, but which make one think of some American Babylon of the

MARY CASSATT
Self-portrait
c.1895

future." The Impressionists, in contrast, were not so much afraid as fascinated by the new lines of Paris. The mile-long perspectives offered by the new boulevards, the St Lazare station in the centre and the railway bridges on the outskirts became the subjects, for example, of Monet's urban paintings.

What "Haussmannization" meant, above all, was the gentrification of Paris, making its centre the exclusive habitat of the bourgeoisie. However, behind these new streets the slums that had been cleared reappeared, only more cramped and squalid. Meanwhile hundreds of thousands of workers had been moved out to new industrial suburbs and slum areas, like Belleville and Menilmontant, where they subsisted much as they had done before, but this time dispossessed of their ancient city.

When the rubble of 1870–71, caused by heavy Prussian bombardment and violent civil war, was cleared away, Paris quickly became *la ville lumière* it had been during the Second Empire. By 1874 it was hard to imagine that dogs and rats had once been on the menu. Although memories of the civil war remained, the economic growth of the Second Empire resumed under a republican guise. Paris reclaimed its place as the centre of European art.

The Impressionists lived in an age of struggle between modernity and a traditional order. We see in their paintings a radical, and, for their time, shocking break with traditional notions of art, the culmination, but not the end, of a series of new ways of seeing. The Abstract movement of the twentieth century stemmed from experiments with existing art just as the Impressionists' innovations grew out of the paintings of Courbet, Corot, Delacroix, Constable, and the old masters who

had gone before in the world of art.

We are surrounded by the art of the Impressionists – the legacy of a relatively brief period in the history of art which has endured in the most diverse of ways. There is scarcely a wall, a mug, a postcard, a jigsaw puzzle or indeed a box of chocolates which has not borne a reproduction of Degas' prima ballerinas, Manet's barmaid, Renoir's girl on a swing or one of Monet's haystacks. These images are perennial because they are windows on a bygone age of leisurely Parisian summers and intensely perceived light which appeal to us in this beleaguered post-modern century. They are also the masterpieces of a crucial period of change and works of art from an optimistic time of endless possibilities. The Impressionists' sense of wonderment at their world has, ironically, become for us a comforting reflection of times passed. Although it would be convenient to think that before Monet, Renoir, Sisley, and Pissarro light could never have been seen and set down in a series of broken, prismatic colours, that shadows were never blue or red, yet in fact these approaches were already becoming possible in the early nineteenth century. It is certainly true, nevertheless, that a short time after these artists had come together, blue shadows and green skies were, and have remained, commonplaces in the vocabulary of art.

The Impressionists were named in jest by a hostile critic; collectively they never published a manifesto – their name is a catch-all for a fragile movement of men and women briefly united in their belief that the time had come for a new art to be seen and appreciated. They came from different social backgrounds, from the patricians Manet and Degas to the working-class Renoir, and in the

BERTHE MORISOT
By Manet
c.1869

end their friendships broke up and they scattered across France. All of them, however, were in Paris during a critical period in French history; they knew and worked with each other and often lived in each other's pockets. Some – Monet, Sisley, and Pissarro, for example – were overwhelmingly attracted by the landscape and were driven to depict it. Others – Degas, Manet, and Renoir – were more concerned with the human figure and the life of the city and its suburbs. In their time they were all accused of being revolutionary; their supporters held them up as the iconographers of a new, modern age; their critics claimed they were subverting a set of artistic ideals and methods which had obtained for centuries.

In some ways the Impressionists were revolutionaries – in their use of colour, for example, or choice of subject and methods of exhibition, and in their assertion of the right to recreate the world as they saw it. The history of the Impressionists is full of contradictions. Edouard Manet (who together with Degas we should be wary of calling an Impressionist in any case), a generous and devoted supporter of the younger artists such as Monet, Renoir, and Sisley, never exhibited in the series of Impressionist exhibitions which shook the Parisian art world. However, he had caused a sensation a decade before with *Luncheon on the Grass* (*Déjeuner sur l'herbe*), and though he was considered to be their leader, he sought distinction through the Salon – a reluctant revolutionary. Degas, of the same generation as Manet, exhibited in all eight of the Impressionists' shows from 1874 to 1886. Monet, Renoir, and Sisley all dropped out of the group's exhibitions in the late 1870s, whilst the most politically revolutionary of them all, Pissarro, would not abandon

Degas (politically an arch-Conservative and anti-Semite) or the Impressionist exhibitions even when the others begged him to. Despite all of these contradictions there existed for a short period in late nineteenth-century France a movement, a loose and informal "academy" whose members learnt from one another and changed the course of art.

When Claude Monet died in 1926, Impressionism was firmly enshrined in the past – new forces had been at work since the 1880s. In the lifetime of Monet and most of the Impressionists France had seen two revolutions, the rise and fall of the Second Empire and the establishment of the Third Republic. An industrial revolution had taken place and Paris had been rebuilt almost from scratch. The Impressionists' own revolution was intimately tied up with that of the world they inhabited. Innovations as seemingly mundane as the mass manufacture of oil paint in tin tubes and the portable easel had freed the artist from his or her studio. Monet's *Boulevard des Capucines* was painted from the window of Nadar's studio high up in the same boulevard, introducing literally a new angle on traditional views of Paris.

By the last years of the nineteenth century the Impressionist style had spread and prospered, evolving into Neo- and Post-Impressionism. But the shock waves of Impressionism continued to reverberate. In 1900, over a quarter of a century after the first Impressionist exhibition, the academician Gérôme, one of the most successful artists of his century, was guiding Président Loubet of France around the Exposition Universelle when he stopped him at the entrance to the Impressionist Room with these words: "*Arrêtez, monsieur le Président, c'est ici le déshonneur de la France!*"

MONET
The Artist's Garden at Argenteuil
oil on canvas
1872. 61 × 74 cm

THE BIRTH OF IMPRESSIONISM

SEVERAL INFLUENCES IN THE earlier part of the nineteenth century are crucial to the development of Impressionism. In the first three decades of the century the inspiration of Dutch and English landscapists began to have an important effect on French landscape painting and art in general. Eugène Delacroix – who was to influence many of the Impressionists, especially Renoir – had brought a new brilliance of colour and virtuosity of brushwork to his paintings of exotic subjects and was a keen admirer of Constable, as were the Barbizon School of *plein-air*, or open air painters attempting a new naturalism in and around the Fontainebleau Forest. The latter were the precursors of Monet and Pissarro, who were also deeply influenced by the landscapists Eugène Boudin and Johan Jongkind working on the Normandy coast. By mid-century the Realists had come to prominence headed by Gustave Courbet, who had rejected the fanciful nature of Delacroix's Romanticism and was painting down-to-earth contemporary and allegorical subjects. All of these trends were significant in creating a world of art where Impressionism could flourish.

In 1863 the Salon was so oversubscribed that an exhibition of the thousands of rejected works was mounted after a popular outcry. Edouard Manet caused a scandal with his *Luncheon on the Grass* which portrayed its classical subject in a modern idiom to shocking effect and he became the reluctant leader of the younger generation of Monet, Renoir, Sisley, and Bazille who had come together the year before at the atelier of Charles Gleyre and formed the nucleus of the Impressionists.

COROT
Landscape at Mornex, Savoy
oil on canvas
undated. 40 × 61.5 cm
(*DETAIL*)

1820–1863: From the English Landscape to the Salon des Refusés

. . . I did not really see a less negative colour, but I felt as if it
were an effort towards a less negative colour, the pulsation of a
hesitant ray struggling to discharge its light.

Marcel Proust, Swann's Way

The Impressionists *par excellence*, Monet, Pissarro, Sisley, and Renoir, met in Paris in the early 1860s and were bound together in their admiration for the work of an older generation of landscape painters who had left their studios to paint in the open air in the countryside near Paris. Tracing the immediate origins of Impressionism, a phenomenon which began in the French countryside, takes us back to the English landscape and the excitement felt by early nineteenth-century French Romantic painters, such as Eugène Delacroix and Théodore Géricault, on encountering the experiments and achievements in oil and watercolour of the English landscape painters John Constable, J.M.W. Turner, and Richard Bonington.

In 1820 the French writer Charles Nodier, whose drawing room in Paris was an important place for the dissemination of news and ideas in the arts, was in London at the Royal Academy summer exhibition. In Nodier's journal, entitled *From Dieppe to the Mountains of Scotland*, he offered the following opinion of the summer exhibition:

In painting, landscapes and sea views are the pieces in which the English have the fewest rivals in Europe . . . the palm of the exhibition belongs to a large landscape by Constable to which the ancient or modern masters have very few masterpieces that could be put in opposition. Near, it is only broad daubings of ill-laid colour which offend the touch as well as the sight, they are so coarse and uneven. At the distance of a few steps it is picturesque country, rustic dwellings, a low river where little waves foam over the pebbles, a cart crossing a pond. It is water, air and sky . . .

When Eugène Delacroix saw *The Hay Wain* at the Paris Salon of 1824 he was so impressed by the natural transparency and brilliance of colour in Constable's sky, trees, earth, and water that he immediately set about reworking his own *Massacre at Chois* (*Massacre à Scio*), a painting which he had almost finished, adding glaze and thick patches of pure pigment in various colours in an attempt to emulate the effect of the Englishman's work. Delacroix's radical use of colour and his technique of *flochetage*, using large flakes (*floches*) of colour to heighten his forms, was later to be developed further by the Impressionists.

Théodore Géricault, a fellow Romantic of Delacroix's, had seen *The Hay Wain* in London, two years before Delacroix's encounter with it at the 1824 Salon, and had expressed his astonishment to Delacroix and others on his return to Paris. With the enthusiasm of Nodier, the shock experienced by the critic Délécluze, who admitted that in comparison to *The Hay Wain* French landscape painting of the 1820s was "heavy, insensitive, and false", and the practical interest of Delacroix and Géricault in the English landscapists' work, an important step had been taken along the road which was eventually to lead to Monet and Pissarro.

During the 1820s and 1830s the sketches of Constable, Turner, and Bonington were of particular interest to Delacroix and his contemporaries. In order to capture "with a pure apprehension of natural effect," the incessantly changing qualities of light and colour, Delacroix observed that in the natural world "light and shadow never stand still." Consequently, the French Romantic painters developed the habit of making quick, but by no means cursory, sketches of a particular scene in oil and watercolour. These sketches, although they were not considered to be "finished" by the authorities and Salons of the

time, are of importance in the development both of the artist's way of seeing the world and the technique of depicting it. They display to a remarkable degree the totality of the artist's vision and observation, and are nowadays often more highly prized than the "finished" work they frequently preceded. In fact, Delacroix and many others of his generation agreed that the vitality of outdoor sketches suffered from being transferred and reworked into studio compositions.

Until Constable and his fellow English landscapists had made their dazzling impact on the French art establishment in the 1820s, French landscape painting had enjoyed an honourable, if dull history. It is often, though quite wrongly, assumed that the Académie in

BONINGTON
The Large Pond, Palace of Versailles
oil on canvas
c.1820. 43.5 × 54.5 cm
Above Avoiding the popular aspects of Versailles, Bonington indicates the obvious touristic elements of the scene as sketchy masses in the background. Everything here is subordinated to the depiction of space and volume.

CONSTABLE
A Cottage among Trees with a Sand Bank
oil on paper on canvas
c.1830
Left An example of Constable's direct approach to landscape. The sketchy nature of works such as this was particularly influential in France.

Paris at this time had no interest in the promotion of landscape painting. A major quadrennial competition in historical landscape painting, the Prix de Paysage Historique, had been instigated at the Ecole des Beaux-Arts in 1817 after many years of agitation by landscapists for the genre to be recognized within the school's establishment. Although the competition for the Prix de Paysage Historique was abolished in 1863 – a date central to the history of Impressionism as it marked the first Salon des Refusés – the teaching of landscape painting at the Ecole was at a significant level of development by the time Constable showed *The Hay Wain* at the 1824 Salon in Paris.

It is important to note that the Prix de Paysage Historique was precisely that – a competition for historical landscape, not landscape after nature or *paysage champêtre*. To compete, students had to choose a classical or biblical theme "of the noble and historical type" for their subject, and figures to be set in the landscape were not to exceed a prescribed height and disturb the proportions of a picture which was, after all, to be devoted to landscape. Despite this, the teaching of landscape after nature at the Ecole was surprisingly advanced, echoing some of the dicta of Constable and vaguely foreshadowing the loose theories of the Impressionists. J.B. Deperthes, who published his *Théorie de paysage (Landscape Theory)* in 1818, advised students of landscape painting that their aim in depicting nature was to paint it "in the light that falls on it at the exact moment when the painter sets out to capture the scene." According to the landscapist Pierre-Henri Valenciennes (who was partly responsible for the Prix de Paysage Historique), under whom Deperthes had studied, a study (*étude*) for a

landscape painting made "from Nature should be done within two hours at the outside, and if your effect is a sunrise or a sunset, you should not take more than half an hour." Neither of these two instructions would have been out of place in a hypothetical manual of the art of Impressionism. Yet landscape painters such as Constable, Bonington, Valenciennes, and Deperthes were confined by tradition to their studios for the completion of their works of art. Painting outdoors did not lead to acceptably "finished" pieces of art. Indeed, Constable, as he was working in his London studio on *The Hay Wain*, was forced to dispatch an underling to the depths of East Anglia to make drawings of the eponymous cart. After the apprentice returned with the drawing Constable then completed the composition of the picture. This was the most practical approach.

CONSTABLE
The Hay Wain
oil on canvas
1821. 130 × 185.5 cm
OPPOSITE The quintessential English landscape, admired by Delacroix and Géricault for its dramatic naturalism. Delacroix reworked his own painting The Massacre at Chios *after he had seen Constable's great landscape at the Salon of 1824. This and other works by the English landscapists were a source of inspiration to the Barbizon School and their successors, the Impressionists.*

(GELÉE) LORRAIN
Landscape with Ascanius Shooting the Stag of Sylvia
oil on canvas
1682. 120 × 150 cm
BELOW Claude Lorrain was the great master of the "obedient" landscape, which aimed for a perfectly harmonious rendering of nature.

COURBET
Entrance to the Straits of Gibraltar
oil on canvas
1848. 18 × 26 cm
*Below Small, hastily executed
sketches were not made for public
consumption, but the aesthetic
of the sketch or study was
gaining ground amongst
French landscapists in the
mid-nineteenth century.*

COROT
The Roman Campagna with the
Claudian Aquaduct
oil on canvas
c.1826–28. 21.5 × 33 cm
*Right The Roman countryside
was the classical landscape taught
in the Ecole des Beaux-Arts. In
an idealized form it provides the
background for countless
academic paintings of the time.*

TROYON
Evening near Barbizon
oil on canvas
1859. 66 × 88 cm
*The young Monet was
particularly interested in the
effects of light depicted in works
such as this. On one of his first
visits to the Salon Monet wrote to
his friend and teacher Eugène
Boudin that Troyon's landscapes
had delighted him especially.
Troyon was a friend of Boudin
and he advised Monet to enrol in
Thomas Couture's atelier, advice
which Monet summarily rejected.*

The move into the country and the de-velopment of the idea that a sketch made outdoors, *en plein-air*, was a legitimate end in itself came with a group of painters known as the Barbizon School. Barbizon is a village in the Fontainebleau Forest to the southeast of Paris. The Fontainebleau Forest and the near-by plain of Chailly had been locations for painters since the mid-eighteenth century, and had been suggested by Valenciennes as useful substitutes for the Roman Campagna, a landscape held in great esteem for its classic-al associations. Between 1830 and 1850 a group of landscape painters, which included Constant Troyon, Théodore Rousseau, Vir-gile Diaz de la Peña, François Daubigny, François Millet, and Jean-Baptiste Corot, made use of the area around Barbizon and often settled there for long periods. Daubigny was a devoted *plein-air* painter who built a studio boat in order to paint *in situ* on the river Oise (an example later followed by

DELACROIX
The Sea from the Cliff-tops at
Dieppe
oil on canvas
This is the landscape of the
Normandy coast that Monet was
to make his own. It is interesting
to see that Delacroix was not only
interested in exotic and
Romantic figures.

Monet). In 1891 Frédéric Henriet, in his biography *The Campaigns of a Landscape Painter* (*Les Campagnes d'un paysagiste*), describes Daubigny's struggle with the elements:

> Daubigny attached his canvas to some posts solidly planted in the ground. And there it stayed, continually exposed to the horns of cattle and the pranks of naughty children until it was completely finished. The painter had specifically chosen a turbulent sky filled with large clouds chased by the angry wind. He was constantly on the alert for the right moment and ran to take up his work as soon as the weather corresponded to that of his painting.

DAUBIGNY
Spring
oil on canvas
1857. 96 × 193 cm
*A perfect example of
the Barbizon landscape,
Daubigny's painting was
exhibited at the Salon of 1857
which was transferred that year
from the Salon D'Apollon in the
Louvre to the larger Palais de
l'Industrie.*

MILLET
The Potato Harvest
oil on canvas
1858. 54 × 65 cm
RIGHT The dignity of peasant labour was Millet's great, if somewhat sentimental theme. Pissarro, and later van Gogh, were influenced by Millet's depictions of the arduous life of the peasant. Millet's work did not find favour with the establishment which preferred idealized landscapes and peasants.

ROUSSEAU
The Village of Becquigny
oil on canvas
1857. 63.5 × 100 cm
RIGHT The composition may be a coincidence, but artists were assiduous museum-goers and learnt much from their predecessors. Baudelaire, however, was critical of Rousseau's lack of a personal vision: "He wants", he said "to be precise and to make something striking. A highly coloured photograph must be his ideal."

The Barbizon School was as indebted to the English landscapists as Delacroix although in historical terms the art being created around Barbizon quickly came to represent a strong reaction against the Romanticism of Delacroix and Géricault, who were not particularly interested in landscape or *plein-airisme* as a genre or method of painting. Just as the Romantics had rebelled against the ingrained Neo-Classicism of the Académie, as exemplified by David and Ingres and taught in the Ecole des Beaux-Arts, so the painting of nature for its own sake amounted to a rejection of both the erudite Neo-Classical and the flamboyant Romantic subject matter. The Barbizon painters, as well as admiring the English landscapists of their own era, were much taken with the eminent seventeenth-century Dutch School of landscape painting,

HOBBEMA
The Avenue, Middelharnis
oil on canvas
1689. 103.5 × 141 cm
*ABOVE This was of course painted
in the studio, but seventeenth-
century Dutch artists were also
concerned with studying their
surroundings at first hand.
Ruysdael warned his students that
light and shadow never stand
still; a sentiment close to Monet's
heart in his later career.*

RUYSDAEL
The Waterfall
oil on canvas
17th century
*LEFT ABOVE The seventeenth
century Dutch landscapists were
the first great exponents of the
genre. This scene is typical of
their approach. Although it is
highly formalised, great attention
is paid to the details of movement
in the torrent of water.*

particularly the works of Ruysdael and Hobbema. In this the Barbizon School was supported by the Director of the Académie, Théophile Thoré, who had commissioned Rousseau and made an extensive study of Dutch art. On the other hand the Comte de Nieuwerkerke, the Director-General of National Museums after 1849, spoke for many when he described the Barbizon School in the following incandescent and patronizing terms: "This is the painting of democrats, of those who don't change their linen and who want to put themselves above men of the world. This art displeases and disquiets me."

Thankfully the Comte de Nieuwerkerke and the French authorities were increasingly disquietened to find their stranglehold on matters of taste weakening. The clear line of development from the Dutch to the English artists, and thence the French landscape painters and their attempt to capture "the exact moment", was leading to the art of Monet and his fellow Impressionists.

Capturing the landscape meant being in it, with all the attendant dangers and inconvenience of being away from the controlled environment of the studio. In 1841 John Goffe Rand, an American portraitist living in London, had invented the first collapsible paint tube, an idea quickly taken up by the colour merchants Winsor and Newton. As Pierre-Auguste Renoir is reported by his son, Jean, to have said, "Without paints in tubes there would have been no Cézanne, no Monet, no Sisley or Pissarro, nothing of what the journalists were later to call Impressionism."

Before the arrival of these new tubes, made of inert tin so as not to react with the various chemicals in the pigment, the ground pigment was supplied by the colour merchant, mixed with oil by the painter and kept in a small pouch of pig's bladder. To use the paint, the artist had to make a small hole in the wall of the bladder and squeeze it out. For centuries these bladders had been the only way of dispensing a ready mixed combination of pigment and oil, but paint could not be kept for long in them before the oil began to oxidize. Once opened, the life of the paint – made up of expensive pigments – was considerably shortened. The tin tube was a revolutionary device by comparison, both for the colour merchant, who had a new product with which to service an increasing clientèle

The four pictures here have been enlarged to show the details of the brushwork of the four master Impressionists – Manet, Pissarro, Monet, and Renoir. The essential similarity between them, and the obvious comparison to be made with the refined, concentrated brushwork of the classical schools and the conventional artists of the time, is the looseness and immediacy of the strokes.

MANET
An Italian Woman
oil on canvas
Private collection

of amateur or "Sunday" painters littering the banks of the Seine on summer days, and the serious artist, who could now venture outdoors confident that the paint was in a stable condition and swiftly to hand. The tube paint had the consistency of fresh butter, which made it ideal for application to the canvas in thick impasto brushstrokes, or even with the palette knife – both methods used by the Impressionists and after them to particularly remarkable effect by Vincent van Gogh. The paint could still of course be further tempered with linseed, walnut, or poppy oil, or diluted with turpentine.

To fill the new tubes a whole new range of bright, stable colours with well-understood drying properties began to appear on the market. The advancement of mineral and organic chemistry in the early part of the century had heralded new colours such as cobalt blue, artificial ultramarine (previously made of lapis lazuli, very expensive and available only in small quantities), chromium yellow with its shades of orange, red and green, emerald green, zinc white and a stable lead white. By the 1850s the artist had at his or her disposal a palette more brilliant, stable and convenient than ever before.

In 1839 the French chemist Eugène Chevreul, director of dyeing at the Gobelins tapestry workshop, who had begun an investigation into why some dyed colours seemed less brilliant than others, published his study *On the Law of Simultaneous Colour Contrast and the Arrangement of Coloured Objects* (better known as *The Principles of Harmony and Contrast of Colours*), which explained the phenomenon that when two colours are placed touching one another the differences between them are perceived to be at their greatest. From this he codified a theory of colours which says that certain pairs of colours, such as green and red, or violet and yellow, complement each other. This gives rise to the phenomenon of "negative or complementary after-image" where the complementary colour of a red, i.e. green, can be seen as an aura around the colour when staring at the red for a moment and then looking away. As the German poet and scientist Johan Wolfgang von Goethe had already observed in his *Theory of Colours* written in 1810, a deep red sunset produced the complementary colour of green in the shadows cast by the sunlight; likewise, the yellowish tinge of snow produced shadows of a violet hue. Delacroix had used coloured shadow in his work, and the Impressionists were to exploit their own perception and Chevreul's theory further with the bright new colours available to them, whilst the Neo-Impressionists were to take this phenomenon to its logical extreme.

PISSARRO
The Farmyard
oil on canvas
1877. 55 × 65 cm
Left

RENOIR
The White Hat
oil on canvas
1890. 55.5 × 46 cm
Below

MONET
The Red Road
oil on canvas
1884. 65 × 81 cm
Left

MILLET
Bringing Home the New-born Calf
oil on canvas
1857–61. 81 × 99 cm
RIGHT Like The Potato
Harvest, *this painting was
ridiculed by some contemporary
critics, who considered Millet's
subjects to be vulgar and
unworthy of fine art.*

COURBET
Joseph Proudhon and His Children
oil on canvas
1853. 147 × 198 cm
*RIGHT BELOW This composition
seems perfectly natural to us, but
it was far too informal for the
taste of the time.*

Meanwhile, the Realism developed by François Millet and Gustave Courbet, which was a complete rejection of Neo-Classical and Romantic styles, began, in the late 1850s and early 1860s, to have a strong influence on young painters like Monet. Millet's great achievement was to paint the peasantry as he found and remembered it, being himself the son of a Normandy peasant farmer. Although paintings such as *The Gleaners* (*Les Glaneurs*) and *Angèlus* show the peasantry at back-breaking work and pious rest, and do not appear today to be particularly realistic, their very subject matter was a cause for fierce controversy at the time among those traditionalists who thought agricultural labour a subject unfit for "proper" representation, and those at the other extreme who believed Millet's work to be the embodiment of socialist values. Despite the claims of the right and the left, Millet remained resolutely apolitical.

Not so Gustave Courbet, the son of a wealthy wine grower from Ornans near Switzerland. Courbet's art, like his politics, was uncompromising. His choice of subjects eschewed everything that had previously been thought suitable for fine art. They were, as Bernard Denvir observes, "unheroic, un-historical, and entirely unconcerned either with religious symbolism or patriotic propaganda." Courbet was a friend and *comrade* of the printer Pierre Joseph Proudhon, the title of whose work of 1850 *What is Property?* (*Qu'est-ce que la proprieté?*) was answered with the immortal words: "It is theft" (*"C'est le vol"*). Courbet's staunch socialism ensured him a spectacular career in politics, eventually landing him in jail for taking part in the destruction of the Vendôme Column, a huge victory memorial in the heart of Paris. But in spite of his radicalism in painting and politics

COURBET
A Spanish Woman
oil on canvas
1855. 81 × 65 cm
As usual, Courbet does not try to prettify his sitters.

COURBET
The Burial at Ornans
oil on canvas
1849–50. 315 × 668 cm
ABOVE Courbet received a medal at the Salon in 1850, but not for this painting. The massive, dark, unconventional composition showing the lower echelons of society provoked outraged criticism. Courbet's Realism was deeply influenced by the political ideas of Pierre Joseph Proudhon, of whom he was a supporter. Courbet's rejection of historical and religious subjects made him a champion of the new generation of the "painters of modern life".

COURBET
The Artist's Studio
oil on canvas
1855. 360 × 600 cm
RIGHT This painting is subtitled an "Allegory of Realism", and the artist has indeed filled his picture with symbols and contemporary figures. Right, seated on the table: the poet Baudelaire. Right, centre: Champfleury. Right, third from left: another friend of Courbet's, the socialist writer Proudhon. In the shadow to the left, seated in profile: the barely disguised figure of Napoleon III, much disliked by Courbet and his radical friends. Left, seated, wearing a top hat: a right-wing journalist. Standing, left: a figure identified as the banker Fould. The woman nursing a child is Irish; she represents poverty and destitution. The dummy behind the easel has been symbolically discarded in favour of a real woman.

he exhibited two works, *The Stone Breakers* (*Les Casseurs de pierre*) and *The Burial at Ornans*, at the Salon of 1850. "I hold", Courbet wrote in 1861, "that painting is essentially a concrete art and does not consist of anything but the representation of real and concrete things". Five years later, at the Exposition Universelle in Paris, Courbet erected his own Realist Pavilion (Pavillion du Réalisme) where he rivalled the official Salon by showing forty pictures including the massive *The Artist's Studio* (*L'Atelier du peintre*), which depicts in "an Allegory of Realism" the artist and the influences at work on him.

In the decade after 1850 French painting underwent an unparalleled fragmentation of styles, partly tolerated but never promoted by the authorities. The experiments of the Barbizon School and the Realists were encouraging the young painters who had been born in the 1830s and 1840s along a path which was artistically a logical progression but which was to appear to the public and the arbiters of the Salon shockingly revolutionary. By the time the Impressionists began to show in the mid-1870s, the Barbizon artists were readily accepted by the Salon and their work was beginning to fetch high prices.

COROT
The Forest of Fontainebleau
oil on canvas
c.1855. 39 × 54.5 cm
*The archetypal Barbizon
landscape.*

PISSARRO, MANET, AND DEGAS

Camille Pissarro, Edouard Manet, and Edgar Degas, born in 1830, 1832, and 1834 respectively, were in their twenties when the 1855 Exposition Universelle was proving to be the delight of Paris. The work of Delacroix, who was now fifty-seven and achieving great popular acclaim, was the main attraction, having been eloquently lauded by the poet and art critic Charles Baudelaire (who was later to befriend Manet). Work by Daubigny, Corot, and Millet was also to be seen hidden amongst the thousands of paintings on show, but it would have been difficult to miss Courbet's spectacular sideshow.

Pissarro, the third son of Franco-Jewish parents, had arrived in Paris from St Thomas, a Danish colony in the Virgin Islands where his father was a merchant. Camille had been to school in France, but after returning to St Thomas to work in his father's store, he had gone to Venezuela in 1853 to work with the Danish artist Fritz Melbye. Eventually his parents decided to send him to Paris to study art. He arrived in 1855, as the Exposition was in progress, to attend the Ecole des Beaux-Arts. He soon left the Ecole for the Académie Suisse, a studio in the quai des Orfèvres, run by an ex-model, which charged small fees, offered no teaching, but had models and equipment for young artists to study life drawing and painting as they wished. At the Exposition Universelle, Pissarro was particularly impressed by the six Corots on show – the young Pissarro had become a landscapist under the influence of his friend Melbye and later went to visit Corot in search of guidance. A couple of years later he was found by Claude Monet to be "peacefully working away in Corot's style"; ten years after the Exposition Universelle, Pissarro was officially exhibiting at the Salon as Corot's pupil. At that time it would be hard to imagine that he would become, with the exception of Claude Monet, perhaps the most influential of the landscape Impressionists.

In contrast to Camille Pissarro, Edouard Manet, twenty-three at the time of the Exposition, was the son of a Parisian magistrate, a member of the *haute bourgeoisie* and blessed, as was his slightly younger contemporary Edgar Degas, with the security of independent means. He had enrolled in the school of Thomas Couture in 1850, where he studied painting for six years. Couture had been a pupil of Paul Delaroche, whose *The Execution of Lady Jane Grey* exemplified the conservative but popular qualities of the Davidian academic style. The painting had delighted the Salon of 1834 where visitors are reported to have wept. They were no doubt moved by the sight of the young English noblewoman with her head on the block, a fate close to the hearts of all French citizens not so long after the mass executions that followed the 1789 Revolution.

COROT
Dardagny, near Geneva, Morning
oil on canvas
1853. 826 × 47 cm
A plain and simple landscape before photography influenced Corot's style. It is worked in large planes of colour with little or no detail to distract from the broad composition.

GÉRÔME
In the Harem
oil on canvas
1848. 150 × 200 cm
This is a good academic piece, with smoothly modelled bodies "à la Ingres" and a subject which lent itself to an acceptable form of voluptuousness.

Couture had caused controversy and ensured himself his own place in the popular imagination of the French public and critics with his huge painting *The Romans of the Decadence* (*Les Romains de la décadence*), a sprawling depiction of a Roman orgy which shocked and titillated Parisian society when it was shown at the Salon of 1847. In the same year, doubtless to make the most of his new-found notoriety, Couture had opened his own private art school in Paris, advertising it as offering "teaching based above all on the great art of ancient Greece, the Renaissance masters and the admirable Flemish school." Couture, in order to clarify his view further, declared himself against the "spurious classical school which reproduces the works of the past in a banal and imperfect fashion," and "hostile to that abominable school, known [as] Romantic."

COUTURE
The Romans of the Decadence
oil on canvas
1847. 466 × 775 cm
Couture, the teacher of Manet,
scored an immense success with
this work at the Salon of 1847.

GLEYRE
The Apostles about to Embark on
Their Evangelical Mission
oil on canvas
c.1844–45. 197 × 294 cm
*The style of Gleyre's painting is
derived directly from Raphael
and Titian, but this sort of
attempt to emulate past masters
was exactly what the
Impressionists rejected.*

MANET
Copy after Delacroix's Dante
oil on canvas
1855. 33 × 41 cm
LEFT Manet went to see the deeply respected Delacroix with his friend Antonin Proust, and asked permission to copy his work.

All this was true to the spirit of Louis Philippe's *juste milieu*, and linked Couture to his contemporaries such as Charles Gleyre and Alexander Cabanel, who were in fact content to use those elements of Classicism, Romanticism and even Realism which would make up an acceptable picture. As an allegory of contemporary hedonism veiled in the skimpy tunic of Classicism, *The Romans of the Decadence* stands in ironic contrast to the *juste milieu* professed by all and which was to continue after the fall of Louis Philippe and well into the Third Republic. The burgeoning French middle classes of the 1850s would have been outraged if Couture had depicted the contemporary French male bourgeoisie at one of its favourite leisure activities, the brothel. Yet, this is exactly what Couture's

DELACROIX
Dante and Virgil in Hell
oil on canvas
1822. 189 × 246 cm
LEFT Manet and the Impressionists were profound admirers of Delacroix's individualistic style. This spectacular work is also commonly known as the Barque of Dante.

pupil Edouard Manet set out to do eight years later at the Salon des Refusés of 1863 with his *Luncheon on the Grass* (*Déjeuner sur l'herbe*). That painting scandalized Paris and pushed

DEGAS
Self-portrait
oil on canvas
1854–55. 81 × 64.5 cm
One of many self-portraits the artist painted in his youth.

Manet reluctantly into the forefront of what became the Impressionist movement.

During his time as a young "apprentice" at Couture's atelier Manet was less concerned with shocking Paris than studying his master's teaching and pondering how literally to reverse the academic technique to his own ends. He also spent many hours in the Louvre studying and copying the techniques of the old masters. The Spanish artists Velazquez, Murillo, and Ribera particularly interested him; an influence which can be seen in his later paintings. During his time spent copying in the Louvre he also absorbed elements of a number of other masters including the French Le Nain brothers. Manet was in effect a pivotal force in the long tradition of European

art. His wish was to evolve from the old masters, not reject what he had learnt from them. He was also significantly in awe of Delacroix, so much so that in 1855 he wrote to him asking permission to copy his *Barque of Dante* (*La Barque de Dante*).

Edgar Degas was the youngest of his generation of artists to study in Paris in the mid-1850s. He spent only one semester at the Ecole des Beaux-Arts, however, before an extended tour of Italy where part of his family lived. Degas was the son of Franco-Italian parents who had made their fortune in banking. He registered with the painting and sculpture section of the Ecole des Beaux-Arts on 6th April 1855 after passing an entrance competition at which the painter Henri Fantin-Latour was also successful. (Fantin-Latour, however, was found wanting and left three months later.) Degas' teacher during his brief studies at the Ecole was Louis Lamothe, who inspired him with his own deeply held respect for Ingres, whose pictures in any case Degas had been copying in the Louvre and at the homes of wealthy family friends for some time. In 1856 Degas was in Naples visiting his relatives, painting their portraits and touring the great museums of other Italian cities, absorbing all the Renaissance masters he could feast his eyes on. Although he was to be a prime mover in the *Société anonyme* just under a decade later, the relationship of Degas' work to the other Impressionists was to be marked both by his experiences in Italy and by his abiding interest in the human form as opposed to the landscape.

THE NURSERY OF IMPRESSIONISM

In 1862 France annexed Cambodia, Victor Hugo published *Les Misérables*, Edouard Manet painted *Music in the Tuileries Gardens*

The teachers of the Impressionists were men raised in an academic ethos of painting which stretched back to principles laid down in the seventeenth century. To prepare for entry into the Ecole, aspiring artists in the mid-nineteenth century entrusted themselves (and their purses) to men such as Charles Gleyre and Thomas Couture who ran private independent ateliers where they could receive formal instruction (a system which persists to this day in France). Life at the atelier for a young *rapin*, or new boy, was often fraught with dangers. According to Albert Boime, the eminent historian of the Académie in the nineteenth century, the *rapin* would be first to arrive at the atelier in the morning and busied himself with menial tasks such as arranging the stools, sweeping the floor, washing the brushes, running errands and suffering occasional persecution by the older students.

INGRES
The Princess of Broglie
oil on canvas
1853. 114.5 × 86 cm
LEFT Degas was a thorough draftsman and Ingres' perfection was an abiding model for him.

DEGAS
The Bellelli Family
oil on canvas
1858–60. 200 × 250 cm
BELOW Degas started a series of portraits while visiting his relatives in Italy.

and four unknown young artists met in the Paris atelier of Charles Gleyre, a fifty-four-year-old Swiss artist who had been an instructor at the Ecole des Beaux-Arts. Claude Monet, the eldest son of a grain merchant in the northwestern port of Le Hâvre, Frédéric Bazille, whose family were affluent wine producers in the southern Hérault, Auguste Renoir, previously a porcelain-painter, and Alfred Sisley, at twenty-three the oldest in the group by two years and the son of an English businessman, had little in common except art. Gleyre's atelier had a reputation for being cheap and Gleyre himself was known to be fairly tolerant and kind to his *élèves* (pupils). Although he was neither famous nor a member of the Académie, one painting by him, *Lost Illusions* of 1843, had enjoyed great success at the Salon. The painting won him a medal and substantial respect from the critics of the day.

DEGAS
Study for Semiramis Building
Babylon
pencil and gouache on grey paper
1861. 30.5 × 21 cm
RIGHT

DEGAS
Semiramis Building Babylon
oil on canvas
1860–62. 151 × 258 cm
ABOVE Semiramis *was Degas'
first attempt at a large-scale
history painting, and as this
study and the final version
show, the artist was clearly
working within the academic
tradition, making detailed plans
for the work. Despite the
conventional process followed by
Degas here and to which he
adhered for the rest of his career,
there is nothing stilted and
academic about the bright,
realistic vision of the work, which
manages to blend all that the
young artist had seen in the
museums of Europe with
his own ideas.*

There were frequently initiation ceremonies, or *blagues*, for the hapless *rapins* to endure before they progressed in the social hierarchy of the atelier.

The course of studies pursued at the ateliers relied on a long tradition of ensuring that the student could draw proficiently before he could be allowed to touch a paintbrush. Drawing exercises which started with copying from engravings, then plaster casts of antique sculpture and finally the live models were rigorous and frequently mind-numbing. Only when the student had mastered drawing technique to a high degree would he be allowed to paint copies of the teacher's work or old masters in the Louvre, as did Manet, Degas and a reluctant Monet.

An equally rigorous system of painting was taught in the ateliers and the Ecole with varying nuances of emphasis according to the predilection of the master. The practical work of painting onto the canvas was as strictly taught as drawing. The student was guided towards producing a painting of a nude or model's head known as an *académie*, which displayed the classical technique of applying the oil paint to the canvas in layers of tones from dark to light. These *académies* were often undertaken in shades of grey or with a very limited palette to produce flesh-tones, for colour was considered a distraction, the sort of thing Delacroix was considered too free with by teachers, yet whose pupils revelled in it. The smoothness in texture and gradation of tone in the finished *académie* was of prime importance. Yet however stifling this kind of training might have been, it had served Degas and Manet well.

So in 1862, the young Monet and his friends found themselves sitting on their stools in Gleyre's atelier, perhaps sketching a

GÉRICAULT
Nude Warrior with a Spear
oil on canvas
1810. 93.5 × 75.5 cm
Though it was painted half a century earlier, this type of academic nude was still taught with the same rigor at the Ecole des Beaux-Arts and the independent ateliers such as those of Gleyre and Couture.

MANET
Study for La Toilette
red chalk on paper
1862. 28 × 20 cm
LEFT There is nothing remarkable about this study, which appears quite average in comparison to Degas' finely detailed sketches.

MONET
Honfleur, rue de la Bavolle
oil on canvas
1864. 56 × 61 cm
*RIGHT The free rendering is
reminiscent of Corot's studies.*

BOUDIN
Low Tide near Honfleur
oil on wood
1854–57. 26.7 × 36.5 cm
*BELOW This small-scale work is
reminiscent of earlier
British studies.*

plaster copy of an antique statue as countless young art students had done before them. For Monet, the atelier must have been stuffy indeed. He stayed there for only eighteen months until Gleyre was forced to close, and afterwards attended the Académie Suisse. Monet was the son of a small businessman who had moved his family from Paris to Le Hâvre on the Normandy coast. The sea and the countryside of his youth were to become Claude Monet's natural habitat, not the Louvre or a Parisian atelier, and later years would find him braving the most appalling weather and terrain to capture a scene. He had returned to Paris on the sufferance of his father to study in the traditional way. Monet's artistic talents had already made an impact in Le Hâvre where he had been earning a reasonable living from selling caricatures. There he had met Eugène Boudin, a self-taught local landscapist, who persuaded him (initially reluctant, according to Monet) to take up painting in the open air. Of the four *rapins*, Monet was the most experienced in painting and with the new Realist philosophies – as exemplified in Courbet's paintings of "common" life – being thrown up around it. By the time he had gone to study with Gleyre he had already spent some time in Paris, done his military service in the French colony of Algeria and had been a habitué of the Brasserie des Martyrs at 75 rue des Martyrs, where Courbet, the art critic Jules Castagnary (who was to be a powerful spokesman for Impressionism), Baudelaire, and François Bonvin (a conventional painter with advanced views) would meet, talk, and drink. Edouard Manet's work was much discussed there even though he himself was an infrequent visitor, preferring to hold court in other cafés.

RENOIR
Trees in the Forest of Fontainebleau
oil on canvas
c.1860.
*It would be difficult to guess that
this robust and literal view is by
Renoir, but his interest in the
effects of light, even at this early
stage, is quite evident.*

Auguste Renoir's family were provincial tailors from Limoges who had moved to Paris shortly after he was born. He was apprenticed to a porcelain-painter (who went out of business in 1858) and then, for a living, Renoir painted fans, copying scenes from artists such as Fragonard, Watteau, and Boucher as well as painting blinds and other odd jobs before enrolling in Gleyre's atelier in 1861. Having been trained as an artistic crafts-man, his whole philosophy in art was geared to the acquisition of technique. Like Manet and Degas, Renoir had studied the old mas-ters in the Louvre, something Monet was reluctant to do. As the art historian John House has observed, by deciding to become a painter Renoir was moving from a trade to a profession, from the skilled working class into the middle class, yet from the very

beginning he seems consistently to have thought of himself as a workman in paint, an "*ouvrier de la peinture*". Unlike Renoir, who in the mid–1850s had been painting to live, Alfred Sisley and Frédéric Bazille had been living to paint. Sisley had narrowly avoided a business career in London and Bazille had given up a career in medicine when they met Monet and Renoir at Gleyre's atelier.

Often spoken of as "the nursery of Im-pressionism," Gleyre's atelier became the meeting-place for four of the most important figures in the movement. There is little evi-dence that the four young painters im-mediately sympathized with each other in the cosmopolitan atmosphere of Gleyre's school, but they soon realized they had several in-terests in common one of which was land-scape painting and often went on *plein-air*

MANET
Fishing at St Ouen
oil on canvas
1860–61. 77 × 123 cm
This is an unusual and transitional work showing the influence of past masters.

expeditions into the countryside around Paris. In 1921, five years before his death, Claude Monet recalled the early days:

> At Gleyre's atelier I found Renoir, Sisley, and Bazille. As we were drawing from a model . . . Gleyre criticized my work. "It's not bad," he said, "but the breast is too heavy, the shoulder too powerful, the foot too large." "I can only draw what I see," I replied timidly . . . "Praxiteles borrowed the best elements from a hundred imperfect models to create a masterpiece," retorted Gleyre drily. "One must always think of classical antiquity."

It is tempting to think that the eighty-one year old Monet's memory had perhaps grown somewhat dim (if not bitter) on the subject of Gleyre, a teacher held in the highest respect by Renoir and many other *élèves*. Nevertheless, one evening during his time at Gleyre's Monet gathered together Sisley, Renoir, and Bazille and said *Filons d'ici!* ("lets get out of here!") "We left," Monet said in 1921 "after two weeks . . . We were well rid of the place, because I don't think any of the most promising students in the atelier ever made good." He was wrong on both counts: his memory must indeed have been failing him, for they remained with Gleyre until he closed down in 1864; and he and his friends were the most promising students in the place!

In addition to Monet, Renoir, Bazille, and Sisley, two more young artists who were to be involved in the Impressionist movement, Paul Cézanne and Armand Guillaumin, born in 1839 and 1841 respectively, had also gravitated to Paris by 1862. Twentieth-century art historians revere the former as the creative talent who was eventually to go beyond

Impressionism, while posterity has largely forgotten the latter precisely because he became one of the most faithful exponents of the new genre.

Cézanne had come to Paris in 1861 on the urging of the novelist Emile Zola, a childhood friend from Aix-en-Provence where Cézanne's father was a banker. Cézanne had been studying law but had abandoned this to become a painter, working at the Académie Suisse. It was here that he met Armand

DEGAS
Study for a Portrait of Manet
pencil on paper
c.1864. 41.5 × 28 cm
Degas and Manet had met in the Louvre in 1862. Degas was copying onto a copper plate when Manet interrupted him with the suggestion that what he was doing was impossible.

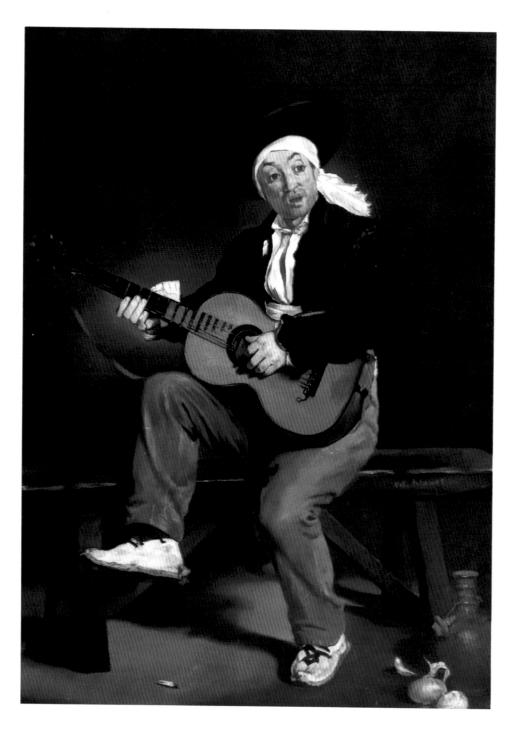

Guillaumin, who was painting during the time off from his job for the Paris-Orléans railway, and Camille Pissarro, who introduced them both to Monet and his friends from Gleyre's atelier.

DEPICTING MODERN LIFE

1862 was certainly a year of coincidental meetings which would have great consequences for art. That year, whilst he was copying Velazquez's *Infanta Margarita* onto a copper plate at the Louvre, Edgar Degas was interrupted in his work by Edouard Manet, signalling the beginning of an extraordinary relationship between the two men. They had much in common; both were of patrician Parisian families, and neither had been greatly influenced by the *plein-air* movement. Degas and Manet were also consciously resisting Courbet's call for a "social realist" art. Despite the fact that circumstances link them very closely with the "true" Impressionists such as Monet and Pissarro, their own artistic concerns in painting *la vie Parisienne* were largely to hold them together and apart from the others.

Manet and Degas were great admirers of one another's work (albeit on occasion very grudgingly), but they differed greatly in matters of politics and philosophy. On the one hand, Manet was staunchly republican in his politics and a considerable intellectual who craved and enjoyed the society of writers and critics involved with the new art such as Champfleury, Duranty, Baudelaire and later Mallarmé. Degas, on the other hand, was an arch-conservative and frequently a peevish anti-intellectual.

At the Salon of 1861 Manet exhibited his *Spanish Singer* (*Le Chanteur Espagnol*) to considerable acclaim. Reminiscent of Velazquez

MANET
The Spanish Singer
oil on canvas
1860. 147.5 × 114.5 cm
OPPOSITE This painting and
The Artist's Parents *were*
accepted at the Salon of 1861 and
received an honourable mention,
a welcome distinction after the
rejection of The Absinthe
Drinker *in 1859.*

FANTIN-LATOUR
Homage to Delacroix
oil on canvas
1864. 160 × 250 cm
LEFT Inspired by a Dutch group
portrait by Frans Hals, the group
includes Whistler standing along
the frame, Fantin-Latour, seated,
wearing a white shirt, Duranty,
Legros, the painter Cordier, the
writers Champfleury and
Baudelaire seated to the right,
Manet standing right of the
frame, Bracquemond and Albert
Balleroy. This is the first of five
group portraits, but Fantin-
Latour destroyed one, keeping
only three of the heads.

and Goya in style and of popular interest in its Spanish subject matter, the painting nevertheless displays the beginnings of the broad brushwork and rich colouration which were to be a feature of Manet's later work. Moreover the *Spanish Singer* disdained the fine finish of the Académic style and showed a sense of Realism which challenged Courbet at his own game attracting a cabal of critics, writers, and painters – Champfleury, Baudelaire, and Henri Fantin-Latour especially – to Manet's door where he welcomed their attentions and the beginnings of fame. Much later Matisse called Manet "the first great modern artist because his free and spontaneous brushwork liberated the artist's instincts."

In retrospect it is tempting to imagine at this time a republican-leaning, critical, artistic avant-garde armed with the desire for the untrammelled, the vigorous, the "real" in art, simply lying in wait for someone like Manet, a skillful, fresh, uncompromising and above all modern artist with metropolitan and cosmopolitan interests to come along and bear the standard of a new art. In many respects this was the case. Baudelaire, who in fact was twenty years Manet's senior, was respected as a rigorous art critic, he was a friend of Delacroix, an admirer of Courbet and lately a close friend of Manet. In 1862 Baudelaire was working on his *The Painter of Modern Life* (*Le Peintre de la vie moderne*) a critique which, as the title suggests, discusses in which direction art should go in the modern

MANET
Baudelaire
etching
c.1869.
Baudelaire and Manet had met in 1858 and they were in frequent and close contact by 1860. The friendship lasted until the death of the poet in 1867. Baudelaire's views on the role of the artist in the modern world, published in 1863 as "Le Peintre de la vie moderne", were an important influence on Manet and his contemporaries.

world of the big city. The subject of *The Painter of Modern Life* is not Edouard Manet, however, who was as yet relatively unknown, but Constantin Guys, an illustrator and watercolourist who had covered the Crimean War for the *Illustrated London News* and whose pictures of Parisian life brought much admiration from artists and critics alike. Baudelaire's critique concerned itself with his own time and demanded an art which could deliver it up in all its present reality, not in anachronistic Neo-Classical allegories:

The past is interesting not only because of the beauty which the artists of the past – whose present it was – have extracted from it, but because of its historical value. The same applies to the present. The pleasure which we derive from the presentation of the present derives from the beauty which it may possess, as well as from its essential quality as the present. Modernity is the transitory, the fugitive, the contingent, which make up one half of art, the other being the eternal and the immutable. This transitory fugitive element, which is constantly changing, must not be despised or neglected. If you do so you tumble into the emptiness of an abstract and undefinable beauty.

Manet was shortly to prove himself to be the painter of this modern life. He was already evolving compositions with subjects such as *The Old Musician* (*Le Vieux musicien*), *The Spanish Dancers* (*Le Ballet Espagnol*) and *Lola de Valence* which, although they were not the *actualités* of Guys, represented real people. Baudelaire considered Manet to "combine a vigorous taste for reality, modern reality – already a good sign – with an imagination

which is both abundant and lively . . . "

In 1859 the Salon had rejected Manet's *The Absinthe Drinker*, a painting of modern Paris in its cups, but had accepted the more innocuous *Spanish Singer* two years later. In 1862 he finished *Music in the Tuileries Gardens*, perhaps the first great painting of "modern life"; its subject matter was on one level completely up to date; the Parisian élite had recently abandoned the Palais-Royale Gardens for the Tuileries, which was larger and closer to their residences. Whether consciously or not, Manet was answering Baudelaire's call; and whilst he was working on the subject of modern life, Degas, Monet, Sisley, Renoir, Bazille, Pissarro, Guillaumin, Cézanne, and Berthe Morisot (who later married Manet's brother, Eugène, and was a very close friend of Manet himself) were also becoming painters of the modern world. Reluctantly Manet was becoming, if not the leader of this wave of artists, then the whipping boy for the sins they were poised to commit in the art world.

Music in the Tuileries Gardens is a painting central to the development of Impressionism in that it seems to embody almost by design the transitory, the fugitive, the constantly changing. It has little in practical terms to do with the increasing desire of Monet, Pissarro, Renoir, and Sisley to find a way of capturing, in Jules Laforgue's elegant words, "nature as she is, which is to say solely by means of coloured vibrations," but it opens up a whole new realm of the possible. It is the view of a fashionable *flâneur*, a stroller in the park taking in the scene, a montage of frozen moments of Parisians at their leisure. We are in the age of photography after all and Manet studied photographs for some of the heads. The painting conveys movement and colour with virtuosic brushstrokes, yet the lighting

MANET
Gypsy Woman Smoking a Cigarette
oil on canvas
c.1862. 91 × 73 cm
*This is probably what the Carmen
in Prosper Merrimé's original
story would have looked like.
However, Bizet's opera was not
performed before 1875.*

is flat, the background has been scraped and smeared with the palette knife to give the impression, and not much more, of foliage; the figures at the extreme edges are real people. Baudelaire himself is there as well as the poet Théophile Gautier, Fantin-Latour, the Inspector of Museums Baron Taylor, the sculptor and poet Zacharie Astruc, Eugène Manet and Offenbach. These people are easily discernable but the woman seated in the centre of the picture exists in a confusion of yellow and violet next to an enigmatic, two-dimensional tree.

Two paintings by Edgar Degas from this period, the *Young Spartans* and *The Gentlemen's Race: Before the Start*, both painted between 1860–1862 (and reworked in the 1880s) continued to answer the broad demands of Baudelaire, and of Edmond and Jules de Goncourt who sought "a line which would precisely render life, embrace from close at hand the individual, the particular, a living human, inward line . . . "

The Young Spartans (*Les Jeunes Spartiates*), despite its classical theme, avoids the stock classical motifs; there are no temples or plane tree groves, the sky is not an attic blue; most importantly the figures are not characterized as Greek, but are modelled on contemporary Parisian boys and girls. The achievement is that of a thoroughly modern history painting. *The Gentlemen's Race* – together with two others, *At the Races* (*Aux Courses*) and *At the Races: The Start* (*Aux Courses: Le Départ*) – reflect the Parisian passion for the new race-course which had opened at Longchamp in the Bois de Boulogne in 1857. The new track was a direct result of the rebuilding of Paris and presented a new venue for the *beau monde* to entertain itself; indeed some of Manet's and Degas' patrons were members of the Jockey Club which organized the races.

DEGAS
Derby Day
oil on canvas
c. 1860–62. 26.5 × 21.5 cm
ABOVE This small picture is reminiscent of English sporting prints of the day.

MANET
Races at Longchamp
oil on canvas
1864. 44 × 85 cm
RIGHT Longchamp was rapidly becoming an important social attraction for the wealthy bourgeois of Paris. Manet and Degas were frequent visitors.

JONGKIND
Entrance to the Port of Honfleur
oil on canvas
1864. 42 × 56 cm
Like Boudin, and later Monet, on
whom he was to have a great
influence, Jongkind was
primarily a self-taught painter
of sea and rivers based
in Normandy.

The new Paris being summoned into exist-ence by Napoleon III and Haussmann was admirably suited to the realization of Baude-laire's project. The increasing wealth and number of people who made up the middle classes, the proliferation of entertainments, the sheer novelty of the new streets and squares with their airy prospects, were the new reality which a painter of modern life had to subsume in his or her work. In retrospect, we can see that the work of Manet and Degas outdoors in the city, and that of the Gleyre students led by Monet, who were escaping Paris to paint in the nearby countryside, would eventually coincide. In his eloquent essay of 1883 Jules Laforgue formulates a definition of *plein-air* painting which declares that "the open air concept governs the entire work of Impressionist painters, and means the painting of beings and things in their appropriate atmosphere . . . " This is what, in a sense, Manet and Degas were already about as early as 1862, strolling through Paris and its environs, sketch-book in hand. In fact Degas' range of vision was much wider than that of Manet, his notebook revealing sub-jects which included mourners and the local undertakers.

PISSARRO
A Clearing in the Woods
oil on canvas
c.1864. 26.5 × 21 cm
*Although this is only a small
study, it is quite clear that the
artist had not yet found
his own style.*

At this early stage in the story of Impressionism, in a year when Monet, Renoir, Sisley, Cézanne, Guillaumin, Morisot, and Bazille were still in their early twenties and searching for something new, the influence on them of the *plein-airistes* and the Barbizon School was still to bear substantial fruit. Monet's links to an older generation of landscape painters increased when he met and became a lasting friend of Johan Jongkind, a Dutch artist whose work is linked to that of Corot, Courbet, and Monet's first real teacher, Boudin. Meanwhile Berthe Morisot, born the same year as Renoir and Bazille, and daughter of the Secretary-General of the Crédit Financier, was working under the encouragement of Corot. He was teaching her landscape painting in Fontainebleau and Auvers where she was in frequent contact with Daubigny whose absolute devotion to *plein-airisme* was uncompromising.

COROT
The Hamlet of Flesselles
oil on canvas
c.1862–65. 33 × 37.5 cm
Camille Corot was perhaps the most influential of the Barbizon painters on the younger landscapists, notably Pissarro, Morisot, Monet, and Renoir. His concern for rendering light and its effects in the landscape is of great importance in the prehistory of Impressionism.

DAUBIGNY
The Marsh at Sunset
oil on canvas
1861. 33 × 57 cm
Daubigny, a devout plein-airiste, *had built a studio-boat to be able to paint from the river, an example later followed by Monet. Some critics said that he produced nothing but sketches and that he was satisfied with a first impression. Others praised his "delicious naivety, simple as a child, adding nothing and removing nothing".*

. . . it is either a young man's idea of a joke, or it is a festering sore, unworthy of comment.

LOUIS ETIENNE, 1863

In 1863 the new railway line from Paris to Deauville was opened by the Duc de Morny, the internal combustion engine was invented, and in August, Eugène Delacroix, the source of so much colourful inspiration for the new artists, died. The 15th January was an ominous day for it marked the announcement by the Comte de Nieuwerkerke, the Director-General of National Museums, that the Salon (which had been held in the vast Palais de l'Industrie since the Exposition Universelle of 1855) was to be reorganized. For established artists, who had won medals at previous Salons, entry was now automatic as they did not have to pass the jury, but they were limited to three works each. The new rules were to present a serious blow to relative newcomers like Manet and Pissarro, whose work the jury was to reject later in the year.

Meanwhile Manet's first major exhibition went ahead at Louis Martinet's gallery in the boulevard des Italiens. It was here that *Music in the Tuileries Gardens* was first shown together with thirteen other paintings including *Lola de Valence* and *The Spanish Dancers*. The exhibition attracted the attention of Monet as well as Bazille who declared in a letter to his parents that one session spent looking at the Manets was worth a month of heavy work.

In April it was becoming clear that the Salon was making heavy work of its new rules. Of the 5,000 works which had been submitted, 2,783 had been rejected by the jury, led by a traditionalist of the history painting school, Emile Signol, who had once been furious with Renoir for using colour in the flamboyant style of Delacroix. In fact Delacroix and Ingres were members of the jury, but were not involved in the selection of works. All three of Manet's submissions, which included *Luncheon on the Grass* were refused entry to the exhibition.

The importance of being shown at the

MANET
Lola de Valence
oil on canvas
1862. 123 × 92 cm
Manet produced a series of Spanish pictures as the ballet company was touring Paris. He had never been to Spain at the time, and did not go there until 1865.

DAUMIER
The Pride of Having One's Portrait at the Salon
lithograph
1845. 26 × 17 cm
ABOVE Honoré Daumier is best known as a prolific and scathing caricaturist of political and artistic events in nineteenth-century Paris. His paintings of contemporary life form a less accomplished background to the work of Manet and Degas – Manet's teacher Thomas Couture had once warned his pupil that he would end up as a Daumier if he carried on in his usual irreverent fashion.

BAZILLE
The Pink Dress
oil on canvas
1864. 147 × 110 cm
LEFT This rich and finely-finished piece – also known as View of a Village *– shows just how much the twenty-three-year-old artist's technique and vision were beginning to mature.*

Eugènie – a more important patron, save the Emperor himself, could not be imagined – and had them rejected. The press seized upon the opportunity offered by the fiasco that the Salon was turning into, and the traditionalists as well as supporters of Manet and the younger artists demanded that something should be done. In the end the Emperor paid a visit to the Salon to judge for himself and, with his wife's rejected commission no doubt firmly in his mind, he too declared that something must be done. However, the jury refused to reconvene and the exhibition had in any case already been hung. On 24th April just three weeks before the opening of the Salon the following announcement appeared in the *Moniteur Universel*:

Numerous complaints have reached the Emperor on the subject of works of art which have been refused by the jury of the Exhibition. His Majesty, wishing to allow the public to judge the legitimacy of these complaints, has decided that the rejected works shall be exhibited in another part of the Palais de l'Industrie. This exhibition will be voluntary, and artists who do not wish to participate need only to inform the administration of the exhibition, which will hasten to return their works to them.

In a sense Napoleon III had pulled off another coup; this time he had succeeded in showing himself as an enlightened liberal ruler concerned with art and ready to listen to public opinion. The press enjoyed a field day on this issue not least because there were few other causes for them to champion under the strict regime of censorship that had then been imposed by the Emperor.

The new exhibition came to be known as

GÉRÔME
Christian Martyrs
oil on wood
1863–73. 88 × 150 cm
Gérôme was one of the most popular Salon artists of his day. His taste and technique in classical and biblical subjects was not shared by the Impressionists.

Salon for artists at this time cannot be underestimated. There were certainly well over a hundred independent galleries like Martinet's, but the Salon was the only marketplace with an assured audience of thousands; *le tout Paris* would be certain to be there, and failure to show at it meant another year without significant exposure to the public, the commissioning authorities, the dealers, and the critics. Although Manet had been rejected before, in 1857 and 1859, he was well aware of the benefits of appearing at the Salon and continued to strive to be accepted there as did the younger artists such as Monet and Renoir. To make things worse, several regular exhibitors had also fallen at the new hurdles, artists with official commissions already behind them who would in the normal course of events be expected to show at the Salon. One artist had even submitted works done for the Empress

MEISSONIER
French Campaign, Napoleon
oil on canvas
1864. 49 × 75 cm
*BELOW Edifying subjects, whether
religious or heroic or both, were
the staple diet of the Salon during
the second half of the century.*

CABANEL
Birth of Venus
oil on canvas
1863. 130 × 225 cm
*ABOVE LEFT The star of the
official 1863 Salon, Cabanel's
Venus embodies perfectly all that
Manet, Degas and the nascent
Impressionists were trying to
avoid. The highly finished,
quintessentially classical
composition with its hint of
eroticism was bought by Napoleon
III. On show next door in the
Salon des Refusés Manet's
frankly realist* Luncheon on
the Grass *drew outrage
and condemnation.*

the Salon des Refusés, and, when it opened its doors directly adjacent to the Salon proper on 17th May, over 10,000 people came to marvel at it. Amongst the jumble of paintings which had been hung with no particular order or care (of course many pictures which deserved to be rejected were on show) were two which caused an especially violent reaction, James McNeill Whistler's *White Girl* which had previously been rejected by the Royal Academy in London, and Manet's *Luncheon on the Grass*. Whistler's painting was ridiculed by many whilst "Manet in the furthest hall," as the *refusé* Jean-Charles Cazin observed, "went right through the wall with his *Luncheon on the Grass*." If *Music in the Tuileries Gardens* had caused a positive stir amongst his fellow artists and the Spanish paintings had delighted the public, *Luncheon on the Grass* was an instant *succès de scandale*.

Manet's technique aside, the general public was outraged at the depiction of a female nude together with two clothed young bourgeois, and Napoleon III pronounced it to be an offence against modesty. (The Emperor was not too modest however to purchase Alexandre Cabanel's studiously academic but erotic *Birth of Venus* (*La Naissance de Vénus*), which was on show in the official Salon next door to the *refusés*.) Zola defended the picture by drawing attention to the fact that there were several paintings in the Louvre with clothed and nude figures. Zacharie Astruc also leapt to Manet's defence, going so far as to publish a newspaper *Le Salon de 1863* which called Manet "one of the greatest artistic characters of the time," lauding his work for "brilliance, inspiration, power, flavour, surprise." Manet professed himself to be distressed by all this attention, complaining to his friend Baudelaire that abuse was raining down on him like hail.

Manet's painting had ultimately derived from a work of 1510–11 in the Louvre (by Titian, Giorgione, or both) known as *La Fête champêtre*; it also had a respectable precedent in an engraving by Marcantonio after Raphael. Yet the flat yellowish lighting on the central nude depicts her without a trace of the customary *pudeur* so obvious and conventionally appealing in Cabanel's pinkly suffused Venus, the star of the "official" Salon. One critic, Théophile Burger, a friend of Baudelaire's "[failed] to see what could have induced a distinguished and intelligent artist to adopt such an absurd composition." But he admitted that "there are qualities of colour and light in the landscape, and indeed some very fine passages of modelling in the torso." These fine passages were passed over in a pamphlet by Louis Etienne who pronounced what was on everyone's mind, describing the painting as:

A nonchalant *bréda* [a prostitute] . . . completely naked, impudently lounges between two dandies dressed up to the nines. They give the impression of two students on holiday who are behaving outrageously, to try and give the impression of real men . . . It is either a young man's idea of a joke, or it is a festering sore, unworthy of comment.

The prostitute in Manet's painting is referred to by Etienne as a *bréda* after the rue Bréda in the Batignolles district of Paris where the women worked. At the time of the Salon des Refusés Manet lived and worked nearby. It

MONET
Spring Flowers
oil on canvas
1864. 117 × 89 cm
*This early piece proves that Monet
was able to produce commercially
accessible work.*

was in the Café Guerbois at 11 Grande rue des Batignolles that a group of like-minded artists and intellectuals, amongst them Manet, Monet, Pissarro, Bazille, Degas, Renoir, Zola, and Nadar would meet in the coming years to discuss their life and work. They became known as the Batignolles Group.

Zola's view, fortunately the one that has prevailed, was that:

> What you have to look for in the picture is not just the picnic on the grass, but the whole landscape with its bold and subtle passages, its broadly painted, solid foreground, its light and delicate background and that firm flesh modelled in broad areas of light, those supple and strong pigments, and, particularly, that delicate splash of white among the green leaves in the background; in fact to look at the whole of this vast, airy composition, at this attention to nature, rendered with such accurate simplicity.

Festering sore or airy composition, *Luncheon on the Grass* pushed modern life into the Salon and out into the world even though it was literally and figuratively one of the *peintures refusées*. Nowadays we find it extremely difficult to find anything scandalous in this picture, but at the time nudes were only acceptable in certain highly stylized and sanitized forms like Cabanel's. The "real thing" was wholly intolerable.

One more event was to cause uproar that year. In a decree dated 13th November the government announced sweeping reforms of the Ecole des Beaux-Arts, removing it from the control of the Académie des Beaux-Arts, installing a system of ateliers to teach painting within the Ecole which had previously only taught drawing, and abolishing several important competitions, one of which was the Prix de Paysage Historique. Many of the Barbizon landscapists had taken part in the competition; Rousseau and Daubigny had both attempted it and, as art historian Albert Boime points out, Corot and Gleyre had trained their students to compete for it whilst Monet and Sisley were both interested in it. The government had decreed the reforms partly under the pretext that they would foster more originality, but they were popular with neither the Académie nor the students, who feared they would no longer be able to choose which master they worked under in preparation for the Ecole. Sisley was one of those who signed a petition protesting against the changes, proving, according to Albert Boime, that the group of students of Gleyre's atelier had not yet relinquished hope of official recognition through the Ecole's competition structure and the official Salon to which they still aspired, despite the success of the Salon des Refusés.

1864–1866: "OLYMPIA WAKES"

In 1864 the Duc de Morny, who organized the building of a coastal resort at Deauville and connected it to Paris with a railway line so that affluent Parisians could take advantage of it, inaugurated the new race track there. Nothing was unusual about this commonplace development in an era of rapid industrial and economic expansion in France. It is simply another example of the new middle-class prosperity and (expensive) free time which many could now spend in a variety of pursuits. That year the first international victory at Longchamp by a French racehorse was celebrated. Speed was of the moment; the railway had already revolutionized travel and

FANTIN-LATOUR
Flowers and Fruit
oil on canvas
1865. 64 × 57 cm
LEFT Fantin-Latour's paintings of flowers sold particularly well in London where he was seen as the highly desirable face of French art.

MANET
Peonies
oil on canvas
1864. 38 × 46.5 cm
BELOW Manet produced still lifes throughout his career, but no painter could rival Fantin-Latour for the popularity of his flower pieces.

was helping France on its way to becoming a major industrial power.

The Second Empire was attempting to extend its power base in other ways too; in Mexico Napoleon III installed Maximilian of Austria as the puppet ruler, but like so much of the Emperor's foreign policy, this was to prove a disastrous chimera. Meanwhile, Eugène Chevreul published his second work on colour, and Charles Gleyre was forced to close down his atelier due to failing health and lack of funds. In the summer Morisot, Renoir, and Pissarro had work accepted at the Salon which was now to be run annually. Manet, however, was rejected and out of the limelight for a year.

With the demise of Gleyre's atelier, Monet and his friends took off to the country to

FANTIN-LATOUR
Tannhäuser on the Venusberg
oil on canvas
1864. 98 × 130 cm
Fantin-Latour had discovered
Wagner the previous year.
Tannhäuser failed in Paris but
Fantin-Latour adored the music
of Wagner and Berlioz, an
enthusiasm shared by Bazille.

paint. In the early spring Monet had been working in and around Fontainebleau with Renoir and Sisley. That summer Monet returned to the Normandy coast at a farm near Honfleur, where Bazille, Boudin, and Jongkind later joined him. Bazille had returned to Paris when Monet wrote to him from Honfleur, entreating him to come back to the country and declaring that:

It really is appallingly difficult to do something which is complete in every way, and I think most people are content with mere approximations . . . I intend to battle on, scrape off, and start again . . . and when I look at nature I feel as if I'll be able to paint it all, note it all down . . . it's on the strength of observation and reflection that one finds a way. So we must dig and delve unceasingly.

The influence of Boudin and especially Jongkind is clearly evident in Monet's work from this early period. He even admitted to touches of Corot in some of the landscapes he was producing near Honfleur. But *Rue de la Barolle* and *Farmyard in Normandy* (*La Ferme Normande*), both painted at this time, display the beginnings of his rapidly developing technique. At this point he was producing work at a phenomenal rate and he continued to do so for the rest of his life; his head was, as he wrote to Bazille in July 1864, "bursting with the desire to paint." This was just as well, for he lived on the edge of destitution and often had to call on friends like Bazille to help him out of financial difficulties. His diligence paid off in the next year's Salon where two works were accepted, along with Degas' first

successful submission and what proved to be his last history painting, *Scene of War in the Middle Ages* (*Scène de guerre au Moyen Age*).

Monet showed two seascapes at the Salon of 1865, *The Mouth of the Seine at Honfleur* (*L'Embouchure de la Seine à Honfleur*) and *Pointe de la Hève at Low Tide* (*Pointe de la Hève à marée basse*). In both the influence of Jongkind and Boudin is evident, but the critic Gallet was moved to describe Monet as "a young realist who promises much. His two seascapes . . . display the work of a powerful hand uninterested in prettiness and greatly preoccupied with accuracy of effect." Another critic, Victor Fournel, offered a withering dismissal: "What is there to say, for instance, about this *Mouth of the Seine at Honfleur*? The waves are represented by

DEGAS
Study for A Scene of War in the Middle Ages
pencil on paper
1865. 35.5 × 22 cm
ABOVE Degas rigorously followed the tradition of drawing nude figures before painting them clothed in order to obtain accurate volumes.

DEGAS
Study for A Scene of War in the Middle Ages
black chalk on paper
1865. 26.5 × 31.5 cm
LEFT Degas' studies were always carefully worked towards the finished painting; he left nothing to chance, a trait which kept him stylistically apart from the mainstream of Impressionism.

CARAVAGGIO
Ecce Homo
oil on canvas
1606. 128 × 103 cm
*FAR RIGHT Caravaggio's
naturalism was considered
outrageous at a time when most
subjects were idealized and
sanitized; Manet suffered the
same fate.*

MANET
Christ Mocked by the Soldiers
oil on canvas
1865. 191.5 × 148.5 cm
*RIGHT "You are the foremost in
the decrepitude of your art",
Baudelaire wrote in a vitriolic
vein to an extremely unhappy
Manet after the scandal of
Olympia and Christ Mocked
had broken at the Salon. Both
paintings were taken down from
their prominent position and
rehung in the darkest corner of
Room M.*

lumps of earth, the sails of the boats by triangles of black wood: one might well think it had been scrawled by a child of twelve on the cover of his Sunday school book." But both Monet and Degas, as well as Pissarro, who was again successful at the Salon, were to be overshadowed by Edouard Manet and his *Olympia*.

Earlier in 1865 Manet had again exhibited at the Galerie Martinet to some acclaim. In May the Salon opened to a hysterical onslaught. The objects of the critics' scorn and the public's distaste were Manet's two submissions, *Christ Mocked by the Soldiers*

(*Jésus insulté par les soldats*) and *Olympia*. Hanging together, they attracted crowds of curious viewers. The critic Victor de Jankovitz waxed sardonic: "Thanks to his brushwork, *Christ Mocked* by M. Manet, is a picture beneath all criticism. It is Raphael as corrected by a third-rate Courbet." *Christ Mocked by the Soldiers* came away from its confrontation with the critics fairly unscathed in comparison with *Olympia*. Gentlewomen were said to have averted their eyes from the shameful sight. Nevertheless they and their gentlemen-folk crushed into Room M to assure themselves of the veracity of the shocking reports.

Olympia's notoriety quickly transcended that of *Luncheon on the Grass* which, it should be remembered, had been shown outside the official Salon as a work which had been rejected as being unworthy of recognition. The Salon catalogue entry for the painting carried the following verse by the painter's friend Zacharie Astruc:

INGRES
Sleeping Odalisque
oil on canvas
1829. 30 × 47.5 cm
*It might be that Ingres' nude is
more provocative and erotic than
Olympia, but nevertheless she is
devoid of the plain everyday look
of Manet's model, too easily linked
to prostitution by a hypocritical
bourgeois society.*

When, weary of dreaming, Olympia
    wakes,
Springtime arrives in the arms of a
    gentle black envoy;
It is the slave, like unto a night of
    passion,
Who comes to make the day bloom, a
    delight to behold;
The august young girl in whom the
    flame burns.

Everything about the painting – the disposition of its subject, her dishevelled sheets and her scant accoutrements, the black maid, the little black cat, the flowers, the technique, with some passages finely modelled and some blocked in with broad sweeps of the brush – conspired to confuse and dismay its viewers. There was little doubt that this was another *bréda*, a prostitute, weary, not from dreaming, but from a night of work. Paris was awash with prostitutes; from the poorest streetwalker in the rue Bréda to the richest *courtesane*, lavishly entertaining in apartments along the *grands boulevards*. But painting them, other than in the enciphered form of a Venus or some demi-goddess, was unheard of until the first Salon des Refusés and now *Olympia*. Manet had liberated a new territory which others, Degas in particular, were later able to exploit with more or less impunity. Directly based on a pose much used by sixteenth-century Italian painters, the English painter Peter Lely, and eighteenth-century French artists such as François Boucher, *Olympia* did not try to charm the public. Here was a real woman, unashamed, addressing the viewer directly and without pretence or any attempt at seduction.

The Second Empire was all artifice. Away from the massive façades of the new Paris designed by Haussmann, half of the population, which Haussmann himself had described as "living in poverty bordering on destitution," was in the process of being relocated to featureless *faubourgs* (suburbs) or concentrated into areas like Belleville. It is significant that one critic openly described Olympia as *une petite faubourienne*, which is to say a common working-class girl, not as *une cocotte*, the euphemism most commonly used. The hypocrisy of the time may appear to be staggering, but it was a hypocrisy which tolerated its *courtesanes* as long as they hovered above the dirt and grime of reality. Manet broke the silence in this respect so thoroughly that, as T.J. Clark has penetratingly observed, it caused a crisis in the language of art criticism itself. Far from being lost for

words, the arbiters of the nation's taste, from the meanest hack to the loftiest intellectual, were volubly falling over each other to avoid describing *Olympia* in traditional terms. Whilst they were busy likening Olympia's skin to India rubber, all but two of them could not or would not see the obvious reference to Titian's *Venus of Urbino* which Manet had once copied in oil at the Uffizi in Florence. The irony of calling a *faubourienne* "Olympia" was not however lost on them; any one of the several licensed brothels in Paris would have offered up a number of women working under the classical *noms de guerre* of Olympia, Lucretia, Calliope or the most popular, Virginia. The chief problem for the critics and public alike was that *Olympia* had appeared *dans le Salon-même*, and this had stretched their tolerance beyond reason and their reason beyond tolerance. The

TITIAN
The Venus of Urbino
oil on canvas
c.1538. 120 × 165 cm
An archetype for Olympia. *The compositional similarities between this and Manet's painting are obvious.*

outcry against the painting and its companion *Christ Mocked* was so great that they were eventually both removed to the furthest, darkest corner of the huge Palais de l'Industrie. Manet's fame (or infamy) was assured for the rest of his life. His position as the reluctant champion of the new artists of modern life was affirmed once and for all.

In the world at large life and death went on: across the Atlantic Ocean in the United States President Abraham Lincoln was assassinated, in Paris the First Communist International was held and in England a young mathematics don at Christchurch College Oxford, published a story called *Alice in Wonderland*, under the pseudonym of Lewis Carroll.

Encouraged by his own reception at the Salon, albeit mixed, and the example of Manet, Claude Monet had embarked in 1865 on his own monumental *Luncheon on the Grass*,

obviously intended to make a much bigger splash in the Paris art world. Sadly the painting was abandoned in March 1866, when the deadline for that year's Salon expired, and survives only in fragments and an oil sketch of what was once a vast picture almost fifteen feet high by twenty feet wide. Monet left the canvas in Bazille's studio for years as security against unpaid rent before he reclaimed it, by which time part of it had gone mouldy. Monet removed this portion and cut the remainder into two sections. The sketch for the painting indicates that Monet's conception was for a major *plein-air* work, using the relatively novel idea of figures sketched on the spot; these included Sisley, Bazille, and Monet's mistress, Camille Doncieux. By all accounts Monet was obsessed with the massive project and spent the whole of the summer of 1865, as the *Olympia* scandal raged

MANET
Olympia
oil on canvas
1863. 130.5 × 190 cm
This painting caused a storm verging on outrage at the Salon of 1865, and established Manet's reputation and fame, though not, perhaps, in the way he had immediately hoped. It has been referred to as a turning point in the history of modern art, combining with Luncheon on the Grass *to entirely subvert the traditional artistic view of the nude, as it was previously encapsulated in the Titian opposite.*

MONET
Luncheon on the Grass
oil on canvas
1865–66. 130 × 181 cm
A sketch of the unfinished work.

in Paris, devoted to it. He frequently begged Bazille by post to come down to the forest of Fontainebleau and sit for him. Throughout his work on the painting Monet was harrassed: firstly he was hampered by an injury to his leg in 1865 and then, having moved to Bazille's Paris studio in order to finish the picture for the 1866 Salon, he was forced to leave the studio and move across the river to another. Unable to complete the painting,

Monet furiously produced (in four days) a full-length portrait of Camille known as *The Woman in the Green Dress (Femme en vert)*, which in turn proved a success at the Salon.

Luncheon on the Grass was a prodigious undertaking in every respect; and as Andrew Forge has suggested, "It was something as different from Courbet's earthy social analysis as it was from Manet's sophisticated reflections on the erotic in modern life.

Monet was trying to present on an exhibition scale that particular area of painting that was specific to the direct study. He was trying to monumentalize the syntax of a sketch."

Undaunted by his failure to complete *Luncheon on the Grass*, in early 1866 Monet embarked on another large picture, nine feet by six feet in size, the *Women in the Garden* (*Femmes dans un jardin*). He had rented a house near Paris and dug a trench for the painting to be lowered into by pulleys so that he could work without moving his position relative to the subjects in front of him. The idea, ridiculed by Courbet, was to complete the whole picture *en plein-air*. The painting was finished but the Salon of 1867 rejected it, a bitter blow to Monet.

THE BATIGNOLLES GROUP

The year 1866 saw the invention of dynamite by Alfred Nobel. In France Napoleon III ordered the withdrawal of his forces from Mexico, a move that was to have disastrous consequences for the puppet Emperor Maximilian. In his own salvo of explosive prose, Zola published an article entitled "Mon Salon en L'Evènement" defending the work of Cézanne, Bazille, Monet, and Pissarro and supporting a letter Cézanne had written to the Comte de Nieuwerkerke demanding another Salon des Refusés. In it Cézanne had felt obliged to "content myself with pointing out to you again that I cannot accept the unlawful judgement of colleagues to whom I have not personally given the task of assessing me . . . I wish to make a direct appeal to the public and have my work exhibited without any restriction."

A complex network of relationships between Monet, Pissarro, Bazille, Cézanne, Guillaumin, Morisot, Renoir, Sisley, Manet,

MONET
Women in the Garden
oil on canvas
1865–66. 418 × 150 cm
This is Monet's last attempt at a large-scale figure composition. Two possible sources for the picture's inspiration are thought to have been a photograph of his friend Bazille's sisters and a costume illustration from a fashion magazine. Camille posed for no less than three of the figures.

and Degas had already begun to form by this point. During the private view of the 1866 Salon Monet and Bazille had encountered Manet and his entourage leaving the exhibition. Monet's signature on his *Woman in the Green Dress* had been mistaken for Manet's, who had entered the Salon to a chorus of acclaim for his supposed work. Monet recounted the story in 1900 to *Le Temps*:

. . . imagine his consternation when he discovered that the picture about which he was being congratulated was actually by me! The saddest part of all was that on leaving the Salon he came across a group which included Bazille and me. "How goes it?" one of them asked. "Awful," replied Manet, "I am digusted. I have been complimented on a painting which is not mine."

MONET
Quays of Paris
oil on canvas
1866–67. 66 × 94 cm
*RIGHT The Impressionists took
quickly to painting cityscapes from
windows high above the streets.
Apart from the interesting
perspective such a position
offered, it was certainly much
more comfortable than painting
outdoors and they were not
disturbed by passers-by.*

DEGAS
Woman with Chrysanthemums
oil on canvas
1865. 71 × 92 cm
*ABOVE Although he used a
photograph to make this picture,
Degas also made exhaustive
preliminary studies from life.*

The next day Manet is supposed to have refused to be introduced to Monet because he was still bitter about Monet's purely unintentional slight on the young master. But as Monet recalled:

> It was only in 1869 that I saw him again, and then we at once became firm friends. At our first meeting he invited me to join him every evening at a café in the Batignolles district where he and his friends gathered at the end of the day to talk. There I met Fantin-Latour, Cézanne, Degas . . . the art critic Duranty, Emile Zola and many others. For my part I used to take Sisley, Bazille, and Renoir there. Nothing could have been more interesting than the discussions we had, with their perpetual clash of opinions. They kept our wits sharpened, encouraged us to press ahead with our own experiments, and provided us with the enthusiasm to keep on painting for weeks on end until our ideas became clear and coherent . . . we emerged more finely tempered, our resolve firmer, our thoughts clearer and less confused.

1866 marks the beginnings of what came to be known as the Batignolles Group. Whilst Monet, Bazille, Renoir, Sisley, and Pissarro were working in the country, the Batignolles area of Paris was becoming a focus of artistic attention. During Haussmannization this area of Paris had expanded greatly, along with the large new boulevard des Batignolles. Between 1842 and 1866 the population of the district had increased from 15,000 to 200,000. Its position away from the centre of the city but close to the Gare St Lazare made it

PISSARRO
The Railway Bridge at Pontoise
oil on canvas
c.1865. 50 × 65 cm
*Pissarro and his family moved to
live in Pontoise, a village on the
river Oise (seen here) near
Auvers, in 1867, about two years
after this picture was painted.*

popular. The buildings were modern, comfortably bourgeois and the area had become residential but still affordable. A letter of Renoir's to his parents a couple of years later when he and Bazille lived in the rue de la Paix confirms this, "Tell Mama not to worry, the Batignolles is a quiet area and cheaper than the rest of Paris."

Parts of the old village of Batignolles remained, populated by poor immigrants, rag-pickers, and prostitutes, amongst whom Manet found some of his subjects and models. Manet had lived there for some time at various addresses and had recently begun to haunt the Café Guerbois at 11 rue des Batignolles. During the next three years practically everyone of importance to Impressionism began to gather there in the evenings – Thursday nights were the favourite – to talk about art and literature. If Gleyre's atelier had been the nursery of the *plein-air* Impressionists, the Café Guerbois was undoubtedly its common room. Anyone looking for the artistic avant-garde in Paris would need go no further than the Café Guerbois, one of many cafés that had sprung up in the new Paris of wide pavements and rolling boulevards. Manet was certainly the first amongst his peers and held court with aplomb. The writer and critic of Impressionism Armand Silvestre described Manet as a revolutionary with the manners of a perfect gentleman: "he had in the extraordinary vivacity of his gaze and the mocking expression on his lips a very strong dose of the Parisian street urchin. He had a marvellous command of the annihilating and

devastating phrase." Yet he still yearned for official recognition.

1867–1868: LA VILLE LUMIÈRE

The year 1867 brought with it crisis for the Second Empire. Since the proclamation of Napoleon III as Emperor in 1852 France had spent itself into a prosperity that was in essence conservative and favoured the middle and upper classes. The new boulevards and buildings of Paris were symbolic of this prosperity, as were the resorts springing up on the Normandy coast. But they had all been constructed on credit and the equivalent of

BELOW Birds-eye view of the World Exhibition of 1867.

RENOIR
The Park of St Cloud
oil on canvas
1866. 50 × 61 cm
RIGHT An early, surprisingly impressionistic painting by Renoir painted three years before the work with Monet at La Grenouillère.

the modern junk bond. In 1866 the Crédit Mobilier, which had financed a great part of the new Empire, found itself with a monumental liquidity problem. Its shares fell the next year from 1,982 francs to just 140 francs. The Mexican fiasco ended with the death of Maximilian who was abandoned by the French and executed by rebels. Manet, who rightly saw this crisis as a failure of imperial politics, began a painting of the execution, making use of photographs, but also basing part of its composition on Goya's *The Third of May* which he had seen in Madrid in 1865. He was given to understand by the Salon that it would not be admitted on the grounds of its political sensitivity. A lithograph of the picture was officially banned by the censors.

Elsewhere in the world tensions ran high. In an attempt to help the Papal States French battalions were dispatched to Rome to defend them against the revolutionary Garibaldi. As usual relations with Prussia were tense. In January Napoleon III had announced constitutional changes with a move towards representative government for the Empire, but it was to be of no avail. The American Civil War had disrupted cotton trade, and the vineyards were suffering from the phylloxera disease which had appeared in 1863 and taken hold, steadily reducing the crop. The outward success of the Second Empire had, as Alastair Horne claims, "blinded French eyes to the realities beneath the surface. Syphilis was rampant and many of the great Frenchmen of the age were to die of it; Maupassant, Jules Goncourt, Dumas *fils*, Baudelaire [in 1867], and Manet. The dread disease was symptomatic of the Second Empire itself; on the surface, all gaiety and light; below, sombre purulence, decay, and ultimately death."

MANET
The Execution of the Emperor Maximilian
Left Manet was making a habit at this time of challenging the sensibilities of the Salon, which took the precaution of telling him well in advance that this painting would not even be considered due to its political content. Manet drew inspiration for the work from Goya's The Third of May, *which he had seen in Madrid.*

GOYA
The Third of May
oil on canvas
1814. 266 × 345 cm
Below

MONET
The Garden of the Princess
oil on canvas
1867. 92 × 62 cm
ABOVE This was one of three works that the Louvre allowed Monet to paint on its balcony. It shows the influence of photography in the angle of the view and the seemingly arbitrary points at which the subject is cut off by its framing.

MANET
The World's Fair in Paris
oil on canvas
1867. 108 × 196 cm
RIGHT Manet's picture shows a cross-section of Parisian society, from the gentlewoman on her morning ride, to the lower-class figures on the grass. Nadar's famous balloon hovers above the scene.

A visitor to Paris in the summer of 1867, and there were thousands, would have been hard pressed to believe all this doom, for the second Exposition Universelle had taken over a city which was already crammed with hundreds of theatres and cafés, all full of Parisians enjoying themselves. Visitors to the Prussian display of armaments marvelled at the Krupp artillery pieces. The implements of modern warfare certainly looked impressive and if the French had taken more stock of them they might have thought twice about engaging the Prussians in battle a couple of years later. A picture by Manet painted at the time, *View of the Paris World's Fair (Vue de Paris pendant l'Exposition Universelle)* shows the French and English lighthouses erected for the Fair and the photographer Nadar's balloon, known as "The Giant", hovering over the city. Renoir's *Champs-Elysées during the Paris Fair of 1867 (Les Champs-Elysées pendant l'Exposition Universelle de 1867)* depicts leisurely strollers; the women wear summer dresses, the sky is temptingly blue with fluffy clouds. In the background a *tricouleur* flies over the Palais de l'Industrie which had been built for the previous Exposition Universelle when Pissarro had marvelled at the Corots and when Courbet's Realist Pavilion had challenged the establishment.

The same was to occur in 1867. Again Courbet erected a pavilion to rival the official Salon, and Manet, who had boycotted the Salon in disgust at having been rejected again, did the same. Pressure for another Salon des Refusés was strong: Monet, Renoir, Pissarro, Sisley, Jongkind, Manet, and Daubigny had all signed a petition to the authorities requesting one, but the *refusés* request was rejected. Unfortunately, Manet's pavilion did scant business. Times were getting harder for the avant-garde painters. The arbitrariness of the Salon juries who changed their views on what was acceptable from year to year was a cause of intense frustration. In May Bazille had written to his parents outlining a plan which had emerged among the group to:

> . . . rent a big studio every year where we will be able to show as many of our paintings as we want. We will invite the painters we like to send paintings. Courbet, Corot, Diaz, Daubigny and many others with whom you may not be familiar have promised to send their work and strongly approve of the idea. With the latter, and Monet who is better than all of us, we are sure to succeed.

The plan came to nothing; the funds to mount the exhibition could not be found amongst the contributors, but this was essentially the first attempt to launch the *Société anonyme des artistes peintres, sculpteurs, graveurs, etc*, which upstaged the Salon of 1874.

In the meantime Claude Monet had gained permission from the Louvre to paint from one of its second floor balconies. One of the three pictures that resulted is the *Garden of the Princess* (*Le Jardin de la princesse*). This, and the views of the *Quai du Louvre*, and *Saint-Germain l'Auxerrois* mark what Forge has called "crucial experiments in which [Monet] seems to be pushing the principles of Realism to their furthest limits." The *Garden of the Princess* indicates a new vision of the city using the technique Monet had been developing in his landscapes and the two large-scale figure paintings. The angle of the view shows the influence of the framing and distortive effects of photography which tend to "wrap" the field of vision at the edges and cut off the composition at arbitrary points producing a vertiginous sense of height, distance, and space. Monet's landscapist's eye, however, shows the crowds down below as a mobile element of the cityscape rendered with the

MONET
Beach at Sainte-Adresse
oil on canvas
c.1867. 75 × 101 cm
Monet never tired of painting the coast of Normandy in his youth and he worked along this stretch of coastline nearly all his life.

swift brushstrokes later to be denounced as "tongue-lickings". The much altered topography of Paris attracted many of Monet's friends. They could also hope to sell paintings of the new Haussmann boulevards which were not controversial subjects.

Visitors to the Exposition Universelle were seduced and intrigued that year by the exhibition of Japanese prints and artefacts which soon launched an enduring fashion for all things Japanese. Many artists were influenced by the composition of these prints, especially Degas, like Whistler before him. Japanese prints had trickled in to Europe from the 1850s, mainly used to wrap artefacts.

RENOIR
Rose Field
oil on canvas
Undated. 33 × 46.5 cm
*RIGHT Renoir's loose style
was at the vanguard of
Impressionism, but the artist later
found that it was too limiting.*

RENOIR
Le Pont des Arts, Paris
oil on canvas
1867. 62 × 100 cm
*ABOVE This was the new Paris
with the recently cleared
embankments where houses had
stood before.*

Following several centuries of seclusion, at last Japan opened its doors to the West in 1867, and two shops in Paris were selling this new exotica. The studios of Whistler, Manet, Degas, and Monet were graced with Japanese china, fans, and prints, and these feature in several later paintings. Castagnary even called the Batignolles Group "the Japanese of painting". Monet said, that "[the Japanese] refinement of taste has always pleased me, and I approve of their aesthetic doctrine which evokes the presence of something by a shadow; and the whole by means of a fragment." Degas' work was increasingly reinforced by the Japanese print masters' sense of space and (to Western eyes) unusual perspectives and framings, as well as their subject matter which was often urban and refined. This new view was much in keeping with Degas' artistic interests.

Napoleon III's last years in power were marked by an increasing desire on his part to free up the country's moribund political and social system. Accordingly, in 1868 new laws allowed limited freedom of the press and the right to assembly for the first time since the First Republic. In a move symptomatic of the decline of the Second Empire, Baron Haussmann was forced to approach the ruling Legislative Body and request a loan to pay for the rebuilding of Paris which amounted to a quarter of the whole French budget. Haussmann was almost finished, but so was Paris.

Manet, Degas, Morisot, Pissarro, Monet, Sisley, and Bazille all made it into the Salon of 1868 after the dismal failure of the previous year and they had François Daubigny to thank because he had been invited to sit on the jury. Daubigny's inclusion was a sign that *plein-airisme* had finally been accepted by the Salon as a legitimate method of painting, although this did not make it any easier for the avant-garde. To artists like Manet, Bazille, and Degas, who were reasonably wealthy, not selling their work did not ultimately mean starvation.

Monet himself had none of the luxuries of a Manet or a Bazille; he was forced to sell or starve, and since he had few buyers in the late 1860s the latter fate stared him and his wife relentlessly in the face. In 1867 he had been forced by his family (on whom he relied for an allowance) to abandon Camille, then pregnant with a son, Jean. In June 1868 Monet had to ask Bazille (once again) to help him out by sending Camille some money to support herself and the child. In his begging letter he signs himself, "Your loyal and tormented friend," and adds curtly and ominously, "I was so upset yesterday that I was foolish enough to throw myself into the water. Fortunately no harm was done." It seems that Monet was too much in love with painting and life to make a serious attempt at suicide even though his despair was deep.

Despite the collapse of the Crédit Foncier and Haussmann's exorbitant claims on the national budget, *la ville lumière* thrived. Paris in the early part of 1868 was depicted with increasing acuity and originality by artists. Degas, the most consistent of the "slice of life" painters, spent all of his time in the streets, cafés, theatres, and concert halls of the city; noting, sketching, and observing with a sharp eye the effervescent activity around him. Not a *plein-airiste* by any stretch of the imagination, he composed his pictures very

DEGAS
Orchestra of the Paris Opera
oil on canvas
1868–69. 56.5 × 46 cm
A fine example of the new theory of composition that the Impressionists were beginning to shape. The figures are caught as though in a photograph – cut off at seemingly random points, and standing at odd angles to the artist. This is very different from the highly stylized, carefully posed, and fully framed tableaux of the classical schools, and represented a radical departure.

carefully *post hoc* in the studio. His *Orchestra of the Paris Opera* (*L'Orchestre de l'Opéra de Paris*) of 1868–69 is an excellent example of both his devotion to Ingres, his finely detailed technique and a thoroughly modern sense of composition: again the influence of photography is evident, with the figures cropped by the edges of the painting and the double-bassist turning his back to us looking at a conductor "out of shot". One of the second violinists is even captured gazing up at the incandescent tutus of the ballerinas, obviously bored with his part.

Away from the bustle of the city, Bazille was succeeding to a great extent in meshing the forms of landscape and figure painting which had been started and abandoned by Monet. *View of the Village* (*Paysage avec un village*) and *The Family Reunion* (*La Réunion de*

MANET
Study for The Balcony
pencil and wash on paper
1868.
BELOW Manet was a diligent technician, and spent endless days in the Louvre copying the works of the great masters when he was a student at Couture's atelier. His wish to evolve from the masters, rather than to reject them, is reflected here in his use of the classical methodology of producing a careful study for a larger work.

MANET
The Balcony
oil on canvas
1868–69. 170 × 124 cm
RIGHT Berthe Morisot had met Manet two months before she posed for this painting. Their friendship lasted till his death in 1883.

Famille) show the influence of Manet and Monet, but taking a firm grip on the elements of the pictures. Bazille is especially fearless in the use of bright colours applied in flat areas. Berthe Morisot said of the *View*, "He is seeking what we have all so often sought: how to place a figure in outdoor surroundings. This time I think he has succeeded."

Whilst Monet, Renoir, Bazille, and Sisley had been working in and around Paris and on the coast, Camille Pissarro, (older than them by ten years and yet stylistically much more a part of their generation than Manet or Degas), had been living in Pontoise, a town to the northwest of Paris where in 1866 he had settled with his mistress, Julie Vellay. His frequent visits to Paris included the Café Guerbois where he expressed himself openly and eloquently in matters of art and politics: he was a radical republican, an anarchist in fact. Thanks to Daubigny two of Pissarro's views of the *Hermitage at Pontoise* (*L'Ermitage à Pontoise*) were shown at the Salons of 1868 and 1869. They were attacked as being vulgar, coarse, primitive daubings. The paint is certainly applied with vigour and Pissarro's denial of detail and his concentration on structure using planes of colour prefigures the later work of Cézanne. But Zola considered that "the originality here is deeply human, not derived from a mere facility of hand or a falsification of nature: it stems from the temperament of the painter himself and comprises a feeling for truth resulting from an inner conviction."

1869: "ROTTEN SKETCHES"

The French elections of May 1869 produced a massive upsurge of support for the opposition parties – mostly varying shades of republicanism. Government control of the Legislative Body was sharply reduced and the Prime Minister was forced to resign. Haussmann's fortunes continued to wane as his opponents questioned the exorbitantly high cost of his rebuilding of Paris. Napoleon III's "Liberal Empire" was in its last days. A left-wing slogan frequently heard on the streets of the big cities was "Moderation is Death".

The convulsive politics of the Empire must have been on the agenda at the Café Guerbois, but of more prurient interest may well have been the erroneous gossip amorously linking Manet and Berthe Morisot who had been introduced to the clique via Fantin-Latour. At this stage gentlewomen were not in the habit

MORISOT
The Harbour of Lorient, Brittany
oil on canvas
1869. 43.5 × 73 cm
*Morisot was visiting her sister,
who posed for her here.*

of frequenting gentlemen's café societies, so Morisot's acquaintance with Manet would have been consolidated outside the auspices of the Café Guerbois, and thus she would have been denied what Monet had called the "constant clash of opinions" and the lapidary wit-sharpening of Thursday nights.

Nevertheless Manet and Morisot had become very close – Manet's main exhibit at the 1869 Salon shows a moody Berthe on *The Balcony* (*Le Balcon*), for which she had posed a few months after they had met at the Louvre, where she was also a copyist. Manet's ponderous influence on Berthe can be seen in a portrait of her sister, Edma, and her mother which Manet had retouched into what Berthe called "the prettiest little caricature". For her part Berthe, who had been brought up by Corot and Daubigny as a *plein-airiste*, encouraged Manet to take to the outdoors and

lighten his otherwise sombre palette. At this time another woman painter, Eva Gonzalès, the daughter of a novelist, appeared on Manet's horizon and much to Berthe Morisot's dismay he agreed to take Eva as his pupil – the first and last time he chose to teach.

In the spring of 1869 Monet had installed himself in the village of Saint-Michel near Bougival. This was an increasingly popular resort on the Seine linked to Paris by the Paris–Saint-Germain railway and the stop at Chatou. This area had long been a retreat for landscapists such as Corot. Pissarro had meanwhile moved from Pontoise to nearby Louveciennes, where Renoir was staying with him. At a branch of the Seine near Croissy there was a popular floating restaurant and bathing establishment called La Grenouillère (literally "The Froggery") where jaded Parisians would retire on day trips

RENOIR
La Grenouillère
oil on canvas
1869. 66 × 86 cm
*ABOVE Renoir and Monet
painted a series of pictures from
the same viewpoints. The
influence of Monet on Renoir's
work is evident.*

MONET
La Grenouillère
oil on canvas
1869. 79 × 60 cm
RIGHT

during the summer months to eat, drink, and swim. It was so popular that it was often illustrated in gazettes; the Imperial couple had once stopped there in their boat, adding to its fame. It was here that Renoir and Monet spent much of the summer of 1869.

In yet another begging letter to Bazille from this period Monet also mentions that "I had indeed a dream, a *tableau*, the bathing place at La Grenouillère, for which I have made some rotten sketches . . . " The "rotten sketches" that he and Renoir had been working on that summer were a turning point, they mark the first major examples of the Impressionism to come in the next decade. The conditions were right: the two artists, each working with an eye on the other's canvas, were using paint with an unheard of directness and speed to capture all the elements in view in as unmediated a way as possible. We begin to see in his *Bathers at La Grenouillère (Baigneurs à la Grenouillère)* the genesis of Monet's famous advice:

> When you go out to paint, try to forget what objects you have before you; a tree, a house, a field or whatever. Merely think here is a little square of blue, here an oblong of pink, here a streak of yellow, and paint it just as it looks to you, the exact colour and shape, until it gives you your own naïve impression of the scene before you.

Despite the insistence of Monet and Renoir that the Grenouillère paintings were merely *pochades*, or sketches, the distinction between sketch and finished painting was by now becoming blurred. A painting done at La Grenouillère and submitted to the Salon of 1870 (it was rejected and is now lost) appears hardly more "finished" than the *pochades*.

1870–1871: WAR AND THE COMMUNE

In May 1870 the new decade seemed to promise a bright future for the Second Empire. A plebiscite on constitutional changes to establish a cabinet government responsible to parliament was approved by an overwhelming majority of six million. As Cobban describes it, "In the early summer of 1870, though the Empire was in a process of evolution, there seemed not the slightest danger of revolution." By 2nd July the Second Empire was in peril. Following a byzantine and mischievous piece of statecraft on the part of the Prussians, Prince Leopold of Hohenzollern was offered as a candidate for the vacant throne in Spain. France could not tolerate the idea of Prussian involvement within its southern neighbour. The scheme brought back old memories of continual war between the Hapsburg Empire and France. The Prussians withdrew the offer to Spain ten days later, but this was not satisfactory to Napoleon III and the belligerent Empress Eugénie, a Spaniard, who took it upon herself to demand through the government an assurance from Wilhelm I of Prussia that no more claims would be made to the Spanish throne. The French were looking for the diplomatic victory over Bismarck such an assurance would provide, but they were outmanouevred when on 14th July a provocative telegram arrived from Ems which had been written by Bismarck and calculated to infuriate the French. When the telegram was published in the press, France exploded in patriotic fervour and demanded war with the Prussians. Napoleon III was too ill at the time to resist this tide of emotion and five days later, on 19th July, he was forced to declare war on the Prussians.

By August the French armies had suffered heavy defeats on all fronts. The Prussians' Krupps guns, so admired at the 1867 Exposition Universelle, had been used to devastating effect; the French army was ill equipped, badly led and swiftly demoralized. Napoleon III himself was barely able to sit astride his horse through illness. The Prussians, on the other hand, had built up a formidable war machine under Bismarck, who made use of the railways to transport men and artillery to the fronts; they took Alsace and Lorraine in the first week of fighting. A series of humiliating defeats followed for the French. On 1st September Napoleon III surrendered his army at Sedan and was taken prisoner of war. Paris erupted in pent-up revolutionary fervour; the Empress Eugénie and the Prince Imperial escaped out of the back door of the Palais de Versailles to England. The chronicler of Parisian life Edmond de Goncourt attempted to describe the chaotic scene as the bad news hit Paris:

PISSARRO
The Orchard
oil on canvas
1870. 56.5 × 84 cm
This painting was created shortly after Pissarro's move to Louveciennes. He worked consistently outdoors during the period, but also kept a studio in Paris. He did not neglect his association with the rest of the Impressionists, attending regularly the meetings at the Café Guerbois.

MONET
L'Hôtel des Roches Noires, Trouville
oil on canvas
1870. 81 × 58.5 cm
The Monets were not staying at
the luxurious 150-room hotel but
in a modest establishment which
they left without paying. The bill
was settled much later.

Who can describe the consternation written on every face, the crowds collecting at street corners and outside town halls, the siege of the newspaper kiosks, the triple rows of readers gathering around every gas lamp? Then there is the menacing roar of the crowd in which stupefaction has begun to give way to anger. Next there are crowds moving down the boulevards shouting "*A bas l'Empire!*" ["Down with the Empire!"] . . . And finally there is the wild, tumultuous spectacle of a nation determined to perish or save itself by an enormous effort, by one of those impossible feats of revolutionary times.

A republican government of National Defence was proclaimed by the moderates in the Legislative Assembly. Within three months the Second Empire no longer existed.

On 28th November, a year short of his thirtieth birthday, Frédéric Bazille was killed in battle at Beaunes-la-Rolande near Orléans. One of his last paintings, *Studio in the rue de la Condamine*, depicts some habitués of the Café Guerbois, Monet, Manet, Renoir, Zola, the musician Maître and the artist himself (painted in by Manet) in happier, more peaceful times.

Manet had remained in Paris, a lieutenant in the National Guard under the painter Meissonier. Renoir was sent to Bordeaux, in the southwest and thus saw no action. In Paris Manet was to be seen swanning around in his officer's uniform, although neither he, Renoir, nor Degas were involved in any action. Cézanne had fled back to Aix-en-Provence in the south to avoid being conscripted into a war which was largely being fought in the northeast. Pissarro had painted on in Louveciennes until the Prussians advanced towards it. Over 1,100 of his paintings (which shows how prodigious his output was) were badly damaged or destroyed when his house was commandeered by several enemy troops.

As the war raged in the east Monet was at Trouville painting a number of pictures of the beach and seafront, notably the two *Beach at Trouville* (*La Plage à Trouville*) paintings and *L'Hôtel des Roches Noires, Trouville* which confirm his increasingly impressionistic style. In the autumn, with the Prussians advancing westward to encircle Paris, Monet and Pissarro fled separately to London.

If the war had proved fatal for Bazille, Monet's closest friend and as promising an artist as any of the group, it provided Pissarro and Monet with the opportunity to meet Paul Durand-Ruel, an important dealer who had opened a gallery in London and was later to

MONET
Beach at Trouville
oil on canvas
1870. 37.5 × 45.5 cm
*This sketchy picture, an important
step on the road to Impressionism,
can be compared to an enlarged
detail of Boudin's painting of the
same subject. The painters were
working together that summer,
and Mme Boudin is perhaps the
other woman in the picture.*

faithfully champion their work and stage exhibitions of the Impressionists in New York.
"A true picture dealer," said Durand-Ruel,
"should also be an enlightened patron; he
should, if necessary, sacrifice his immediate
interest to his artistic convictions and oppose
rather than support the interest of specula-
tors." Living in the West End of London,
Monet had been introduced to Durand-Ruel
by Charles Daubigny, who was making a
good living painting scenes of the Thames.
Durand-Ruel in turn put Monet in touch with
Pissarro who was staying with his mother in
South Norwood, a quiet, picturesque village
to the southeast of London.

By 20th September 1870 the Prussians had
completely surrounded Paris, cutting it off
from the rest of France. An attack by the
crack Zouaves Regiment had been routed the
day before. Edmond de Goncourt heard a
terrified national guardsman on the street
"relating that the Prussians numbered a hundred thousand in the Bois de Meudon . . .
One senses in these accounts the madness of
fear, the hallucinations of panic . . ." The
Bois de Boulogne had been turned into a
farmyard, siege fortifications had been built
in and around the city which thronged with
soldiers from the National Guard. Throughout the autumn and winter and on into 1871
the war continued, with food supplies running short and starvation becoming rampant.

One of the few links to the outside world
was via hot air balloons. On 8th October,

Léon Gambetta, a fiery and popular orator and Minister of the Interior, had made an heroic escape to Tours in a balloon launched from the heights of Montmartre. Taking advantage of this, Nadar organized letters to be sent by balloon post. One letter from Berthe Morisot to her sister, Edma, describes the noise of the Prussian bombardments which began in November, the corpses lying in the streets and grim warnings from Edouard and Eugène Manet that Berthe would be better off if she lost her hand or became disfigured. On 19th January the Paris garrison attempted to break out of the city and through the Prussian lines, but failed. This attempted *sortie en masse* was the last significant action of the war. Nine days later Paris surrendered to the Prussian army.

In February a republican National Assembly was elected to make peace with Prussia and approve massive reparations. But the National Guard was still armed in Paris and when on 18th March troops loyal to the new republican government attempted and failed to seize the cannon in Montmartre, Paris – led by a coalition of revolutionaries – was at war with the Republic. On 28th March the Paris Commune was elected amid scenes of jubilation that harked back to the days of the Revolution in 1789 and the first Commune. On 2nd April the second siege of Paris began; the Commune held out until the "Bloody Week" which began on 21st May when more than 20,000 Parisians were killed in indiscriminate reprisals as government forces overran the city.

Gustave Courbet, who had been elected chairman of the Arts Commission after the fall of the Empire, was a prominent member of the Commune and became implicated in the destruction of the Vendôme Column,

which stood as a bitter reminder of Napoleonic power to the Communards. When the government "liberated" Paris he was imprisoned and later exiled to Switzerland where he died in 1877.

Amidst the dramatic events of this period Degas' eyesight had begun to deteriorate, Renoir had obtained a pass during the Commune and left to continue his landscape studies and most of the others of the Batignolles Group had fled to safety.

Manet was the only member of the group concerned with depicting the war in Paris and its effects. Standing on the corner of the boulevard Malesherbes, he sketched the dead bodies lying there. The lithograph *The Civil War* (*La Guerre civile*) shows how readily his *Execution of Maximilian* must have come to his mind as he observed the horror in the streets of Paris at that perilous time: the starvation, sheer anarchy, and devastation.

MONET
Green Park, London
oil on canvas
1871. 40 × 73 cm
ABOVE

PISSARRO
Upper Norwood, Crystal Palace
oil on canvas
1871. 40 × 51 cm
OPPOSITE This work by Pissarro and the painting above by Monet were each the product of the artists' voluntary exile in England during the Franco-Prussian war. It was an important time, as it brought the two men together, but was commercially unsuccessful, as the English public was not yet ready for the Impressionists, and the Royal Academy – equivalent to the French Salon – rejected their work.

PILS
The Ruins of the Tuileries Palace
watercolour on paper
1871. 38 × 51 cm
*RIGHT We have to turn to
topographical artists, or to
Meissonier, to find pictures of the
devastation of war. Most of the
Impressionists were out of Paris at
the time and in any case had no
desire to paint such scenes.*

MANET
Civil War
Lithograph
1871. 40 × 51 cm
*ABOVE The artist had seen corpses
lying in the streets near his home.*

DEGAS IN NEW ORLEANS

For illustrations of the Commune we have to turn to photography and the topographic artists who remained in Paris to record the suffering and destruction. None of the Impressionists was interested in the ruins of the Tuileries Palace, which had stood in the heart of the city, an area they had often depicted before the war.

In the end, the war against Prussia and the Commune had little effect on the French economy. France was now a *de facto* republic for the third time in her history. In the climate of expansion which immediately followed the end of the troubles Durand-Ruel began to invest heavily in the Batignolles artists. He bought 30 Monets and paid Manet 51,000 francs for 29 of his paintings, a fantastic sum considering Claude Monet's income the next year was 25,000 francs. For Monet in particular things were looking up at last. From England he had gone to Holland and then to Argenteuil on the Seine near Paris where Renoir frequently joined him as before. Pissarro had returned to Louveciennes and then decamped to Pontoise where Cézanne visited him. The Café Guerbois evenings continued for another year. In November Degas and his brother René arrived in New Orleans to stay with their mother. In a letter to his friend Lorentz Fröhlich, Degas described the effect the new world was having on him:

> Everything attracts me here, I look at everything . . . I accumulate plans that would take a lifetime to complete. I will abandon them in six weeks to return and never again leave my home . . . My eyes are much better.

Ten days later he wrote to Henri Rouart:

> The light is so strong that I have not yet been able to do anything on the river. My eyes are so greatly in need of care that I scarcely take any risk with them at all . . . Manet would see lovely things here, even more than I do . . .

Indicative of his friendly rivalry with Manet he went on:

> . . . but not many more of them. One loves and gives art only to the things to which one is accustomed.

Among the results of Degas' period in New Orleans, chiefly devoted to painting portraits of his family, are two remarkable pictures,

PISSARRO
Horsechestnut Trees at
Louveciennes
oil on canvas
c.1872. 41 × 54 cm
*This evocative snow-scene was
painted close to the artist's home at
Louveciennes, where he had
moved with his family three years
before.*

The *Invalid* (*L'Invalide*) and *Portraits in an Office – New Orleans* (*Portraits dans un bureau à Nouvelle-Orléans*) better known as *The Cotton Market* (*Le Bureau de Coton*). The former is one of Degas' most atmospheric works, conveying what Henri Loyrette calls "the stifling sense of the sickroom" in broad, swift brushstrokes; the latter, making the modern business world a legitimate subject for art, was described by Armand Silvestre as "an exceedingly witty painting that one could spend days contemplating." This painting is perhaps as epochal as Manet's *Music in the Tuileries Garden* had been a decade earlier. After this Degas' failing eyes allowed him to paint few pictures of such acute detail.

1873: SOCIÉTÉ ANONYME

The post-war boom soon gave way to a period of economic recession which lasted for five years and affected the Impressionists, their patrons, and especially Durand-Ruel, forcing him to close his London gallery in 1874. As in 1863 the Salon was hugely over-subscribed but this time the *refusés* succeeded in pressurizing the government to mount another Salon des Refusés. A huge Renoir painting, almost eight and a half by seven and a half feet, the *Morning Ride in the Bois de Boulogne* (*Allée cavalière au Bois de Boulogne*) had been rejected by the Salon but was shown to great acclaim at the alternative exhibition.

RENOIR
Madame Camille Monet
oil on canvas
1872. 61 × 50 cm
*There are hundreds of instances
of the Impressionists painting the
other members of the group and
their families – this is perhaps one
of the finest. It was painted shortly
after the Franco-Prussian war,
when Renoir and Monet
developed the habit of painting
together on trips along the banks
of the Seine.*

Monet's influence on Renoir, after long
months working with him before and after
the war, had led to a brightening of his palette
and more delicate brushwork. Renoir's *Pont
Neuf* of the previous year was one of his most
impressionistic pictures to date; the briefly
sketched-in figures highlighted with dabs of
pure pigment betray the influence of Monet,
as do the complementary colours blue-violet
and yellow in the overall composition, and the
bluish shadows, which create the effect of
colour contrast in brilliant sunlight.

Unlike the events a decade earlier, the
Salon des Refusés of 1873 was remarkably
devoid of scandal. The painter most likely to
cause an uproar, Edouard Manet, was showing two works at the official Salon, a portrait

of Berthe Morisot and *Le Bon Bock* – a
portrait of the engraver Bellot at a table in the
Café Guerbois. The latter proved a welcome
success for Manet, sensitive as ever to the
barbs of the critics. The influence of Frans
Hals, whom Manet had been studying during
a tour of Holland the year before, as well as
the deliberate lack of a scandalous subject
gently reassured the Salon-going public of
Manet's talent.

The Salon des Refusés did little to placate
the rest of the Batignolles Group who were
still desperately looking for outlets for their
work. Ironically, the war had promoted a
deeply conservative streak in the Salon jury
which made Nieuwerkerke's *ancien régime*
appear liberal by comparison. This conspired
against an avant-garde whose influence was
by now becoming widespread. With Durand-
Ruel's business suffering in the recession and
unable to support them they were forced to
look elsewhere. The idea first mentioned by
Bazille in 1867 of forming an independent
organization to stage an exhibition was rekindled. A much heated discussion between Pissarro, who was for a highly complex association based on a social and political union, and
the others in the group, including Renoir and
Monet, who demanded a simpler, looser collective, resulted in a document signed on 27th
December founding the *Société anonyme des
artistes peintres, sculpteurs, graveurs, etc.* Only
Manet refused to join the new body, arguing
in common with Cézanne, that still "the
Salon is the true battlefield." Degas was in
favour, writing to Tissot that "the realist
movement no longer needs to fight with the
others. It is. It exists, it must show itself as
something distinct . . . So forget the money
side for a moment. Exhibit. Be of your
country and your friends."

MANET
The Railway
1872–73. 93.5 × 114.5 cm
Left Also called **The Gare St Lazare,** *we can hardly guess that there is a railway station behind the cloud of smoke. Most Impressionists painted scenes with trains at this time.*

SISLEY
The Seine at Bougival
oil on canvas
1872–77. 38.5 × 62 cm
Above Sisley was interested at this time in the problems of depicting water and sky. His palette was somewhat dark and sombre compared to most of the other Impressionists.

Claude Monet 8

THE AGE OF IMPRESSIONISM

T HE WORKS OF MONET, Renoir, Manet, Morisot, Pissarro, and Sisley, which characterized the Impressionist idiom in its most popularly recognizable form, were painted in the 1870s. Degas, who played an important role in organizing the series of Impressionist exhibitions which marked the 1870s and 1880s, remained resolutely opposed to *plein-air* painting. He nevertheless produced the most striking images of modern Parisian life, taking inspiration from Japanese prints and photography, and, like Manet, basing his technique on a thorough appreciation of the old masters. Towards the end of the 1870s serious rifts began to appear in the group and Monet, Renoir, and Sisley dropped out as Degas and Pissarro exerted more and more control over the exhibitions, replenishing the group with new artists. For most of the Impressionists this was a time of personal consolidation, with patrons and dealers securing them a regular income despite periodic economic recessions. The penultimate Impressionist exhibition – minus Degas – took place in 1882 and essentially represented the fragile group's last stand. The next year Manet died having completed his masterpiece *Bar at the Folies-Bergère*. He had remained highly supportive of the group but never exhibited with them.

By 1886 the final Impressionist exhibition featured the work of Degas, Pissarro, and a new generation including Georges Seurat, Paul Signac, and Paul Gauguin.

MONET
The Sea at Fécamp
oil on canvas
1881. 65 × 80 cm
(*DETAIL*)

COURBET
Beach Scene
oil on canvas
1874. 37.5 × 54.5 cm
*Above Courbet's choice of subjects
from ordinary life and his very
simple artistic philosophy
("Painting is an art of sight and
should therefore concern itself
with things seen") made him a
natural precursor of the
Impressionist movement.*

1874: The First Impressionist Exhibition

*We were all one group when we first started out. We stood
shoulder to shoulder and encouraged each other . . .*

The quotation above was given by Renoir, twenty years after the inaugural collective Impressionist show: the *Société anonyme*'s first (and last) exhibition opened in mid-April, deliberately timed to upstage the official Salon. Situated in Nadar's old studio, it was close to the premises of several dealers and photographers, including Durand-Ruel's gallery. The choice of a *grand boulevard* was in itself a fitting one for the generation of artists who had grown up in Haussmann's Paris painting Baudelaire's *vie moderne*.

The exhibition was immediately a critical *cause célèbre*; not only did it provoke the aspersions of critics such as Leroy, it also rallied the influential theorist Edmond Duranty (with whom Manet had once fought a duel!) to the Impressionists' defence. At the time, Jules Castagnary also showed particular insight in putting his finger on the fact that Monet, Pissarro, Sisley, Morisot, and Renoir were "Impressionists in the sense that they render not the landscape, but the sensation produced by the landscape."

MILLET
Haystacks in Autumn
oil on canvas
1873–74. 85 × 110 cm
*Right Though charmingly done
in their own right, Millet's
haystacks are perhaps of more
interest through their very obvious
foreshadowing of the magnificent
series by Monet.*

However, the exhibition was such a financial disaster that the *Société* was later forced to meet in December to wind up its affairs. Thanks to Louis Leroy's scurrilous satire in *Charivari*, the group, which had laboured under several titles, none of them really appropriate – *la bande à Manet*, the Batignolles Group, the Realists – was now known as "the Impressionists". There were seven more Impressionist exhibitions, the last in 1886, although none of them bore the title "Impressionist", their participants typically preferring the name *Expositions de Peinture*, or on one occasion, an *Exposition des Independants*.

All but forgotten in a new world of painting, Charles Gleyre died that same year. Renoir, for one, maintained to the very end that Gleyre had taught him his *métier*. He recalled a scene at Gleyre's a decade before:

Whilst the other students yelled and broke the windows, tormented the model and distracted the teacher I would quietly sit in the corner, observant and prepared, studying the model and listening to the master. And they accused me of being a revolutionary.

1875: CRITICS AND COLLECTORS

The Salon of 1875 was graced with the results of Edouard Manet's work at Argenteuil where he had spent the previous summer with Monet and Renoir. Manet had helped Monet's family to find new lodgings in this picturesque village on the banks of the Seine and proceeded under the latter's influence to create a series of highly impressionistic figures in landscapes. Liberated from the studio and surrounded by the most devoted of Impressionist *plein-airistes*, Manet's technique underwent a revolution. *Monet Painting in his Studio Boat* (*Monet dans son studio flotant*),

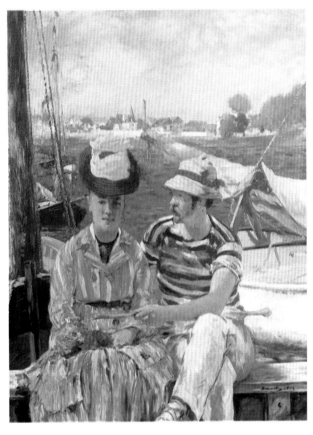

Banks of the Seine at Argenteuil (*Les Bords de la Seine à Argenteuil*) (the two figures are Camille Monet and Jean), and *The Monet Family in their Garden* (*La Famille Monet au jardin*) are remarkable for the breathtaking speed of their execution and the abandonment of Manet's otherwise sombre palette in favour of strokes of pure pigment. The contrast between Monet's insistence on landscape as his *motif* – his reluctance to attempt large figures after *Women in the Garden* some ten years earlier is palpable – and Manet's abiding concern with the human figure is still marked, even at the point where their styles most obviously converge.

The respite offered by Durand-Ruel to the poorest Impressionists, Monet, Renoir, Pissarro, and Sisley (whose father's business had

WHISTLER
The Old Battersea Bridge, Harmony in Blue and Gold
oil on canvas
c.1872–75. 68 × 51 cm
ABOVE The Japanese influence is obvious, but Whistler is not the only artist who succeeded in blending Impressionism with the Japanese style.

MANET
Banks of the Seine at Argenteuil
oil on canvas
1874. 148 × 115 cm
ABOVE LEFT Manet's technique shows the liberating influence of Monet and Renoir; his palette is brighter than ever and his style is at last truly impressionistic.

BOLDINI
Highway at Combes-la-Ville
oil on canvas
1873. 70 × 102 cm
*ABOVE Boldini was one of several
artists whose work was close to
Impressionism for a while,
although most of them did not
persevere in this style.*

BOUDIN
Beach Scene, Trouville
oil on canvas
1873. 15 × 30 cm
*RIGHT One of many scenes of this
kind by Boudin. He deplored the
invasion of tourists but could not
avoid depicting them. Like
Boldini (above), Boudin flirted
with Impressionism, and indeed
his work was included in the first
Impressionist exhibition. Yet he
was a free spirit, refusing to
permanently ally himself to any
specific grouping.*

MANET
Nina de Callias
oil on canvas
1873–74. 113.5 × 166.5 cm
*OPPOSITE She was Anne-Marie
Gaillard, also known as Nina de
Villard, wife of Hector de Callias,
a musician. A warm woman, easy
going but sometimes hysterical,
she held a salon between 1868
and 1884. She became insane in
1881 and went to an asylum
where she died in 1884. She asked
to be buried in this outfit.*

collapsed in the war) had temporarily evaporated; sales had plummeted in the recession. Even Degas was in trouble after the death of his father had entailed the Degas estate. An auction of Impressionist work arranged by Renoir and held at the Hôtel Drouot ended in farce and near riot. So derisory were the bids that the artists were forced to purchase many of their own works. Albert Wolff, the art critic of the important daily *Le Figaro*, had been asked by Manet to promote the sale. His answer was to write "the impression the Impressionists achieve [is] that of a cat walking on a piano keyboard or a monkey who might have got hold of a box of paints."

Gradually, however, patrons were beginning to come to the aid of some of the Impressionists. An eccentric customs official called Victor Chocquet, who had devoted his life to collecting the work of Delacroix and many other objets d'art, had become enamoured of Renoir's work at the Hotel Drouot and began to support the Impressionists. Renoir introduced him to Cézanne, also in need

of more patronage and the result was a series of portraits of M. and Mme Chocquet by the two artists. A comparison of Renoir's and Cézanne's 1876 portraits of the collector shows the difference in the two artists' approach to their subject. Renoir's picture is executed with feathery brush strokes evoking a gentle, kindly, almost ethereal individual; Cézanne's portrait (like the later portrait of 1879–82) shows his increasing concern with structure and volume, and the paint is applied in thick patches and with the palette knife.

The second Impressionist exhibition planned for 1875 was unable to go ahead because there were no available funds to mount it. Although this decline of the *Société anonyme* was only a temporary setback, some serious rifts were already beginning to appear in the group. In August Pissarro and his friend Alfred Meyer set up *L'Union* to carry on the work of the defunct *Société anonyme*. Cézanne and Monet objected to this upstart organization, especially the involvement of Meyer who they believed was plotting against the

COROT
The Waggon, Souvenir of Saintry,
near Corbeil
oil on canvas
1874. 47 × 57 cm
*ABOVE Amidst the excitements of
1874, with the first Impressionist
exhibition, the old war-horse
Corot continued on in his own
inimitable fashion. The group, to
whom he had been both an
inspiration and a supporter, was
greatly saddened by his death in
the following year.*

GUILLAUMIN
The Aquaduct at Arcueil
oil on canvas
1874. 51 × 65 cm
*RIGHT Among the Impressionists
Guillaumin was one of the few to
depict the grim aspects of the
urban industrial landscape.*

artistic objectives of the Impressionists. Although *L'Union* had recruited several minor painters to its ranks, including Guillaumin, it attracted little attention from the critics and eventually faded into oblivion. However much this singular group of artists was identified by the critics, the public and other artists as a homogenous circle their talents and personalities were formidably individual. A mutual struggle against the inflexibility of the art world brought them "shoulder to shoulder", but that alone was not enough to keep the Impressionists together for very much longer.

The death of Camille Corot in 1875, the inspiration for so many of the Impressionists, was an occasion for much sadness in the group, especially for Berthe Morisot and Camille Pissarro who had been closest to him and learnt the most from his work and artistic guidance. "We don't see in the same way; you see green and I see grey and silver," Corot once said to Pissarro, " . . . but this is no reason at all for you not to work at [tonal] values, for this is the basis of everything, and in whatever way one may feel and express oneself, one cannot do good painting without it." Morisot had outgrown Corot's style by the time of the first Impressionist exhibition, as her painting *The Cradle (Berceau)* indicates, but Corot's influence on Pissarro persisted well into the 1870s.

PHOTOGRAPHY AND IMPRESSIONISM

Of great interest to art historians is the fact that over three hundred photographs were found in Corot's studio after his death. These photographs are now lost, but a contemporary source described two hundred of them as being "studies from nature".

The first reliable photographic process had been discovered by Louis Daguerre and announced to the French Académie des Sciences in 1839. (In 1822 Joseph-Nicéphore Niepce had succeeded in fixing a photographic image on glass, and William Henry Fox Talbot in England was developing a rival process which could reproduce from negatives.) The daguerreotype was capable of producing a positive image fixed on a highly polished metal plate and soon became widely available. The new invention had an immediate effect on artists, especially miniature portrait painters: it put many of them out of business. Nevertheless the practical applications of the new medium were apparent to

MANET
Masked Ball at the Opera
oil on canvas
1873–74. 60 × 73 cm
On the left, talking to a masked woman in white, is the composer Chabrier, a friend of several Impressionists. This kind of entertainment was not suitable for the respectable Mme Manet or Berthe Morisot.

MANET
Madame Manet
pastel on paper
1873. 54 × 39 cm
*ABOVE The use of pastel and other
media apart from oil paint was
revived by Manet and Degas in
particular.*

MORISOT
Chasing Butterflies
oil on canvas
1874. 47 × 56 cm
*RIGHT Morisot had work accepted
by the official Salon as early as
1864, when she was only twenty
three: but it was not until 1879,
five years after their inaugural
exhibition, that she first showed
with the Impressionists.*

major artists such as Ingres and Delacroix. The latter made no secret of his admiration, a daguerreotype, he said:

> . . . is a mirror of the object, certain details, almost always neglected in drawings from nature . . . in the daguerreotype take on a great importance and bring the artist into a full understanding of the object's construction. There, passages of light and shade show their true qualities . . .

In fact the daguerreotype was often more prone to distorting reality. Very slow expo-sure speeds in the 1850s meant that gently moving objects like trees were recorded on the plate in a blurred image, the light from the sky eating into the moving edges of the foliage. Corot and the Barbizon School were closely acquainted with the landscape photo-graphers of the time who, as the historian of photography Aaron Scharf suggests, must have been setting up their tripods right next to the painters' easels in the leafy recesses of the Fontainebleau Forest and in other land-scape sites. After 1840 there is increasing and direct use of the "halated" or blurred effect in the outline of Corot's trees as well as the influence of photographic over- and under-exposure in his astute handling of light and dark areas.

By the 1860s "snapshots" with fast exposure times were possible and Talbot's system of producing copies on paper from a negative had made the photograph widely available. Manet's *The Execution of The Emperor Maximilian* (*L'Execution de l'empereur Maximilien*) is partly indebted to photographs taken in Mexico of the doomed Emperor and his aides. As a cultural expression of its time, *The Execution* stands poised between the instantaneous modernity of the photograph with its ability to capture current events, and the art of Goya who had painted his *Third of May* (1808) in the first Napoleonic era.

Describing Monet's painting in 1874 Ernest Chesneau perceptively wrote: "Never has the elusive, the fleeting, the instantaneous movement been caught in its incredible flux and fixed, as it is in this extraordinary *Boulevard des Capucines.*" The previously unseen, blurred forms of moving people and objects which the camera could reveal had now become part of the vocabulary of the Impressionists, whether or not the influence was a conscious one.

In the year Corot died Degas painted the *Place de la Concorde* (now sadly lost). Of his contemporaries it was Degas who exploited the photograph to its fullest potential, later using it to help him with studies of dancers and horses. The view of the *Place de la Concorde* with the Vicomte Lepic and his daughters frozen in motion, sliced off by the bottom of the picture, and an onlooker on the left similarly clipped by the frame, is clearly reminiscent of a snapshot and influenced by the new ways of framing made possible by the camera.

CASSATT
On the Balcony
oil on canvas
1873. 101 × 83 cm
Left An unusual Spanish-style picture for Mary Cassatt who, like Berthe Morisot, had to rely on sitters from among the members of her family.

MONET
Boulevard des Capucines
oil on canvas
1873–74. 79 × 59 cm
Below The picture was painted in the autumn from Nadar's old photographic studio on the second floor. The brand-new Grand Hotel is on the left.

1876–1877: LA NOUVELLE PEINTURE

"None of its members show signs of possessing first-rate talent, and indeed the 'Impressionist' doctrines strike me as incompatible, in an artist's mind, with the existence of first-rate talent. To embrace them you must be provided with a plentiful absence of imagination."

HENRY JAMES, *THE NEW YORK TRIBUNE*
13TH MAY 1876.

The second Impressionist exhibition opened in mid-April 1876 at Durand-Ruel's gallery in the rue Le Pelletier. Some of the more extreme critics had seized the opportunity of likening the group to madmen and syphilitics, so Henry James's criticism seems mild by comparison. Yet it was typical of the prevailing school of thought which still could not accept Impressionism in any form. A critical defence was needed and several writers sympathetic to the Impressionists came to their aid. In his pamphlet *La Nouvelle Peinture*, Edmond Duranty analyzed the "new painting" in some depth. Monet, Renoir, and Pissarro were less than pleased with Duranty's tacit praise of Degas at their expense, but *La Nouvelle Peinture* offers some thoughtful insights into the Impressionists' work. This is what he had to say about the Impressionist use of colour:

Their real discovery consists in the realization that a strong light *discolours* tones, that sunshine reflected off objects tends by virtue of its clarity to blend its seven prismatic rays into a single, uncoloured brilliance which is light. From one flash of intuition to another, they have succeeded in breaking up solar light into its rays, its elements, and to reconstruct

MONET
Impression, Sunrise
oil on canvas
1872. 48 × 63 cm
*OPPOSITE ABOVE This is the
painting which provoked Leroy
into coining the name
Impressionism at the group's first
joint exhibition in 1874.*

SISLEY
Louveciennes, Heights of Marly
oil on canvas
1873. 38 × 46 cm
*OPPOSITE BELOW Sisley painted
this scene in the region of
Louveciennes, very much the
home territory of Pissarro. In this
period, shortly before the first
Impressionist exhibition of 1874,
Sisley was experiencing the life of
the professional painter for the
first time. Up until 1871, when
his father's business collapsed, he
had been very much the leisured,
gentleman painter: now, he
painted to eat.*

PISSARRO
La Côte du Chou, Pontoise
oil on canvas
c.1875–76. 81.5 × 65 cm
*RIGHT At this stage of his career
Pissarro was increasingly being
sought out by his younger
Impressionist colleagues for help
and advice. Cézanne, in
particular, was a frequent visitor
to Pontoise (where Pissarro and
his family had returned in 1872),
and once said that his friend was
"a little like the good Lord."*

it as a unity by the general harmony of the iridescence they spread on their canvases. From the viewpoint of the refinement of vision and the subtle penetration of colours, it has produced an extraordinary result. The most astute physicist could find no fault with their analysis of colour.

Other critics did not agree. One of the fifteen works by Renoir at the second exhibition (several were on loan from Victor Chocquet) was the *Étude*, better known as *Nude in Sunlight*. In his satire on the first exhibition Leroy had conceded that the painter "has a certain understanding of colour"; and Silvestre in *L'Opinion* thought *Nude in Sunlight* "the work of a true colourist." Wolff, however, in *Le Figaro* made a devastating attack focused on Renoir's palette:

> Would someone kindly explain to M. Renoir that a woman's torso is not a mass of decomposing flesh with the green and purplish blotches that indicate a state of complete putrefaction in a corpse . . .

Not to be outdone in similes of corrupt flesh, Louis Enault in *Le Constitutionnel* offered his readers this opinion:

> It is depressing to look at this large study of a nude woman; her purplish flesh is the colour of game that has been hung for too long, and someone really should have made her put on a dress.

Despite these attacks this was, as art historian Phoebe Pool says, Renoir's *annus mirabilis*. Not only do two of his finest paintings, *The Swing (La Balançoire)* and the *Ball at the Moulin de la Galette (Bal du Moulin de la Galette)*, date

RENOIR
Nude in Sunlight
oil on canvas
1876. 81 × 65 cm
LEFT Where Monet concentrated on the overall lighting in a picture, Renoir preferred the contrast of light and shade. The picture was bitterly condemned by critics, one of whom, Albert Wolff, likened it to decomposing flesh. Georges Rivière, a friend of Renoir said of Wolff: "When I see Albert Wolff I can forgive him the harsh words he has written about my friends. Nature has treated him far worse."

SISLEY
Flood at Port Marly
oil on canvas
1876. 50 × 61 cm
BELOW LEFT

RENOIR
The Greenhouse
oil on canvas
Undated. 60 × 74 cm
OPPOSITE

MONET
The Seine at Vétheuil
oil on canvas
1879. 60 × 81 cm
ABOVE This picture was painted during a period when Monet's fortunes were at a very low ebb: personal or financial difficulties never did effect his incredible work-rate.

MONET
The Pond at Montgeron
oil on canvas
1876–77. 172 × 193 cm
RIGHT Working in isolation, Monet's style was developing rapidly.

from this period, but he had the good fortune to meet Georges Charpentier, a wealthy young publisher who became an important patron. Mme Charpentier's salon was an important meeting place for the intellectual and social élite of the day. Renoir's later portrait of Mme Charpentier is described by Proust in *Time Regained (Le Temps retrouvé)* as being comparable to the best of Titian.

It was also around this time that a young painter of independent means, Gustave Caillebotte, became an important force amongst the Impressionists. His *Floor Scrapers (Les Raboteurs de parquets)* and *Le Pont de l'Europe* were shown at the second Impressionist exhibition. The influence of Degas and photography is discernible in the deep perspective, and whilst the style can hardly be called "impressionistic" in the sense of Monet, Sisley, or Renoir, these and several later paintings, notably the *Boulevard Seen from Above (Boulevard vu d'en haut)* have often been mentioned as some of the most memorable urban images of his century. Seven years younger than Renoir and Monet, Caillebotte was soon engaged in organizing the 1877 exhibition and funding the group through the extensive purchase of some of their most important works, with the intention of bequeathing them to the State. (There were sixty in all, including the two by Renoir mentioned above, now in the Musée d'Orsay, in Paris).

As Renoir's fortunes waxed for the time being, Monet's waned. During the years between 1876 and 1880 Monet was consistently forced to rely on the largesse of others. He described himself as being penniless and destitute, although he was still earning (and spending) six times more than the average workman whilst occasionally living in some style. Nevertheless the third Impressionist exhibition held at Durand-Ruel's and funded by Caillebotte, showed that penury could not stop Monet's outflow of work.

In January Caillebotte had rented a small apartment and studio for Monet close to the Gare St Lazare, the main station for points west of Paris, including the Normandy coast, Argenteuil, and Bougival (in 1877 it handled 13 million passengers). With the sort of bravado only a penniless artist like Monet could summon up, he went to call on the Superintendent of the railway who assumed him to be a famous artist and offered him the freedom of the station. A series of twelve paintings was the result, seven of which were shown at the third exhibition. Greeted with astonishment, they proved to be the last of his urban landscapes. Georges Rivière, an art critic of the time held the overall view that "these paintings are amazingly varied, despite the monotony and aridity of the subject. In them more than anywhere else can be seen that skill in arrangement, that organization of the canvas, that is one of the main qualities of Monet's work." Trains and the new railways

MONET
Gare St Lazare, Pont de l'Europe
oil on canvas
1877. 64 × 81 cm
ABOVE The railway bridge seen at train level, a much more animated and interesting composition than Caillebotte's work.

MONET
The Japanese Kimono
oil on canvas
1876. 231 × 142 cm
LEFT The model is Monet's first wife, Camille.

109

MONET
Gare St Lazare
oil on canvas
1877. 60 × 80 cm
*ABOVE Monet put on his best suit,
went to the director of railways
and asked permission to paint
inside the station. Mistaken for a
famous artist, the station was
cleared for him, the engines
stacked to provide abundant
smoke, and he was escorted by
railway officials. He painted
twelve views of the station and
showed seven of them at the third
Impressionist show of 1877.*

CAILLEBOTTE
Pont de l'Europe
oil on canvas
1876–77. 105 × 130 cm
*RIGHT Caillebotte lived in the area
of the St Lazare railway station,
like Manet.*

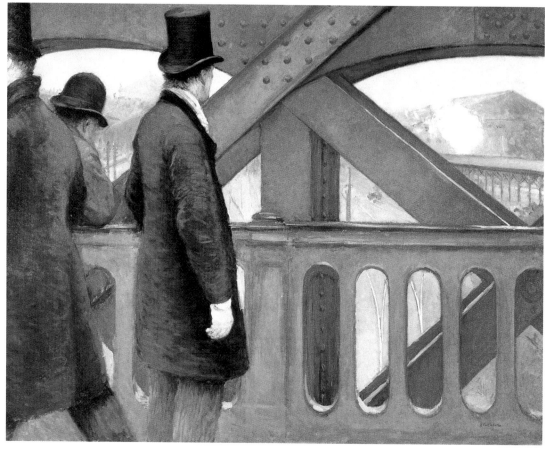

were indeed an important feature in the work of the other artists, notably Pissarro, Sisley, and Manet. Manet's *The Railway* (*Le Chemin de fer*) of 1873 tells us a great deal about the difference between him and Monet. It is primarily a figure painting: the railway itself is beyond the picture and represented by a cloud of steam; the little girl stands (like Degas' double-bass) with her back to us. Manet, unlike Monet, is not primarily interested in the railway as such, but in the relationship between it and his figures. As an icon of its time it is a powerful image, portraying a sense of wonderment (the girl) and banality (the woman) in the modern world.

Looking at this modern world from an entirely different perspective, Degas' contribution to the exhibition included two celebrated images of Parisian vice; *In a Café* (also known as *The Absinthe Drinker*) and *Women on the Terrace of a Café in the Evening* (*Femmes à la terrasse d'un café soir*). Of the latter, the contemporary critic Alexandre Pothey confessed, "the terrifying realism of these painted, faded creatures, exuding vice, who cynically tell each other about their day's activities and accomplishments." The scandal caused by Manet's *Olympia* twelve years before in the long summer days of the Second Empire had been instrumental in clearing the way for Degas' explicit depiction of prostitution and alcoholism, now tacitly acceptable in polite

Third Republic society. If Baudelaire had survived he would have been delighted, for Degas was now the painter of modern life *par excellence*, making art of everything that went on in Paris, from the loneliest bar to the heaving café-concert. His interest in ballet had resulted in *The Star (L'Etoile)* and *Dancers at the Barre*, whilst the café-concert, a sort of vaudeville or music hall at the height of its popularity in the 1870s, was the trigger for several pictures on this subject, as indeed it was for Renoir and Manet.

DEGAS
The Star
pastel/monotype
c.1878. 60 × 44 cm
Left Degas said, "People call me the painter of dancing girls. It has never occurred to them that my chief interest in dancers lies in rendering movement and in painting pretty clothes."

DEGAS
Three studies for a Fourteen-year-old Dancer
chalk and charcoal on green paper
c.1876–80. 48 × 63 cm
Above The exhaustive studies for this sculpture demonstrate both Degas' determination to master his subject completely, and his cautious move into a new medium, that of sculpture, which became increasingly important in later years when his eyesight began to fail.

1878–1881: BEGINNING OF THE END

*We are far from the moment when we are able to do without
the prestige attached to the official exhibitions.*

ALFRED SISLEY, 1878

In 1878 an important patron of the Impressionists, Ernest Hoschedé, the director of a
Paris department store, was in serious financial difficulties which later forced him to sell a
sizeable collection of works he had accumu-
lated after the first Impressionist exhibition in
1874. Monet in particular was affected by the
impending fall of Hoschedé; he had made
extensive use of Hoschedé's country house at
Montgeron near Paris and had produced
some important work for the collector. The
loss of a patron was bad enough; Monet and
Camille now had a second child to support,
they had recently been forced to leave their
house in Argenteuil, relying on Edouard
Manet to find them lodgings at Lavacourt
near Vétheuil, a village over thirty miles from
Paris. The Monets were already desperate,
as Camille was ill with cancer of the uterus,
and to make things worse, the Hoschedés
were ruined, and they came, with their
six children, to stay. To complicate matters Claude had been having a secret liaison
with Hoschedé's wife, Alice, for some time.
Thus began a strange *ménage à douze*. From
around this time Monet began to be more and
more isolated from the other Impressionists,
rarely venturing into Paris.

One of the founding members of the *Société
anonyme* who had already cut himself off from
the group to a certain extent, pursuing his
own aims and methods, was Alfred Sisley.
He was becoming a recluse; some years later
he crossed the street to avoid Renoir who had

once been one of his closest friends. Eight
years earlier Sisley's father's business had
crashed during the Franco-Prussian War and
from this time to his death in 1899 his life was
a continual struggle to support his family. His
finest work dates from the mid-1870s. Sisley
had lived near Argenteuil in the earlier part of
the decade and between 1875 and 1877 he had
gone to Marly-le-Roi to continue his landscapes. In 1878 he got his work into the Salon
along with Renoir; both artists had now
officially left the Impressionists. Sisley told
Duret that:

DEGAS
Women on the Terrace of a Café in
the Evening
pastel/monotype
1877. 41 × 60 cm
OPPOSITE

MANET
Women Drinking Beer
pastel on paper
1878. 61 × 51 cm
*LEFT Manet and Degas were the
resolutely urban painters of the
group. Scenes of modern Parisian
life were just the sort of thing that
Baudelaire had in mind when he
demanded a new art.*

SISLEY
Snow at Louveciennes
oil on canvas
1878. 61 × 50.5 cm
Right Like Monet and Pissarro, Sisley was concerned with capturing the blue winter light on the snow. Renoir hated it and painted only one snow scene.

PISSARRO
The Kitchen Garden
oil on canvas
1879. 55 × 65 cm
Below Whereas Renoir had a longing to be accepted by high society, Pissarro remained staunchly loyal to his principles and continued to paint humble subjects.

It is true that our exhibitions have served to make us known and in this they have been very useful to me, but I believe we must not isolate ourselves for too long. We are far from the moment when we are able to do without the prestige attached to the official exhibitions. I am therefore determined to submit to the Salon.

Underlying this dissatisfaction was the increasing dominance that Degas (and Caillebotte) seemed to be exerting on the group. A benign example of Degas' influence can be seen in his patronage of a young American, Mary Cassatt, who had been living in France since 1866 and had shown twice at the Salon. But other, lesser artists were now to be drafted into the Impressionist exhibitions to make up for the loss of Renoir, Sisley, and later Monet himself. Clearly the Impressionist exhibitions had partially succeeded in promulgating the "movement" but the Impressionists themselves could not expect to live on the proceeds. Chocquet, Charpentier, and other patrons (Manet and Caillebotte also fulfilled this role) were still vital to their livelihood, and, as frustration with the relative failure of the independent shows grew, Renoir, Sisley, and Monet in particular looked once again to the Salon. The radical Pissarro would not countenance this and in 1878, a year when there was no Impressionist exhibition, he rented a room in the Montmartre quarter of Paris to exhibit his own pictures, which were ironically less radical than ever before, to potential clients. Pissarro, like Monet, had recently lost a friend and patron, Ludovic Piette, a landscapist of some talent who had exhibited with the Impressionists and had died in 1877, depriving Pissarro of an important source of income.

"A BANAL SCHOOL"

The fourth Impressionist exhibition opened on 10th April 1879 at 28 avenue de l'Opéra in Paris without Sisley, Renoir, Morisot (who was pregnant) and Cézanne, but it had works by Cassatt, Forain, Zandomeneghi (all protégés of Degas) and an as yet unknown painter by the name of Paul Gauguin, who had been befriended by Pissarro. For once it was a success and the irony was that as the crowds flocked to see the exhibition there were precious few of the major Impressionists on view. The Salon was now the place to see works like Renoir's *Portrait of Madame Char-* *pentier and Her Children* (*Madame Charpentier et ses enfants*) and Manet's *Boating* (*En Bateau*), both of which received considerable acclaim. That April Georges Charpentier published the first edition of *La Vie Moderne*, a magazine of style, science, comment, and criticism aimed at the well-to-do Parisian. *La Vie Moderne* instituted a series of exhibitions at which Renoir in 1879, and Manet and Monet in 1880, were to have hugely successful one-man shows. As Monet's work finally began to receive the praise he had longed for he was at his most isolated, declaring, "I am still and always intend to be an Impressionist — but very rarely see the men and women who are

MANET
At the Père Lathuille
oil on canvas
1879. 93 × 112 cm
The Impressionists challenged not only the technique but also the subject matter of the academic style as taught in the Ecole. Manet, although not radically different in technique, turned his eye away from the traditional, classical content of painting by depicting the modern life of Paris. Here he has chosen a restaurant in the Batignolles area near where he lived as the setting for what could have been an ordinarily bourgeois scene.

CASSATT
Young Lady in a Park
oil on canvas
c.1880. 71 × 90 cm
RIGHT In his essay in Le Figaro
*entitled "The Painter of Modern
Life", a seminal influence on the
Impressionists, Baudelaire set
forth his views on the status of
women in this new art. "Woman",
he wrote, "is for the artist in
general . . . she is divinity, a star
. . . a glittering conglomeration of
all the graces of nature,
condensed into a single being . . .
she is an idol, stupid perhaps, but
dazzling and bewitching . . . "
Clearly this attitude had little to
do with the lives and work of
Cassatt and Morisot, who could
not walk the streets of Paris, or
even copy in the Louvre, without
being chaperoned.*

CASSATT
Mother and Child
pastel on paper
Undated. 55 × 45 cm
*OPPOSITE Mary Cassatt, who
had no children, nevertheless
made motherhood and child-
rearing her personal artistic
domain. As this pastel shows,
she was influenced by Degas,
her initial mentor, and treats
her subjects with the
detailed observation not to be
found amongst her truly
impressionistic contemporaries.*

my colleagues. The little church has become a banal school which opens its doors to the first dauber that comes along."

Camille died in September 1879. As he watched her growing cold, Monet could not resist painting her portrait for the last time. 1880 marked the beginning of a new decade and the end of an era. Duranty, Flaubert, and Offenbach had died. Manet's illness was now seriously affecting him, making a trip to the Café de la Nouvelle-Athènes, which had replaced the Café Guerbois as Manet's haunt, a rare occurence. Of the original subscribers to the *Société anonyme* only Degas (who had appeared in every show so far), Pissarro, and Berthe Morisot were to exhibit in the Im-

pressionist exhibitions of 1880 and 1881. Renoir was moving in a higher strata of society and was now financially secure although an artistic crisis was looming for him. Degas' increasing grip on the Impressionist exhibitions in which he included more and more of his followers drove Pissarro and Caillebotte to beg him to allow Monet, Renoir, and Sisley back into the fold. Caillebotte finally turned against Degas, bitterly attacking him in a letter to Pissarro:

This man has gone sour. He doesn't hold the big place that he ought to according to his talent and although he will never admit it, he bears the whole world a grudge. One could put together a volume from what he has said against Manet, Monet, you . . .

Pissarro would not be swayed and remained faithful to Degas to the last. The 1881 exhibition opened at the boulevard des Capucines where seven years earlier Monet's *Impression, Sunrise* had given the history of art a new *-ism*. Caillebotte did not participate. A new generation of Impressionists joined Degas, Morisot, Guillaumin, and Pissarro; this was the third Impressionist show for Mary Cassatt, the second for Paul Gauguin; the others included Rouart, Vidal, Vignon, and Zandomeneghi.

Meanwhile the dying Manet had been awarded the *Légion d'Honneur* by a Third Republic which had finally come to terms with him. The pronouncement of Gambetta, the hero of the Siege of Paris in 1870, that "You are revolutionaries, that's the trouble . . . It is better for the Republic to live with bad painting than to die for the sake of great art . . . " had been overturned. The love-hate relationship between the Salon and Manet, the continual rejections and occasional triumphs, had at last resolved itself in favour of the artist. Manet had always tried to play both sides against the middle, encouraging and supporting the Impressionists in their darkest hours whilst resolutely maintaining that he was neither a revolutionary nor an Impressionist. Astruc had said of him in 1867, "M. Manet . . . has no intention to overthrow the old methods of painting or to create new ones. He has merely tried to be himself and no one else." Hearing that he had won the *Légion d'Honneur*, Manet complained with typical barbed wit, "It would have made my future once, but now it is too late to make up for twenty years of failure."

In 1882, with the notable absence of Degas and Cassatt, the Impressionists held their penultimate exhibition in the rue Saint-Honoré. Although there was to be another show in 1886, this was in reality their last stand. For a final time, and with great difficulty, Caillebotte and Pissarro (with the aid of

GAUGUIN
The Sculptor Abbi and His Son
oil on canvas
1882. 53 × 71 cm
*ABOVE An almost conventional
double portrait, with no overt
symbolic content, although the
composition is strangely
disconnected by the vertical join in
the centre of the picture.*

RENOIR
The Terrace
oil on canvas
1881. 100 × 81 cm
*RIGHT Renoir was still painting
landscapes, but portraits were a
favourite subject.*

summation of his adventure as a "painter of modern life". It shows a barmaid, blank-faced, before a mirror reflecting the incessant nightlife of Paris; there is an improbable reflection of her and her customer to the right which touches the borders of surrealism: we might be that customer. In the top left hand corner the legs of an acrobat are bizarrely severed by the frame. A moment of staggering insignificance captured in the very heart of the City of Light.

Manet died on 30th April 1883, at the age of fifty-one. A sale of his work in 1884 realized the modest sum of 116,637 francs for 167 paintings, an average of less than 700 francs per work, far below anything paid for an official Salon painting, or even the Barbizon School which had now become highly collectable.

1883–1886: THE LAST SHOW

Renoir was in the throes of a crisis: "I had come to the end of Impressionism. I was reaching the conclusion that I didn't know how either to paint or draw. In a word, I was at a dead end." In 1882 he had been travelling in Italy and Sicily where he had painted a portrait of Richard Wagner; from there he had joined Cézanne at l'Estaque on the Côte d'Azur and fell seriously ill with pneumonia. His journey to Italy was mainly a quest for classical art and technique. He studied the wall paintings of Pompeii and even more so the perfect smoothness of Raphael's works in Rome, which led him to work in a tighter, more refined and precise style for a while, before he returned to his instinctive, less disciplined brushwork. The conflict of his styles heightened a personal and artistic crisis which is eloquently demonstrated in his painting *The Umbrellas (Les Parapluies)*,

Durand-Ruel) had gathered together the work of Monet, Morisot, Renoir, and Sisley (with Gauguin, Guillaumin, and Vignon) under one roof. At the last moment Edouard Manet was struck with indecision about whether to join the group. At any rate he was now in the final stages of his illness, a form of locomotor ataxia it is believed, which was steadily paralyzing him. His appearance with the others would have been a fitting conclusion to a decade he had spent devoted to them. Nevertheless his last great masterpiece, *A Bar at the Folies-Bergère* (*Le Bar aux Folies-Bergère*) was shown at the Salon of 1882 as he received for the last time the official recognition he so desperately desired.

The painting can perhaps be seen as a

MONET
The Cliffs at Varengeville
oil on canvas
1882.
A favourite subject for Monet, the cliffs along the Normandy coast provided him with a spectacular mixture of land- and seascape.

SIGNAC
Port-en-Bessin
oil on canvas
1884. 68 × 127.5 cm
Although Signac claimed some credit for the Pointillist technique that Seurat developed, it is clear in this work that he was not yet using it himself. He later codified the aims and methods of Pointillism, or Divisionism, in his book From Delacroix to Neo-Impressionism *(1899).*

reworked during the 1880s and left unfinished. Cézanne's powerful influence is evident in Renoir's solid handling of the umbrellas; the group on the right is painted in the delicate, feathery style associated with his high Impressionist period, whilst the girl on the left shows the beginnings of a brief flirtation with classical purity of form and line. A series of *Bathers* illustrates well the more restrained rendering which he tried to apply in later years to commissioned portraits.

In 1883 Monet, Alice Hoschedé and their respective children settled in Giverny, a small village near the Seine and close to Rouen. Ernest Hoschedé had gradually been estranged from his wife and had left the double household. After years of poverty,

moving from house to house, relying on others to pay his way, Monet was now firmly established with a decent income; his pictures were fetching excellent prices, especially in America. He could now devote himself to exploring the *enveloppe* of light he perceived to hold the world together. For the next forty-three years he lived at Giverny, established and tended his celebrated garden, and painted more than ever before. Foreign artists, many of them American, settled nearby; others frequently visited him. The other Impressionists had spread out across France: Pissarro had moved north of Paris to Osny, Cézanne rarely left Provence, and Renoir had decamped to Essoyes in Burgundy with his mistress (later his wife) Aline Charigot.

MONET
Giverny in Winter
oil on canvas
1885. 64.5 × 88.5 cm
*At this time Monet was
exploring the area where he was to
live until his death in 1926. No
weather was cold enough to
discourage him.*

The last Impressionist exhibition took place in 1886. Degas was back with his protégés, but their thunder was stolen by the Neo-Impressionists, or Divisionists, Seurat and Signac, who had already begun to influence Pissarro, after he, like Renoir, had reached a stylistic dead end. Seurat's huge painting *La Grande Jatte* caused a storm at the exhibition, and closed the decade of Impressionism with a new form of painting as controversial as that which had begun it.

The great age of Impressionism lasted barely more than a decade. By 1886 it had permeated the entire world of art, spawning Impressionist movements in the United States, Britain, Germany, and Scandinavia which were to continue for many years to come. Impressionism as an innovative force was still influential, but was also beginning to be challenged, especially by Gauguin, and in 1886 a thirty-three-year-old Dutchman, Vincent van Gogh, arrived in Paris to study at Félix Cormon's atelier . . .

VAN GOGH
The Weaver
oil on canvas
1884. 67.5 × 93 cm
LEFT Despite the important influence of the Impressionist and Neo-Impressionist use of colour on van Gogh's palette, he was no more an Impressionist than the renegade Gauguin. Van Gogh arrived in Paris in 1886, just in time to catch up with the last days of the movement.

SEURAT
Study for La Grande Jatte
oil on canvas
1883. 71 × 104 cm
ABOVE This is one of several finely detailed studies for the finished painting which Seurat made. Pissarro said of him: "he has something new to contribute . . . I am totally convinced of the progressive nature of his art and certain that in time it will yield extraordinary results . . . " Seurat died at the age of thirty-two in 1891 before he could witness the profound influence his work was to have on the Post-Impressionists.

SECTION TWO

◆

THE LIFE AND WORKS

C. Pissarro. 1896.

CAMILLE PISSARRO
Self-portrait
1873
ABOVE

TALENTED ARTISTS as diverse as Gauguin, Cassatt, and Cézanne held Camille Pissarro in the utmost reverence as a teacher and a man of integrity. His selfless devotion to the cause of art and his fellow artists endeared him in a way that few, if any, of his contemporaries could claim. His openness enabled him to transcend his (at best theoretical) anarchist convictions and get on with the likes of the extremely reactionary Degas and the innately conservative Renoir, whilst he was a natural friend and ally to Monet and Sisley, who both struggled, as indeed Pissarro did, long and hard to secure their place in the art world.

Although Pissarro was able to instil confidence in others, he was himself deeply uneasy about his own ability and only settled into a mode of expression which began to satisfy him very late in his life, following a brief but productive flirtation with Neo-Impressionism.

PISSARRO
Sunset at Eragny
oil on canvas
1896. 54.5 × 65 cm
OPPOSITE

LIFE AND WORKS: CAMILLE PISSARRO (1830–1903)

Remember that I have the temperament of a peasant, I am melancholy,
harsh and savage in my works. It is only in the long run that I can expect to please,
and then only those who have a grain of indulgence.

CAMILLE PISSARRO

Camille Jacob Pissarro, "the First Impressionist" as Cézanne referred to him, was born on 10th July 1830 on the island of St Thomas in the Danish West Indies (now the U.S. Virgin Islands), the fourth son of Abraham Pissarro, a French Jew from Bordeaux, and Rachel Manzana-Pommié, a Creole from Dominica who had been widowed and was seven years older than her second husband. Abraham Pissarro ran a general store in Charlotte Amalie, the capital and port of St Thomas.

Though he and his family lived on a tiny island thousands of miles from France, Abraham Pissarro was keen to bring up his children in the French manner, so between the ages of twelve and seventeen Camille attended a boarding school, the Académie Savary in Passy, a suburb of Paris. M. Savary, the director of the Académie, is said to have encouraged the boy's artistic leanings by imploring him to draw coconut palms from nature when he returned to the West Indies. In 1847 Camille was back in St Thomas working in his father's store and he must have indeed followed M. Savary's advice in his spare time, for nine years later (in Paris again) he was painting tropical landscapes from memory.

Camille remained with his family in St Thomas until 1853 when, after five years of working as a clerk, its charms were no longer able to detain him. He decided he had to see more of the world and took off without parental consent to Venezuela with the Dan-

ish artist, Fritz Melbye. For the next two years they rented a studio in Caracas where Pissarro practised drawing and attempted his first watercolours under the thoughtful eye of Melbye who had studied at the Copenhagen Academy and was able to teach his friend the basics of the Academic Style. By the time he had obtained his father's blessing and sailed to Paris to study with Melbye's brother Anton, Pissarro was already an accomplished landscape painter.

The Exposition Universelle of 1855 was in its last few days when Pissarro arrived in Paris. Courbet's Realist Pavilion was creating a stir, but Pissarro was more interested in the few landscapes by Corot on show and later introduced himself to the master landscapist. During the next couple of years Pissarro worked as Anton Melbye's assistant, took some private lessons at the Ecole and studied at the free Académie Suisse where he met Claude Monet; he was also an occasional pupil of Corot, describing himself as such in his first submission to the Salon in 1859.

Pissarro passed the Salon hurdle at the first attempt. His parents had recently returned to France and settled in Paris, and were suitably impressed (and no doubt relieved) that their youngest son had begun to make his mark in the art world. The Salon was the summit of exhibitions and Pissarro's carefully worked landscape of Montmorency had enough of Corot in it to succeed in academic terms, but it also proved that Pissarro's talent was to be uncompromising. The move from the exotic Virgin Islands and South America to what the art historian Linda Nochlin calls "the infinitely civilized" French countryside had produced in Pissarro a lighter, more naturalistic vision than that of Corot. In the years to come he was frequently to be accused of painting vulgar and unaesthetic landscapes far from Corot's comparatively idealized works.

From his earliest drawings in St Thomas to his death in 1903, Pissarro's style and method were in a continual state of flux. As the art historian John House has said, "to chart Pissarro's stylistic evolution . . . we meet in turn Corot, Daubigny, Courbet, Jongkind, Monet, Cézanne, Renoir, Millet, Seurat, Turner, and Monet again." Although he was the oldest of the Impressionists, Pissarro never ceased assimilating the work of others in an artistic evolution which is unparalleled among his contemporaries. In the late 1850s and early 1860s the Salon and the French art world were in a deep debate about the acceptability of Daubigny's sketchy *plein-airisme* and the consequences of Courbet's realism. Having succeeded on the safer ground of Corot, Pissarro began to appreciate the attempts of Daubigny and Courbet to paint what they saw and wanted to see. At the age of twenty-nine Pissarro met Monet, ten years his junior, at the Académie Suisse and soon became part of a new generation of artists fired by the example of Courbet and Daubigny, impatient with the academic landscape.

COROT
Dardagny, Morning
oil on canvas
c.1853. 26 × 47 cm
Pissarro had seen the few Corots on show at the 1855 Exposition Universelle and a year later went to see the master landscapist. Corot's style was a profound influence on Pissarro for many years. This small, sketchy picture displays the freer side of Corot which suited Pissarro's early vision.

Unlike Monet, Renoir, Sisley, and the other budding Impressionists with whom he was soon to have a remarkable relationship, Pissarro's view of the world had already become deeply politicized. The glory of the Second Empire was skin deep as far as he could see and the dehumanizing effects of rapid industrialization hidden behind the glittering façade of the Empire were not lost on him. He grew increasingly attracted to the extreme radicalism of Proudhon and Prince Kropotkin. Proudhon had said that "art should show us exactly as we are, not in a mediated fantasy that no longer represents us." The artist he had in mind for his project was Courbet; Pissarro was already well acquainted with Courbet's work in the late 1850s and had read Proudhon's huge tract *On Justice in the Revolution and the Church*, published in 1858. Somewhat anarchic by nature, Pissarro began to espouse some of Proudhon's anarcho-federalist ideals and was to become more avowedly anarchist as the years went by. (Proudhon was, as the art historian Ralph Shikes points out, "a passionate advocate of Justice, Liberty, and Equality, yet his Equality did not embrace universal suffrage; blacks, whom he regarded as inferior; and women, equally inferior, whose place he felt was in the home.") The task of the artist, as Pissarro was to say many years later, echoing Proudhon, "is to seek with our own senses the elements of what surrounds us. This can only be achieved by observing

MILLET
The Gleaners
oil on canvas
1857. 83.5 × 111 cm
Millet was also an important early influence on Pissarro, who was attracted to subjects like this and continued to paint them throughout his career. Millet's plain and sentimental paeans to peasant life were criticized for the "vulgarity" of their subject matter, but formed an important model for artists such as Pissarro and later van Gogh.

nature with our own contemporary sensibility. It is a serious mistake to believe that every form of art is not closely linked to its time."

In 1860 when it seemed little could shake the foundations of the Second Empire, Proudhon's views were considered dangerous but tolerated. Despite his growing convictions, Pissarro's talents clearly lay in the reality of nature and agriculture, in landscapes with figures – what one critic has called humanist landscape – not social realism, although the two could combine successfully to a certain extent in his *Railway Bridge at Pontoise (Le Pont de chemin de fer à Pontoise)* of 1860, and yet prove stilted and sentimental in *Donkey Ride at La Roche-Guyan (Promenade à l'âne à La Roche-Guyon)*, what Shikes calls "the only canvas of his career with an overt social message."

Several important relationships developed for Pissarro in 1860. Working in the country-side around Paris one of his constant companions was Ludovic Piette, a landscape painter four years older than Pissarro who had studied at the famous atelier of Couture and then at the Académie Suisse. Pissarro struck up a life-long friendship with Piette, who was moderately well off and had a farm at Mont-foucault in Brittany which in future years became indispensable to the penniless Pissarro. At about this time Pissarro became closely attached to Julie Vellay, the daughter of a viticulturist from Burgundy, who had found employment as his mother's maid. There had been no Salon in 1860, but after his initial success two years earlier the vagaries of the Salon were against Pissarro this time. The jury was severe and rejected his entry but accepted Manet's *Guitar Player (Le Joueur de guitare)* with an honourable mention. Pissarro continued to work in Paris, copying at the

PISSARRO
Woman Reading
oil on canvas
1860. 26.5 × 29 cm
The sitter is Julie Vellay, the maid of Pissarro's mother, whom he met the same year, and who was quite a few years younger than him. They had seven children and married ten years later, in 1870, while they were in London.

Louvre and working at the Académie Suisse where he met two important allies, Paul Cézanne, on whom he was to have a great influence, and Armand Guillaumin.

1863 was the year of the Salon des Refusés and the scandal of Manet's *Luncheon on the Grass (Déjeuner sur l'herbe)* which over-shadowed the contributions of Pissarro, Cézanne, Jongkind, and Guillaumin and laun-ched the reluctant Manet as a figurehead of the avant-garde. The year had begun auspi-ciously for Pissarro and Julie Vellay; in Febru-ary the first of their seven children, Lucien,

PISSARRO
Banks of the Marne in Winter
oil on canvas
1866. 92 × 150 cm
*The influence of Corot is manifest
in this bare work, which was
shown at the Salon, where the
subject was found vulgar and the
painting ugly. It was indeed not
decorative enough for its time, but
Pissarro was never concerned
by prettiness.*

was born (Julie had in fact suffered a miscarriage the year before). Pissarro was a devoted father to his children; his extensive correspondence with Lucien, who moved to London in the 1890s to set up a book illustration press, forms a large part of our knowledge about Pissarro's later life.

Two years later Abraham Pissarro died, precipitating a financial crisis for Camille Pissarro and his growing family – they now had a daughter, Jeanne. The Salon of 1864 had accepted two landscapes from the artist, described in the catalogue as a pupil of Corot and (Anton) Melbye, and Pissarro appeared in the Salon until rejected along with Renoir, Sisley, and Monet in 1867.

Despite this relatively steady success rate at the most important of art markets, Pissarro's sales were few and far between; he was already beginning to call upon the largesse of friends such as Ludovic Piette whose farmhouse in Montfoucault he had visited in 1864. At this time he also began to fall out with Corot who did not approve of the increasing influence of Courbet in Pissarro's work and thereafter Pissarro stopped calling himself a pupil of Corot. The painting Pissarro showed at the 1866 Salon, *Banks of the Marne in Winter*

(*Les Rives de la Marne en hiver*) drew the praise of Zola for its modernity, whilst another critic said: "M. Pissarro is not commonplace for want of the ability to be picturesque, he has used his robust and exuberant talent to depict the vulgarity of the modern world." The influence of Corot and Daubigny in Pissarro's use of dark and subdued pigments, as well as Courbet's palette knife technique is evident here, but even at this early stage in his development Pissarro's choice and control of his admittedly banal subject stands out as an intensely personal vision of the countryside (near Pissarro's home at the time, La Varenne-Saint-Hilaire) that he painted.

By 1867 Pissarro and his family had moved to Pontoise, a village on the river Oise near Auvers, where they remained until 1869 and then settled in Louveciennes. Pissarro worked consistently outdoors at landscapes during these years but kept a studio in Paris and was close to the rapidly growing movement that met in the Café Guerbois. The 1867 Salon which coincided with the Exposition Universelle was particularly conservative in its selections and Pissarro, one of the many *refusés*, had joined Renoir, Sisley, Monet, Bazille, and Cézanne in signing a petition

PISSARRO
Springtime in Louveciennes
oil on canvas
c.1868–69. 53 × 82 cm
The Pissarros had recently moved to Pontoise, a small town on the banks of the Seine not far from Marly, where Sisley lived, and Bougival, where Monet worked. This landscape is still close in style to Corot, especially in the rendering of the trees on the right.

PISSARRO
The Diligence at Louveciennes
oil on canvas
1870. 25.5 × 35.7 cm
Pissarro has at last found his own style: the brushstrokes are less unified and he captures well the atmosphere of a rainy day. The diligence was the public coach transporting local passengers, here seen on its slow round.

demanding another Salon des Refusés. There was now talk of an independent exhibition amongst the Gleyre students and Pissarro, Cézanne, and Degas. Pissarro was by now deeply involved in the emerging group and was to play an increasing role in its future development. Daubigny's inclusion on the Salon's jury the next year secured the exhibition of two of Pissarro's Pontoise landscapes, moving Zola to pronounce Pissarro "one of the three or four true painters of our day. I have rarely encountered a technique that is so sure . . . *C'est là la campagne moderne* [this is truly the modern countryside]." Sadly this praise was of little avail to the Pissarro family, now in financial straits. Their income was so erratic that Camille was occasionally forced to join with Armand Guillaumin decorating shop fronts and blinds.

A brief period of relative calm and consolidation ensued in Louveciennes, where Pissarro's researches into landscape continued. He was joined by Claude Monet, who had been working with Renoir at La Grenouillère (Pissarro had briefly worked there as well during the summer). In the winter of 1869–70 under varying weather conditions both artists painted similar views of the road to Versailles where Pissarro's house stood.

The outbreak of war on 19th July 1870 forced the Pissarro family to move to safety, first to Piette's farm in Brittany and then in December they crossed the English Channel to a suburb of London where Pissarro's mother was already living. There he finally married Julie Vellay, already pregnant with their third child.

Monet had fled to London as well, and through the auspices of the sympathetic dealer Durand-Ruel, also a refugee in London, Pissarro made contact with him: "Monet

and I were very enthusiastic over the London landscapes," recalled Pissarro in a letter of 1902. "Monet worked in the parks whilst I, living in Lower Norwood, at that time a charming suburb, studied the effect of fog, snow, and springtime. We worked from nature . . . We also visited the museums. The watercolours and paintings of Constable and Turner and the canvases of Old Crome [i.e. John Crome, 1768–1821, leading artist of the Norwich School of landscapists] have certainly had an influence upon us. We admired Gainsborough, Lawrence, Reynolds, etc., but were struck chiefly by the landscape painters who shared more in our aim with regard to *plein-air*, light and fugitive effects." As the art historian Phoebe Pool notes, Pissarro's initial delight at the English landscapists was grudgingly tempered. In the last year of his life he

PISSARRO
The Pink House
oil on canvas
1870. 46 × 55 cm
Pissarro's subjects are always factual and completely unpretentious, true to his own temperament. Like most true Impressionist artists, he was satisfied to choose a spot and to paint it. Monet joined Pissarro at Louveciennes, where they painted the local streets side by side.

wrote to Lucien saying, "Turner and Constable . . . showed us in their work that they had no understanding of the analysis of shadow, which in Turner's painting is simply used as an effect, a mere absence of light. As far as tone division is concerned, Turner proved its value although he did not apply it correctly and naturally."

The important contact with Durand-Ruel aside, Pissarro's fortunes did not improve in London; the public were not keen to buy his paintings and the Royal Academy's annual exhibition refused both his and Monet's work. Twelve paintings and some studies survive from Pissarro's time in London,

ranging from the highly impressionistic *Fox Hill, Upper Norwood* and *Dulwich College* to the more highly polished *The Avenue, Sydenham*, which Durand-Ruel eventually bought in 1871, but which Pissarro must have hoped to sell to the London market.

The net result in artistic terms of Pissarro's exile in London, his contact with Monet and the English landscape school, was a freer handling of brighter pigments, using the swiftly applied patches of colour which Monet had been developing since La Grenouillère and was now employing to great effect in his views of the Thames. Compared to Monet, now approaching Impressionism

PISSARRO
Dulwich College
oil on canvas
c.1870. 50 × 61 cm
Save the rather systematic
rendering of the branches, the

careful if plain rendering of some
of Corot's work has now
disappeared from Pissarro's.
Dulwich College was and remains
one of the landmarks of the area.

par excellence, Pissarro's ongoing debt to the first of his mentors, Corot, as well as to Daubigny and Courbet is still evident in *The Avenue, Sydenham*. Solidity and consonance of composition characterize his work in comparison to Monet's search for "fugitive effects" in light and water.

The fall of the Paris Commune and the end of war in 1871 allowed Pissarro and his family to return to Louveciennes. What they saw when they got there horrified them. The Prussians had commandeered their house and used it as a butchery. Of the 1,500 paintings the artist had stored there, only about forty remained; the rest had been ripped from their stretchers and placed on the ground for the soldiers to walk on. Pissarro found the abused canvases discarded on the compost heap. Undeterred, Pissarro carried on painting as prodigiously as before. In November their second son, Georges, was born. In 1872 they moved back to Pontoise where they remained until 1882. Cézanne, invited by Pissarro to continue his landscape studies in Pontoise, arrived in the winter of 1872 with his companion Hortense Fiquet and their son Paul. They took up residence in a local hotel, later

CEZANNE
Dr Gachet's House at Auvers
oil on canvas
1873. 46 × 38 cm
FAR LEFT Cézanne worked with Pissarro between 1872 and 1874, and his technique improved considerably under Pissarro's tuition. Here we can see how Cézanne emulates Pissarro's style, abandoning a thick impasto worked with a palette knife for a lighter and more sober rendering.

CEZANNE
Self-portrait
oil on canvas
1873–76. 64 × 53 cm
LEFT He has depicted himself tormented and scruffy, seeking himself and not often pleased with the result of his efforts.

PISSARRO
Self-portrait
oil on canvas
1873. 56 × 46.5 cm
RIGHT Pissarro was only forty-three when this portrait was made, but he looks much older by our standards. Renoir complained of being old at the same age.

PISSARRO
Early Frost
oil on canvas
1873. 65 × 93 cm
RIGHT Pissarro was the only Impressionist to share with the previous generation a taste for pastorals, peasants and villages, and he preferred orchards and kitchen gardens to the cultivated gardens dear to Monet. This composition is sophisticated in its simplicity and it is remarkably well balanced and delicate.

PISSARRO
Red Roofs
oil on canvas
1877. 54.5 × 65.5 cm
BELOW Pissarro painted **Red Roofs** *during the winter of 1876–77. It was a cluster of houses at the bottom of the Côtes des Boeufs, very near Pissarro's house.*

moving to nearby Auvers-sur-Oise. Cézanne's *House of the Hanged Man at Auvers* (*La Maison du pendu à Auvers*) from this period is greatly influenced by Pissarro's increasingly impressionistic style.

Pissarro's fortunes were temporarily looking up. Auctions in Paris were fetching high prices, whilst the influential, sympathetic and extremely wealthy journalist and art critic Théodore Duret, the Comte de Brie, was beginning to champion the work of Pissarro and others in the group. The soon-to-be-named Impressionists, including Pissarro, were thrashing out the details of the new *Société anonyme* that they were about to form in order to launch their first exhibition. Pissarro was deeply involved in organizing the new venture, foreseeing a sort of cooperative or collective bizarrely based on the

PISSARRO
La Côte des Boeufs at the
Hermitage, near Pontoise
oil on canvas
1877. 115 × 87.5 cm
*This year Cézanne had returned
from the south of France to work
with Pissarro. Here we find a
similar view of cottages seen
through trees, and a hill blocking
part of the background. Pissarro
was beginning to apply thicker
coats of paint, giving more texture
to his canvases.*

PISSARRO
The Garden at the Hermitage
oil on canvas
1877. 55 × 46 cm
Above Abandoning for once the open country, Pissarro depicts two of his children in the family garden, which does not look as well cared for as Monet's.

PISSARRO
The Seamstress
pastel on canvas
1881. 25 × 20 cm
Right In this small study, Pissarro depicts the humble life of a peasant woman in the peace of her home.

principles of the Pontoise bakers' union and the *Association des artistes, peintres d'histoire et de genre, etc* which he had joined thirteen years before. Renoir, Monet and the rest of the group found the complexities of Pissarro's plan too much and eventually a joint stock company was founded with the fifteen artists as equal shareholders. Further tension was created by Pissarro insisting on Cézanne and Guillaumin joining the *Société*'s exhibition but Pissarro had his way. Duret was against the whole idea of an independent exhibition and urged Pissarro to follow Manet's example and stick to the Salon. This Pissarro ignored and thus remained faithful to the concept of the Impressionist exhibitions; he went on to contribute to all eight.

April 1874 was an eventful, albeit traumatic

PISSARRO and GAUGUIN
Respective portraits
c.1879–80.
Gauguin, self-centred and opinionated, was one of the young artists who profited from Pissarro's benevolent tuition. Gauguin was to find Pissarro's world all too simplistic and pursued his own very different quest. He turned against his mentor but later acknowledged how much he owed him.

SEURAT
Alfalfa Field near St Denis
oil on canvas
1885. 65 × 81 cm
*Seurat had been experimenting
with Pointillism for several years
when he painted this landscape.
His teachers at the Ecole in Paris
had found him hardworking, an
essential quality for the
painstaking technique he evolved.*

month for Pissarro. In the Impressionists' first exhibition Pissarro's innovative landscapes were condemned along with the others. When the exhibition closed Pissarro was forced to appeal to Piette for help. Following his critical failure Pissarro's nine-year-old daughter, Jeanne, died the same month.

Pissarro was now almost forty-five years old. Fifteen years later in 1890 he wrote a letter to his niece, Esther Isaacson, summing up his career thus far: "I began to understand my feelings and know what I wanted in my forties – but only vaguely; at the age of fifty, in 1880, I conceived an idea of [artistic] unity without being able to render it; at sixty I am now beginning to see the possibility of rendering it." Pissarro's career was indeed a long and arduous search for the perfect method of expressing himself and his ideas. Until his sixty-second year when Durand-Ruel mounted a hugely successful retrospective of his work he was permanently in dire straits as his family continued to grow. Yet

despite these pressures, he never begrudged anyone advice and encouragement. Younger painters, beginning with Cézanne in 1872, Gauguin in 1877, and later Matisse and Picabia sought him out. Cézanne revered him, saying he was like a father to him, *"un peu comme le bon Dieu"* ("a little like the good Lord"). Mary Cassatt thought he was such a good teacher he could have taught the stones to draw.

By the time of the last Impressionist exhibition in 1886 the great teacher was himself in an artistic crisis. The intervening years had seen him contribute to every Impressionist show and often cajole the other members of the group into accepting the works of younger artists such as Gauguin. He had been helped along by commissions from the successful patissier Eugène Murer, who had also bought a hotel room for him in Rouen where he spent considerable periods painting the cityscape. A printing partnership with Degas and Mary Cassatt had been successful, Durand-Ruel had supported him when and as he could, and so he had managed to get by. In 1884 the Pissarro family had moved to Eragny where they eventually bought the house they had leased (with the aid of a loan from Monet which Pissarro scrupulously repaid). Meanwhile Pissarro's interest in the human figure, especially the peasant women who were so much a part of the landscape, had come to dominate his work as a fundamental expression of his humanism. As Ralph Shikes observes:

Often he paints the grubby kitchen gardens, quite understandably paintings of little appeal to a self-conscious middle class. His agricultural workers – members of the peasant family or day labourers – carry

PISSARRO
Haymakers, Evening
oil on canvas
1893.
While retaining his familiar
subject matter, which Seurat had
also treated in small studies,

Pissarro is now adapting
Pointillism to his own style, and
the woman in the foreground has
lost the soft and natural posture
of his earlier figures.

143

PISSARRO
Landscape at Eragny
oil on canvas
1895. 60 × 73.5 cm
*Another example of Pissarro's late
Pointillism. This is an
afterthought – he had renounced
the technique a few years earlier,
and it has none of the dogmatic
coldness seen in Seurat's works.*

buckets of water, herd the cows, feed the chickens. They are mostly women performing lowly chores. They are not heroic figures, but simple humanity observed in the cadenced rhythm of the seasons . . . as they perform their [daily] tasks.

But the method of expressing all this had become problematical. The web of comma-like brushstrokes which had now become his trademark seemed to have reached its logical conclusion and he was casting about for new ways of painting. A harder edge was called

for. Impressionism seemed to have had its day; Renoir for example had recently found himself in a similar stylistic dead-end and was developing an overtly linear, Neo-Classical style; years before, Cézanne had abandoned a softer vision of the world and was absorbed in lines, volumes, and planes. In October 1885 Pissarro met the young Georges Seurat who was developing a new technique, Divisionism, based on several theories going back to Chevreul. Pissarro too had read the new colour theories proposed by the American colour theorists Charles Henry and

Ogden Rood, and with Paul Signac he found common cause in Seurat's juxtaposition of small dots of pure pigment to create the forms of a painting. "I am totally convinced of the progressive nature of this art," he wrote to Lucien, "and certain that in time it will yield extraordinary results. I do not accept the snobbish judgments of romantic Impressionists in whose interest it is to fight against new tendencies. I accept the challenge, that's all."

At the age of fifty-five Pissarro became a Neo-Impressionist; his anarchism had also become more fervent. Writing later to Lucien, he said: "I firmly believe that our anarchist philosophy is linked to our work and therefore disagreeable to current thought." Signac and Seurat were also sympathetic to the aims of anarchism, although it is difficult to see any concrete link between these amorphous aims and their work. In any case Pissarro's Neo-Impressionism was to last barely five years, and was resisted on the one hand by Durand-Ruel who refused to buy his Divisionist works and on the other by Impressionists who were loath to exhibit in the company of Divisionists. Nevertheless Pissarro secured what amounted to a separate Divisionist Room in the final Impressionist exhibition of 1886, where he, his son Lucien, Signac, and Seurat showed work which attracted both acclaim and horror.

The tedious physical process of painting in what was variously called the Neo-Impressionist, Pointillist, or Divisionist technique of dots took its toll on Pissarro and reduced the number of canvases (normally high) which he could finish. In May 1889 his mother died at the age of ninety-four. The same year Pissarro began to suffer from an eye infection, forcing him to work indoors, but not inhibiting his flow of work. He

abandoned the limitations of Divisionism the next year and began a phase of painting urban and quayside landscapes in Paris, Rouen, Le Hâvre, and Dieppe, as well as in London. The years between 1889 and 1900 were perhaps the most productive of his life; in 1896 he was earning sufficient sums to begin paying back the money he had borrowed from Monet. Truly anarchic to the end, Pissarro became more committed to the cause as he approached his seventies. Back in the days of the Café Guerbois he had once suggested burning down the Louvre; now, in 1894, his

PISSARRO
Paris, Place du Hâvre
oil on canvas
1893. 60 × 73 cm
Dissatisfied with Pointillism, Pissarro looked instead for a different kind of subject and produced many cityscapes in his later years, most of them seen from the window of rooms high up above Paris, Rouen and Dieppe.

PISSARRO
Roofs of Old Rouen (*DETAIL*)
oil on canvas
c.1866–1902. 102 × 76 cm
*ABOVE Closing the circle, the old
painter, who died the following
year, chose to re-work a painting
executed when he was very much
under Corot's influence.*

PISSARRO
Boulevard Montmarte, Paris
oil on canvas
1897. 72 × 91 cm
*RIGHT Renoir was very critical of
Pissarro's cityscapes. He might
more justly have said that
compared to Monet, Pissarro's
style had not evolved as much.
There is indeed no marked
difference between some of
Monet's cityscapes of 1876 and
this painting, made twenty
years later.*

anarchist sympathies forced him to spend four months in Knocke, Belgium after the knifing to death of Président Sadi Carnot by an Italian anarchist. During the Dreyfus Affair, which practically tore *fin de siècle* France apart, he came out staunchly on Zola's side and against the entrenched anti-Semitism of the French military which had clumsily framed an innocent Jewish captain-of-the-guard and led to his exile and imprisonment.

Camille Pissarro died in Paris on 13th November 1903 of blood poisoning caused by an abscess of the prostate: his homeopathic doctor had attempted to cure it without an operation. His last years were marked by international honour and widespread public acclaim. Of all the Impressionists he was perhaps the best loved and respected by his friends, fellow artists, and protégés. After Pissarro's death Gauguin said of him, despite the severe criticism he had received from Pissarro: "*Ce fut un de mes maîtres. Je ne le renie pas.*" ("He was one of my masters. I cannot renounce him.")

PISSARRO
Boulevard Montmarte by Night
oil on canvas
1897. 53.5 × 65 cm
Both pictures were painted from the Hôtel de Russie at the corner of the boulevard des Italiens and of the rue Drouot in Paris, in an area familiar to the Impressionist group. The night view presented a challenge which seems to have stimulated the artist, and Pissarro met it with great success, in a decidedly impressionistic way, giving life to the flicker of street lights and to the reflection of the rain on the pavement.

manet

E DOUARD MANET WAS the figurehead of a generation of artists who saw him as a champion of
experimental and non-conformist art. As a conventional member of the bourgeoisie who desired
nothing better than to be acclaimed by society at
the Salon, Manet's career was marked by mis-
understanding from both sides. As a friend of Baudelaire, he was
at the very forefront of the artistic avant-garde, yet he remained
personally conservative and eager to please. It was his ability to
create something new from the most conventional of subjects
that ensured his continuing fame as well as a deeply felt ambiva-
lence amongst his critics, who until recently have expressed
contradictory views that he was both a genius and lacking in
imagination. His achievements lay in the ambiguity and unrivalled originality with which he portrayed the Paris of his day, as
epitomized in the *Bar at the Folies-Bergère* and the *Corner in a
Café-concert* – two paintings which more than any of his contemporaries' encapsulated impressions of an age of decaying and
transitory brilliance.

EDOUARD MANET
By Fantin-Latour
1867
ABOVE

MANET
The Walk
oil on canvas
c.1880. 92.5 × 70.5 cm
OPPOSITE

LIFE AND WORKS: EDOUARD MANET (1832–1883)

. . . a revolutionary painter who loved society and had always dreamt of the success only Paris can offer – the flattery of the ladies, the warm embrace of their salons, a life of luxury hurtling through admiring crowds.

EMILE ZOLA

MANET
Copy of Tintoretto's Self-portrait
oil on canvas
61 × 50 cm
ABOVE This is one of the numerous old masters copied by Manet. He was a registered copyist at the Louvre, but also worked in the Rijksmuseum of Amsterdam, and in Florence, Rome and Venice. Manet was a vital pivot in a long tradition which he sincerely acknowledged.

Edouard Manet was born in Paris on 23rd January 1832, the oldest son of August Manet, Head of Personnel at the French Ministry of Justice, and Eugénie Désirée Fournier, a diplomat's daughter.

Manet could have become a successful lawyer, which is what his father had in mind for him, but it was perhaps the influence of his artistic mother Eugénie and his uncle Edmond Fournier, a great connoisseur of art, that quashed the idea early on. From the age of fifteen Manet and his friend at the exclusive Collège Rollin, Antonin Proust, received special drawing lessons and were taken on instructive tours of the Paris museums by Edmond Fournier. At sixteen Manet rebelled against his father's wish to enter him in the Faculty of Law, declared his desire to be an artist, forced a compromise with his father (it was more of a ruse than anything) and joined the Navy. He failed the Naval entrance examinations but set sail nonetheless on 9th December 1848 at the age of sixteen as an officer cadet on the ship *Le Hâvre et Guadeloupe* bound for Rio de Janeiro.

On his return to France the next year Manet failed the Naval examinations once again and finally swayed his father to his artistic ambitions. The baggage Manet brought back from the Americas was crammed with drawings to prove his vocation.

In the Paris of the 1850s there were several independent ateliers where a budding artist could study, and Manet chose one of the most celebrated, that of Thomas Couture in the rue de Laval (now the rue Victor-Massé). Couture had beguiled the Salon of 1847 with his epic painting *The Romans of the Decadence* and was famous both as a painter and as a liberal teacher. Manet remained at Couture's from 1850 to 1856, studying the master's teaching, copying (amongst other things a Velazquez) at the Louvre and occasionally causing trouble in the atelier, as Antonin Proust remembered: "On Mondays, the day when a pose was to be struck for the rest of the week, Manet would invariably fight with Couture's models . . . Mounting the podium they would assume their traditional and exaggerated poses. 'Are you incapable of being natural?' Manet would cry, 'Is that how you stand when you're buying a bundle of radish at the greengrocer's?' " Proust described another incident which sheds some light on Manet's developing wit and his relationship with Couture: "One day Manet had managed to make Gilbert (a model) assume a natural pose, half dressed. Couture walked into the atelier and threw a fit in front of the clothed model. 'So you pay Gilbert to *keep his clothes on*? Who is responsible for this stupidity?' 'I am,' said Manet. 'Come now, my poor boy,' said Couture, 'you will never be anything but the Daumier of your time.' " Later Manet is supposed to have told Antonin, "The Daumier of my time! At least that would be better than being the Coypel of it." (Coypel was not a fashionable painter at that time.)

Despite these frivolities Manet was greatly indebted to Couture, an opponent of the all-pervading academic style and its constrictions. Couture's advice to his students was: "Make sure first of all that you have mastered material procedures; then think of nothing and produce with a fresh mind and hearty spirit whatever you feel like doing." This was exactly what Manet was to do, building on a complete mastery of technique and a deep appreciation of the old masters in order to make his revolutionary (or evolutionary) mark. A foretaste of what was to come is supplied by Antonin Proust, who remembered Manet drawing a picture in 1851 which showed the identification of bodies in the

MANET
The Absinthe Drinker
1859. 177.5 × 103 cm
LEFT Absinthe had far too bad a reputation to be an acceptable subject for the Salon. Manet found his low-life models in the Batignolles area where he lived. The model here is the ragpicker Colardet.

MANET
The Parents of the Artist
oil on canvas
1860. 110 × 90 cm
OPPOSITE The austere M. Manet does not indeed look like the sort of father a son could confide in about his illegitimate offspring. Manet never told his father about Léon, born to his twenty-year-old piano teacher Suzanne Leenhoff, and married only after his father's death.

Montmartre cemetery, victims of the December *coup d'état* by Louis Napoleon. Manet was already a fierce republican; he had written to his father from Rio de Janeiro: "Try to keep a good republic for us against our return; I'm afraid Louis Napoleon is not a very good republican." How right he was; the corpses in Montmartre proved that Manet's fears for the Second Republic were well founded – it had lasted barely two years after his return from South America.

In January 1852 a son, Léon, was born to Suzanne Leenhoff, Manet's twenty-year-old piano teacher with whom he had been having

MANET
Young Woman in Spanish Costume
oil on canvas
1862. 95 × 113 cm
*RIGHT The pose is that of Goya's
Maja. Whereas Goya painted both
a nude and a dressed-up version,
Manet chose to dress her as
a torero. (DETAIL)*

MANET
The Spanish Dancers
oil on canvas
1862. 61 × 91 cm
*BELOW All things Spanish
appealed to the French Romantics
in ascendence during Manet's
youth. Manet could not resist the
opportunity of painting members
of a ballet company that was
touring Paris in 1862. The
group in this picture includes
Lola de Valence.*

an affair since 1850. Eugénie Manet knew of the illegitimate birth, but she and Manet conspired to keep this from the austere and conservative Auguste Manet, passing the child off as Suzanne's brother and Manet's godson, even after Suzanne and Manet's marriage. Manet's strict adherence to form held sway, as it would in other matters, and Suzanne, like so many other mistresses, companions, and courtesans, was set up in an apartment to keep her out of harm's way until it was safe for her to emerge into society.

Manet left Couture's atelier around Easter 1856 and moved into a studio in the rue Lavoisier with another painter, Albert de Balleroy. He then made a tour of Holland, Germany, Austria, and Italy ending in Venice, visiting museums and studying the old masters. In 1859 Manet made his first submission, *The Absinthe Drinker (L'Absinthe)* to the Salon. It was summarily rejected on several counts, notably those of immorality and vulgarity; only Delacroix voted for it. The next year Manet made the acquaintance of the poet and art critic Charles Baudelaire, eleven years his senior, who had published his masterpiece, a collection of poems called *Les Fleurs du mal (The Flowers of Evil)* in 1857. The poems had caused outrage and several were banned. Flaubert's *Madame Bovary* had suffered a similar fate in 1856. The early years of Louis Napoleon's reign were difficult ones for literature and the avant-garde, of which Manet was rapidly becoming an important if somewhat reluctant member. He was now moving in two social milieux; upper middle-class salon society and the Bohemian demi-monde of Baudelaire and his friends where revolutionary new ideas were inspired and thrashed out. Baudelaire, with whom Manet became very close, died in agony of the

MANET
The Old Musician
oil on canvas
1862. 187.5 × 248.5 cm
This painting is a very large
composition which retains a
stillness typical of many of
Manet's works. Again, he found
his models near his home: he re-
used the figure of The Absinthe
Drinker, *who stands on the right,*
wearing a top hat. The old man
was the gypsy Jean Lagrène. The
cut-off figure along the right edge
of the picture represents the
Wandering Jew. All these people
are poor, but Manet did not
attempt to depict them in a
romantic or sentimental manner,
rather he displays the detachment
from his subject matter which was
later to bring accusations of
coldness and impersonality.

LE NAIN
Landscape with Figures
oil on canvas
c.1645. 54.5 × 67.5 cm
This painting was not in a public
collection, but Champfleury,
whom Manet knew, wrote about it
in his book Les Frères Le Nain,
published in 1862. Manet is
known to have worked from
reproductions and he may
have used this picture as the broad
base of his own picture The
Old Musician.

MANET
Battle of the *Kearsage* and the *Alabama*
oil on canvas
c.1865. 139 × 130 cm
ABOVE Always interested in current events and no doubt recalling his own days at sea before he became a painter, Manet painted two scenes of this remarkable episode in the American Civil War which took place off the coast of Boulogne. In the second picture, the Kearsage *is seen damaged and moored along the jetty.*

MANET
The Execution of the Emperor Maximilian
oil on canvas
1867–68. 35 × 26 cm & 89 × 30 cm; 190 × 160 cm; 99 × 59 cm.
RIGHT The first sketch, which Degas tried to piece together after Manet's death. Manet had acquired photographs of the execution which were available in Paris and noticed that the soldiers wore uniforms resembling that of the French army, except for the white gaiters. One of Manet's friends, the commandant of a local barrack, lent him a squad of soldiers as models.

effects of aphasia and syphilis in 1867. His anguished romanticism can be heard in these lines from *Les Fleurs du mal*:

> – *Ô douleur! ô douleur! Le Temps mange la vie,*
> *Et l'obscur Ennemi qui nous ronge le cœur*
> *Du sang que nous perdons croît et se fortifie!*

> – O agony, agony! Time eats away at life,
> And the obscure Foe which gnaws on our hearts
> Grows ever stronger on the blood we lose!

Manet's close friendship with Baudelaire inspired his art in other ways, however. It is noticeable that after *The Absinthe Drinker*, and Manet's encounter with the extraordinarily decadent Baudelaire, the artist avoided further images of rank dissolution. The less decadent side of Baudelaire, his penetrating art criticism and demand for an urban "painter of modern life", was of more interest, in fact, to Manet than the last torments of a dying genius.

Manet's early interest in politics did not abate and he remained keenly aware of current events throughout his life. In June 1864 he went to the port of Cherbourg to witness a bizarre incident of the American Civil War playing itself out. A corvette of the Union Navy, the *Kearsarge*, was attacking and pursuing a Confederate privateer, the *Alabama*, which had been detained in the French docks. Manet painted a gripping picture of the scene. Three years later he painted the first version of *The Execution of the Emperor Maximilian*. The painting was banned as being too sensitive a political subject for exhibition at Manet's pavilion in the place d'Alma during the 1867 Exposition Universelle. Indeed, from

MANET
The Execution of the Emperor
Maximilian
oil on canvas
1867. 195 × 259 cm
In this advanced study, the firing squad is wearing Mexican outfits and the faces of the victims are featureless. The news of the execution had just reached Paris and to Manet the incident illustrated all too well the bankruptcy of Napoleon III's regime.

MANET
Olympia watercolour study
1863.
*BELOW Manet undertook
several studies for the
scandalous painting.*

MANET
Olympia
oil on canvas
1863. 130.5 × 190 cm
*BELOW The older Courbet was
critical of Olympia: "She looks
like a Queen of Spades on a
playing-card: not enough
modelling." Manet, himself
declared: "There is only one
important thing: put down what
you see the first time. If that's it,
that's it." Manet painted with the
light in his studio falling from
behind him, which flattened the
volumes of the figures in the
painting and brought the
artist violent criticism.*

the scandal of *Luncheon on the Grass* at the Salon des Refusés of 1863 onwards Manet was constantly (and it must be said unwillingly) at odds with the authorities, both artistic and political. Manet's subject matter was at the forefront of modernity and strained the limits of the acceptable. He had side-stepped the social realism of Proudhon and Courbet and worked initially under the aesthetic veil of *l'art pour l'art* (Art for Art's Sake), as exemplified in its most frivolous literary form by these two stanzas from a poem by Théophile Gautier:

> *Que tu me plais dans cette robe*
> *Qui te déshabille si bien,*
> *Faisant jaillir ta gorge en globe,*
> *Montrant tout nu ton bras païen!*
> *Frêle comme une aile d'abeille,*
> *Frais comme un coeur de rose-thé*
> *Son tissu, caresse vermeille,*
> *Voltige autour de ta beauté.*

> How you please me in this dress
> Which undresses you so well,
> Letting your breast burst forth,
> Showing quite nude your pagan arm!
> Fragile as a bee's wing,
> Fresh as the heart of a tea-rose,
> Its tissue, a vermillion caress,
> Flutters about your beautiousness.

> *A une robe rose* (To a Pink Dress)
> FROM *EMAUX ET CAMÉES*, 1852

Apart from its concision – brevity was becoming Manet's own stylistic watchword – and its eroticism, *A une robe rose* also gives us a taste of just how small the Bohemian world of Paris was; the poem is dedicated to Apollonie Sabatier, delectable courtesane, and the *Présidente* of the infamous Club des Hashishins frequented by Baudelaire and Gautier, an object herself of extreme (and unrequited) passion from Baudelaire who immortalized her in a cycle of poems within *Les Fleurs du mal*. (She was also given permanent fame in other ways; the sculptor Clésinger made a cast of her body and then modelled it in marble to the delight of the 1847 Salon.)

The influence of Baudelaire's ideas in the early part of Manet's career can be seen in his painting, *Music in the Tuileries Gardens*, which answers the call for a painting of modern life by doing just that; depicting the bourgeoisie

outdoors on a summer's day together with a smattering of Bohemians. Baudelaire and Gautier are among the strollers.

By 1865 *Olympia* had turned the art world upside down, and Manet was the focus of the younger artists' admiration. In that year he began to frequent the Café Guerbois, where contemporary accounts testify to Manet's *sang-froid* and incisive wit in the midst of his colleagues Bazille, Whistler, Nadar, Astruc, Renoir, occasionally Degas, Monet, Cézanne, and Pissarro. But his personality and his aims (if he had any other than simply to paint as well as he could) remain unclear. He was full

MANET
The Bullring
oil on canvas
1865–66. 90 × 110.5 cm
The public reaction to Olympia prompted Manet to travel abroad, and he went to Spain, where he continued to sketch. It was not until the mid-1870s and the influence of Monet and Berthe Morisot that Manet became an open-air painter. This work, like all the others, was done in his studio.

CHARDIN
Still Life with Plums
oil on canvas
c.1730. 45 × 50 cm
RIGHT The French writer Diderot praised Chardin's magical realism and colour harmonies. Others admired the varying effects of light on household objects, and scenes such as this one. It is easy to see how a diligent student and copyist of the classics like Manet would have been strongly influenced by work such as this.

MANET
Still Life with Peaches and Melon
oil on canvas
1866. 69 × 92 cm
BELOW This again illustrates how attached Manet was to tradition. He painted a number of still lifes, some with oysters, which were one of the seventeenth-century Dutch artists' favourite subjects. Manet's work is never plagiaristic, no more than was Bach's borrowing of Vivaldi's musical themes.

of disingenuous advice to younger painters along the lines of "paint what you see as soon as you see it," but his technique was in a class of its own. Few artists could wield a brush with as much nervous energy and accuracy as Manet; few artists (apart from Degas) would dare to choose the subjects he did; few artists had the thorough grounding of five years at Couture's and countless hours copying in the great museums of Europe; few artists had the leisure to paint (his father had left him a more than generous inheritance); ultimately few of his contemporaries (except Degas again) had the ineffable, ambiguous sense of a picture that Manet had. He was modest in triumph, self-effacing in defeat and did not have the inclination of a Pissarro to teach. What went through his mind is difficult to discern.

MANET
Madame Manet at the Piano
oil on canvas
c.1868. 38 × 46.5 cm
Mme Manet was an accomplished
pianist and the couple often
organized musical evenings with
their friends. Now a bourgeoise,
officially respectable since her
wedding, she accepted her
husband's passing affairs.

MANET
The Folkestone Boat, Boulogne
oil on canvas
1869. 60 × 73 cm
*ABOVE Manet spent the summer
in Boulogne with Degas, and
painted six landscapes, the only
ones he executed outside Paris in
the 1860s. The scene shows
passengers about to cross the
English Channel.*

at the end of his tether, desolated by the unheard of ferocity of the critics towards him. The year before Baudelaire had drawn the artist's attention to the fact that *Agnes at Christ's Tomb* depicted the Saviour's spear wound on the wrong side of his body. He wrote to Manet: "You will have to change the position of the wound before the exhibition opens. And don't give those spiteful people a chance to laugh at you." During the *Olympia* scandal Manet wrote to Baudelaire in despair:

I wish you were here, my dear Baudelaire; they are raining insults on my head . . . I should have liked your sane verdict on my pictures, for all these cries have set me on edge . . . something must be wrong . . .

However we do know that in some respects Manet was highly sensitive. In 1860 he moved his studio to the rue Victoire after the young boy who cleaned the brushes and scraped the palettes for him, the subject of *Child with Cherries* (*L'Enfant aux cerises*), hanged himself in the atelier, inspiring a short story from Baudelaire and sending Manet into depression. The artist had threatened to send the boy back to his parents, but had not foreseen the tragic effect of his reprimand. In the next two or three years as Manet's personal fame and ability to create scandal increased he found himself the subject of an irritable reprimand from Baudelaire. The poet had supported him loyally through the *Luncheon on the Grass* episode in 1863, but when the *Olympia* scandal erupted in 1865, Manet was

MANET
Madame Manet and Her Son Léon
at Arcachon
watercolour
1871.
*Right A sketch of peaceful
domesticity, the soothing
atmosphere Manet needed to
restore his shattered spirits. The
crushing of the Commune had
been merciless and bloody, and
most people in Paris were affected
by these tragic events.*

MANET
Emile Zola
oil on canvas
1868. 146.5 × 114 cm
*Left Manet met the
writer and journalist Zola, a
childhood friend of Cézanne, in
1866. Zola was to become
somewhat critical of
Impressionism as he was the
advocate of Realism. Zola wrote
that: "The individual element,
man, is infinitely variable. If
temperament had not existed, all
paintings would have of necessity
to be simple photographs."*

MANET
The Queue at a Butcher's Shop
During the War
engraving
1871. 23 × 16 cm
Right

MANET
Monet Painting in His Studio Boat
oil on canvas
1874. 82.5 × 104 cm
*ABOVE Renoir and Monet
spent the summer of 1874
painting at Argenteuil, then a
small town along the Seine, not
very far from Paris. Manet joined
them and produced four boating
pictures. It is certain that the
younger Monet influenced
his style.*

Baudelaire's withering rejoinder reads:

I am afraid I am again forced to speak to you
about yourself. I shall have to apply myself
to demonstrating to you just what your
value is. What you ask is quite ridiculous.
People are making fun of you, you say; their
jokes set you on edge, etc, etc . . . Do you
think you are the first man who has ever
been in this position? Are you more of a
genius than Chateaubriand or Wagner? Have
people made fun of them, I wonder? They
have not died of it. And in order not to
inflate you with too much pride, I would
add that these men are models, each in his
own field, in a rich world, and that you, you
are simply the foremost in the decrepitude of
your art. I do hope you won't take this
amiss. You know how dear you are to me. I
wanted to have M. Chorner's personal impression [of *Olympia* and *Christ Mocked*], at
least insofar as a Belgian can be considered a
person . . . What he said tallies with what
several intelligent men have said about you:
"There are faults, weaknesses, a lack of
aplomb, but there is an irresistible charm." I
know all this, I was the first to understand it.
He added that the picture of the nude, the
Negress and the cat (is it really a cat?) was far
superior to the religious picture.

Manet's technique, as poor M. Chorner
observed, and Baudelaire knew, was the least
of his worries. Since his years at Couture,
when he would draw objects perfectly but
upside down for fun, he had developed *peinture claire*, described by the art historian Bernard Denvir as

A method of painting . . . which creates a
high-key colour configuration by first

MANET
Couple Boating
oil on canvas
1874. 97 × 130 cm
*The man is his brother-in-law
Rodolphe Leenhoff, wearing the
outfit of a fashionable sailing
club. Manet showed the painting
at the Salon of 1879.*

MANET
The River at Argenteuil
oil on canvas
1874. 61 × 100 cm
RIGHT ABOVE Manet was much less interested in the effects of light than Monet and Renoir. Manet's brushwork is much smoother and more controlled than the other two artists'.

MANET
The Monet Family in Their Garden
oil on canvas
1874. 61 × 100 cm
RIGHT The Monets received the Manets and the Renoirs during the summer of 1874, and both artists painted the Monets in their garden. Mme Monet and her son Jean have such similar poses that the pictures seem to have been done at the same time.

applying loose-flowing and *grasse*, or fat, pigment onto the canvas, and then, whilst the paint is still wet, adding the half-tones and darker passages . . . the reverse of the accepted Academic process. The resulting effect is one of sparkle and vitality . . .

The problem for contemporary critics was that he had applied this bold and innovative technique to a fundamental reinterpretation of some of the icons of western art. By reinventing the nude in *Luncheon on the Grass* and *Olympia*, with explicit reference to past masters, he had appeared to rupture a series of seemingly inviolable traditions. To the budding Impressionists he was an iconoclast; to his own mind he was simply carrying on in the tradition he was falsely accused of breaking.

By the age of thirty-eight, and the outbreak of the Franco-Prussian War in 1870, Manet had painted several masterpieces and as Zola had said in 1866 in *L'Evènement*: "Our fathers

MANET
The Plum
oil on canvas
1878. 73.5 × 50 cm
*RIGHT This young woman is
holding an unlit cigarette and has
ordered a plum in brandy. The
picture shows the unique stillness
of many of Manet's sitters.
Various interpretations have been
suggested, but she is probably
just a working girl passing
the time before she returns to
her small lodgings.*

laughed at M. Courbet so we went into raptures over his work. Now it is we who laugh at M. Manet and it is our children who will be in raptures at his canvases." Manet was now probably the most famous (and infamous) artist of his day, but by the end of the Commune his nerves were shattered and he went to Boulogne in August 1871 to recover. Despite his ubiquitous fame he had sold very few paintings in the 1860s. This was scarcely a problem financially, but his self-esteem demanded buyers for his work, and success at the Salon. Durand-Ruel, the saviour of Monet, Pissarro, Renoir, and Sisley now stepped in and (with as great foresight as ever) bought 50,000 francs worth of paintings. Manet refused, however, to part with *Music in the Tuileries*, *Luncheon on the Grass*, *Olympia*, and *The Execution of Maximilian*, which Durand-Ruel had valued together at a total of 76,000 francs, an astronomical

MANET
The Tub
pastel on canvas
1878–79. 54 × 45 cm
*RIGHT Manet did not paint
many nudes, and this one is
reminiscent of the poses more
familiar in his friend Degas'
work, although the approach is
quite different. The woman, like
Nana and Olympia, is aware of
the gaze of either the viewer or the
painter, whereas Degas's women
are oblivious to any presence
near them.*

sum. *Olympia* was eventually purchased for the French nation by a subscription organized by Monet in 1890, seven years after Manet's death. For seventeen years the Louvre refused to hang the picture until Monet sought the aid of Président Clemenceau in 1907 and had it transferred from the Musée de Luxembourg to the Louvre – the whiff of scandal lingered around the painting for decades.

In December 1874 Manet's close friend Berthe Morisot married his brother Eugène. Thereafter there were no more languorous paintings of her pictured as she is in *The Balcony* (*Le Balcon*) or *The Sofa*. Whatever their relationship had been before – it had certainly been intense – she sat for him no more. In 1876 Manet met Méry Laurent, on whom Marcel Proust's character Odette

MANET
Study for the Beer Waitress
oil on canvas
1878–79. 77.5 × 65 cm
*ABOVE The model is a waitress
Manet knew, but she would only
pose in the presence of her
boyfriend, who is seated. In this
study, the woman is also aware of
an external presence,
and looks at us.*

MANET
The Beer Waitress
oil on canvas
1878–79. 97 × 77.5 cm
*LEFT Manet has enlarged the
composition to place the two sitters
in a wider environment, and we
can see more of the performer on
stage. The setting was the cabaret
Reichshoffen, on the boulevard de
Rochechouart, but the painting
was done in Manet's studio.*

MANET
At the Café-concert
oil on canvas
1879. 47 × 39 cm
RIGHT Another café-concert scene with a young woman very similar to the sitter in The Plum, *who is also holding a cigarette. The man is like many characters of the time, not quite chic but of a relative bohemian elegance. We also find an example here of reflection in a mirror, which is most strikingly exploited in the later* Bar at the Folies-Bergère.

MANET
In the Winter Garden
oil on canvas
1879. 115 × 150 cm
ABOVE The sitters are Jules Guilleme and his American wife. Conservatories, which had first been fashionable among the very wealthy, were now adopted by the bourgeoisie.

Swann was based, a formidable courtesan and the lover of the poet Stéphane Mallarmé. It is possible that Manet had an affair with her; certainly they were devoted to one another in the last years of his life and she is the subject of his last work. The Symbolist poet Mallarmé and Manet had become friends in 1873 and developed a close and constant friendship to rival that with the late Baudelaire. Mallarmé was far removed from the decadence of Baudelaire (who was forced to borrow money from Manet and still owed him 500 francs when he died). He held salons on Tuesday nights crammed with the literary and artistic lions of his day, including Manet and the Impressionists. Manet's association with Mallarmé resulted in illustrations for the poet's translation of Edgar Allan Poe's *The*

MANET
Georges Clémenceau
oil on canvas
1879–80.
ABOVE Gustave Manet, the painter's younger brother, was a friend of the famous French politician, then a deputy in the Parliament. Manet made two portraits of him and a pastel portrait of his wife.

MANET
Portrait of Irma Brunner
pastel on canvas
1882. 53.5 × 44 cm
LEFT ABOVE The sitter was of Viennese origin and was introduced to Manet by his friend Méry Laurent in 1882. Manet liked profile portraits of women wearing dark hats providing a strong background for the sitter's features.

MANET
The Artist's Garden
oil on canvas
1881. 65 × 81 cm
LEFT BELOW In bad health, Manet rented a villa in Versailles during the summer of 1881, intending to paint the classical gardens of the castle, but he was not able to fulfil his project.

MANET
Autumn (Méry Laurent)
oil on canvas
1881. 72 × 50 cm
*RIGHT The sitter was Méry
Laurent, a "grande cocotte" he
had met in 1876 when she came
to see the show he had set up in his
studio after two of his paintings
had been turned down by the
Salon. It was a huge success and
people queued in the street to see.
They were casual lovers and
remained very good friends. This
picture, commissioned by Antonin
Proust, was to be one of four
symbolizing the seasons, a theme
which had been popular
throughout the centuries, but
Manet did not complete the series.*

MANET
Still Life with Carnations
and Clematis
oil on canvas
c.1882. 56 × 35.5 cm
*FAR RIGHT Méry Laurent would
send flowers to her dying friend
Manet, and he used some of them
in still lifes such as this one.
Despite the appalling nature of his
illness, which made it difficult for
him to hold a pastel and almost
impossible to hold a paint brush,
Manet's technique remained
remarkably controlled, and he did
not reduce the size of his canvases.*

rejected by the Salon on the grounds of impropriety and in 1881 he was damned with faint praise when the Salon awarded him a *seconde médaille* for his *Portrait of Pertuiset*. Finally his childhood friend Antonin Proust, who had risen to the rank of Arts Minister, secured Manet the *Légion d'Honneur*. Although he was working flat out on his last masterpiece, the *Bar at the Folies-Bergère*, he was in considerable pain, finding it increasingly difficult to hold a paintbrush. On 6th April 1883 he could no longer walk and was confined to bed. Two weeks later his left leg was amputated to stop the spread of gangrene. He died on 30th April and was buried in Passy cemetery on 3rd May.

Raven as well as a remarkable portrait of Mallarmé which shows Manet under the increasing influence of his Impressionist friends. Indeed, the summer Manet had spent with Monet and his family at Argenteuil in 1874 had released his rather sombre style into a much more colourful, impressionistic idiom. His paintings of Monet, Camille, and Jean in the open air are some of the liveliest documents of the heyday of Impressionism. Manet's new-found interest in light and colour continued to produce sparkling canvases when he visited Venice the next year.

By the end of the 1880s Manet was beginning to feel the effects of the disease locomotor ataxia, which was to kill him before long. The official recognition he so strongly desired was still eluding him; yet he was still capable of causing a stir. In 1876 *Nana* had been

MANET
Study for Bar at the Folies-Bergère
oil on canvas
1881. 47 × 56 cm
LEFT In this large sketch, nearly half the size of the finished work, the waitress is off centre, looking sideways, and the mirror seems to be immediately behind her, while the male customer is very small.

MANET
Bar at the Folies-Bergère
oil on canvas
1881–82. 96 × 130 cm
LEFT In the finished painting, Manet returns to his instinctive preferences and the waitress is facing us, but seems to look through us rather than at us. The foreground forms in itself a very beautiful still life, but Manet was much criticized for his handling of the woman's back and the customer reflected in the mirror. It is indeed inaccurate, but does it matter?

Degas

I N A FAMOUS STATEMENT, Edgar Degas likened his art to the perpetration of a crime; "make counterfeits," he said "and add a touch of nature." Degas never painted *en plein-air* and had nothing but scorn for painters who did, preferring to make sketches of his subjects – primarily the human figure in motion – and use whatever means at his disposal, including photography, to ensure the accuracy of his observation before working in the studio. Thus, until his later experiments with pastel and gouache, Degas had very little to do with the Impressionism of Monet, Renoir, or even the later work of Manet. But, like Manet, his inspiration grew directly out of an intense admiration for past masters.

Despite his uncompromising refusal to espouse the style of his Impressionist colleagues, Degas was instrumental in the foundation of the *Société anonyme* and all the subsequent Impressionist exhibitions except one.

EDGAR DEGAS
Self-portrait
c.1855
Above

DEGAS
Dancers at the Barre
pastel on paper
c.1877. 66 × 51 cm
Opposite

LIFE AND WORKS: EDGAR DEGAS (1834–1917)

*A painting is a thing which requires as much trickery, malice,
and vice as the perpetration of a crime; make counterfeits and
add a touch of nature.*

EDGAR DEGAS

Edgar Degas, like Manet, was born into the higher echelons of Parisian society; in fact he came into the world on 19th July 1834 above a branch of his family's Neapolitan bank in the rue Saint-Georges. But unlike Manet, Degas did not have to fight his parents to become an artist. Amongst the Degas' friends were several eminently wealthy art collectors and government officials who encouraged Edgar, already self-taught, by allowing him to study and copy their art treasures. The Valpinçons, for example, owned Ingres' *Odalisque au turban*, a source of enduring delight and inspiration to the young Degas; and Achille Devéria, Keeper of the Cabinet d'Estampes, the Prints and Drawings Room at the Bibliothèque Nationale, allowed Edgar to peruse the collections and copy the works in them. By the time he was eighteen Degas had also obtained permission to copy at the Louvre. In a comfortable family environment, free of untoward pressure, with a father devoted to him (his mother died when he was fifteen), Edgar Degas was able to indulge his talents with the help of the finest public and private collections in Paris. In 1854 he was to visit wealthy uncles, aunts, and cousins in Naples and Florence where, as one biographer puts it, he undertook an orgy of museums and copying the old masters – Raphael, Mantegna, Bellini, Pollaiuolo, Botticelli, and Giotto. "Draw lines, young man, draw lines," Ingres is said to have advised his young devotee in 1855 when Edouard Valpinçon took Degas to visit the French master, and this he did, and continued to do.

By July 1856 Degas had finished his brief academic studies, having gained a place at the Ecole des Beaux-Arts the year before, studying with a disciple of Ingres, Louis Lamothe. Degas' ability was by now considerable; deep

INGRES
Odalisque
oil on canvas
1826. 32 × 25 cm
This is the purity of line the young Degas admired. Friends of the Degas family had an odalisque similar to this which fascinated the young Degas.

DEGAS
Young Spartans
oil on canvas
c.1860. 109 × 154.5 cm
*Degas was inspired by his reading
of classical authors for this
unusual subject. In contrast to
more academic painters he
deliberately left out classical
elements such as Greek buildings.*

immersion in old masters of every conceivable school, but particularly the Italians, was producing polished results. He then set off for an extended tour of Italy which lasted until April 1859, where he continued to devour the old masters and paint family portraits. In November 1858 Degas' father Auguste, having just received a packing case from his son, wrote to him in Florence with some pride:

> I have unrolled your paintings and some of your drawings. I was very pleased, and I can tell you that you have taken a great step forward in your art; your drawing is strong, the colours are right. You have rid yourself of the weak, trivial, Flandrinian, Lamothian manner of drawing and that dull grey colour. My dear Edgar, you have no reason to go on tormenting yourself, you are on the right track . . . You have a great destiny ahead of you . . .

Auguste Degas seems to have had the measure of his son's potential; the portraits, self-portraits, genre paintings, copies of frescos and old masters produced in Degas' youth bespoke a solid if somewhat unexciting future for the artist. The abundance of self-portraits at such an early age testifies to Degas' single-minded obsession not only with art, but with himself; he resolutely remained a bachelor for the rest of his life.

On his return to Paris, Degas continued his steady self-improvement by copying in the Louvre, gaining permission to do so by listing his friend Emile Lévy as his fictitious master. That was where Edouard Manet first met him in 1862, interrupting him in the

DEGAS
Edmond and Thérèse Morbilli
oil on canvas
c.1865. 117.5 × 90 cm
ABOVE Thérèse was Degas' sister; she had married her first cousin in 1863.

DEGAS
Manet Listening to His Wife
Playing the Piano
oil on canvas
1865. 65 × 71 cm
RIGHT Manet did not like the way Degas had depicted his wife, Suzanne, in this double portrait, and cut part of the canvas off, much to Degas' horror. Degas intended to restore it but never did, perhaps because Manet executed a similar portrait later on.

DEGAS
On the Cliff-top
pastel on paper
c.1869. 30.5 × 45 cm
OPPOSITE Although Degas was a virulent anti-plein-airiste he painted around a hundred landscapes in brief periods during the 1860s and the 1890s.

process of copying Velazquez's *Infanta Margarita* onto a copper plate. At this time Degas was trying to finish his first important history painting, *Semiramis Building Babylon*, and, with the usual friendly rivalry which marked their relationship, Manet was to jest a decade later in the Café de la Nouvelle-Athène that "Degas was painting *Semiramis* when I was painting modern Paris." Manet had certainly completed *The Absinthe Drinker*, *Music in the Tuileries Gardens*, and the epochal *Luncheon on the Grass* by this time and was practically reinventing art, as his critics saw it, but

Degas, only two years younger than Manet, was not far behind: *The Gentleman's Race: Before the Start*, with its highly original composition, dates from 1862.

The relationship between the two artists is described in several tantalizing anecdotes by their friends (and enemies), but remains clouded in a certain amount of mystery. We do know that they admired each other greatly and were in frequent contact; at one point in 1869, for example, Manet wrote to Degas asking for the return of two volumes of Baudelaire. One incident in particular tells us

DEGAS
Races in the Country
oil on canvas
1869. 36.5 × 56 cm
*This is a portrait of Degas'
boyhood friend Paul Valpinçon,
with his wife leaning over the
nurse who holds their new-born
son. Degas did several portraits of
his friend and family, and often
stayed with them in Normandy.*

a great deal about their strange relationship. Between 1868 and 1869 Degas painted a double portrait of Manet with his wife, Suzanne, at the piano. It survives with a piece of canvas attached to the place where half of Mme Manet used to be before M. Manet slashed it off in a fit of pique. In 1924, with dubious accuracy, but with much wit, the dealer Ambroise Vollard recounted the tale Degas had told him in this way:

Vollard: Who slashed that painting?

Degas: To think it was Manet who did that! He thought that something about Mme Manet wasn't right. Well . . . I'm going to try to restore

DEGAS
Racehorses before the Stands
oil on canvas
1866–68. 46 × 61 cm

DEGAS
The Cotton Market
oil on canvas
1873. 73 × 92 cm
*R*ɪɢʜᴛ *The painting was*
executed while Degas was staying
with relatives in New Orleans,
and he thought it could sell in
Manchester, a cotton-spinning
centre. In fact it was exhibited in
1878 in the French southern
city of Pau, which bought it
for its museum.

Mme Manet. What a shock I had when I saw it at Manet's . . . I left without saying goodbye, taking my picture with me. When I got home I took down a little still life he had given me. "Monsieur," I wrote, "I am returning your *Plums.*"

Vollard: But you saw each other again afterwards?

Degas: How could you expect anyone to stay on bad terms with Manet?

By the early 1870s Degas had emerged from his deep and intensive involvement in the past and its forms and, following the example of Manet, he was beginning to apply himself to painting the world of modern Paris, in particular its people (and horses) in motion. Unlike the Impressionists with whom he was to be deeply involved, Degas had shown little interest in landscape. Vollard remembers him wryly pronouncing: "If I were the government, I would have a squad of gendarmes to keep an eye on these people painting landscapes from nature. Oh! I don't wish anyone dead. I would, however, agree to spraying them with a little bird-shot, for starters!" But the landscapes he produced in the late 1860s are delicate, imaginary pastels done in the

DEGAS
The Dancing Lesson
oil on canvas
1873–75. 85 × 75 cm
Left Degas' dance pictures are set in the old Opera House, which burnt down in 1873. He made numerous studies of the dancers.

DEGAS
The Ballet Master Jules Perrot
oil on paper
1875. 48 × 30.5 cm
Above Perrot, who retired when this picture was made, had been a star dancer and had taught for ten years in St Petersburg.

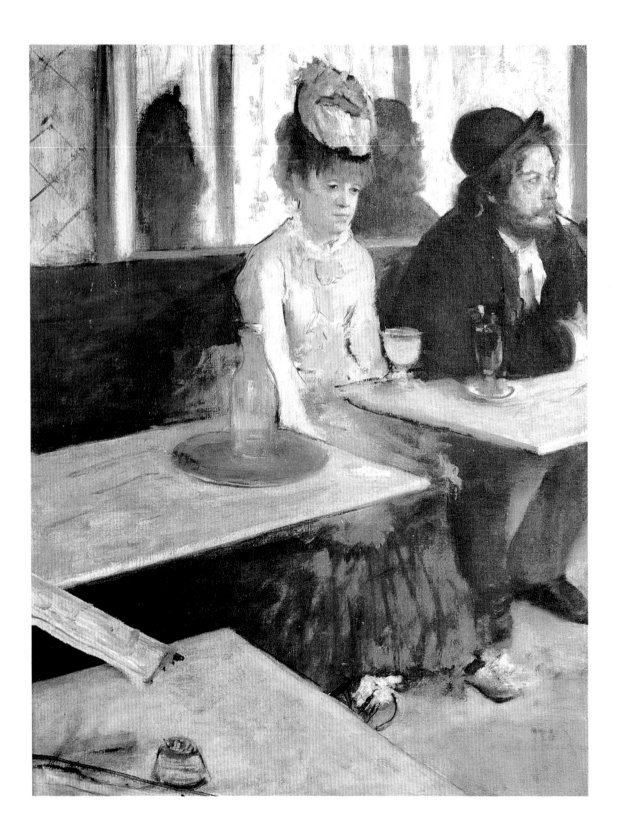

DEGAS
The Absinthe Drinker
oil on canvas
1875–76. 92 × 68 cm
Left The sitters are the actress Ellen Andrée and the painter Marcellin Desboutin, both friends of Degas. When Walter Crane saw it in 1893, he said it was a study in human degradation, male and female.

DEGAS
Dancer Bowing on Stage
pastel and gouache on paper
c.1877. 72 × 77.5 cm
Right Strong sunlight affected Degas' eyesight, but he loved the effect of artificial light. He also liked to experiment with mixing different media, as in this picture.

DEGAS
Aux Ambassadeurs
pastel/monotype
1877. 37 × 27 cm
Far right Degas started to make monotypes towards the mid-1870s. The process consists of applying greasy printer's ink or oil paint on a metal plate. The plate is then printed on paper and can be coloured with a variety of media, mainly oil or pastel. Café-concerts were a favourite haunt of Parisians and they varied in price and quality.

studio, whilst the monotypes of the 1890s are even more imaginary, appearing almost completely abstract.

The range of the subjects he tackled in the ensuing years is formidable: ballet dancers in rehearsal and before, during, and after performance; racehorses – before, during, and after the race; café-concerts and their singers in performance; the opera; acrobats; prostitutes; businessmen; milliners; a pedicurist, musicians; a billiard room. No nook or cranny of Paris in the 1870s and 1880s was immune from his fastidious gaze or his notebook. These notebooks, which have survived, allow us an important insight into the artist's mind. "Draw all kinds of everyday objects," reads a note from 1876, "placed, accompanied in such a way that they have in them the life of the man or woman – corsets which have just been removed, for example, and which retain the form of the body, etc, etc." Another note reads:

On bakery, *Bread* – series on baker's boys, seen in the cellar itself, or through the basement window from the street – backs the

colour of pink flour – beautiful curves of dough – still lives of different breads, large, oval, round, etc. Studies in colour of the yellows, pinks, greys, whites of bread . . . 2 panels on birth – delicate mother,

DEGAS
Portraits at the Stock Exchange
oil on canvas
c.1878–79. 100 × 82 cm
*Right Ernest May in the centre.
He was a wealthy financier,
patron and friend of Degas and
had a collection of Corots and
Impressionist works. The painting
was exhibited at the Impressionist
shows of 1879 and 1880,
although it was not for sale.*

DEGAS
The Name Day of the Madam
pastel/monotype
1876–77. 26.5 × 29.5 cm
*Below It is easy to believe that
Degas made these pictures for his
own and his friends' amusement.
The same was probably true of
Picasso, who owned this picture.*

fashionable – food – large wet-nurse – large behind – enormous ribbons. Lilac coloured dress fluted like a pillar . . .

He had inherited both the dark and corrupting Paris of Baudelaire with its accursed denizens –

*You who wander, stoic, without complaint,
Across the chaos of the living city,
Mothers with bleeding hearts, courtesanes
    or saints,
Whose names in former times were on the lips
    of all . . .*

(from *Les Fleurs du Mal*)

– and the sparkling life of *la ville lumière*, the only place he really felt at home, with its ordinary working people, its ever-increasing number of cafés, concerts, operas and ballets, stars and starlets.

Above all Degas was concerned with the female form: women dancing, women singing, women ironing, women before, during, and after the bath, women sleeping, combing and braiding their hair.

Degas has another comprehension of life, a different concern for exactitude before nature. There is certainly a woman there, but a certain kind of woman, *without the expression of a face*, without the wink of an eye, without the décor of the *toilette*, a woman reduced to the gesticulation of her limbs, to the appearance of her body, a woman considered as a female, expressed in her animality . . .

DEGAS
Edmond Duranty
pastel and tempera on paper
1879. 101 × 100.5 cm
*Duranty was a wealthy literary
and art critic. Degas made three
preliminary drawings for this
picture, which was executed a year
before Duranty's death.*

DEGAS
Brothel Inmates
pastel/monotype
c.1879. 14 × 20.5 cm
*Degas did about fifty such works,
which have always puzzled his
admirers and critics as well as
scholars, who offer various
interpretations for this choice of
subject and the manner in which
it is treated.*

DEGAS
Study for Miss La La at the Cirque
Fernando
pastel on paper
1879. 61 × 48 cm
*ABOVE Degas attended
performances at the circus in
January 1879, and made several
studies, of which this is the last.*

resemblance to Renoir's in their rotundity. Renoir depicts his women "*with the expression of a face*", and all that implies. Increasingly Degas' women at their toilette are, as the 1890s wear on, studies of line and colour; indeed the coloured line, possible with pastels, opened up new avenues for experimentation. As he put it to Sickert, "They [his contemporaries, the Impressionists] are all exploiting the possibilities of colour. And I am always begging them to exploit the possibilities of drawing. It is the richer field." And none could draw with the mastery, and ultimately the abandonment, of Degas.

Degas' sheer energy, his urge to capture fleeting movement in its countless nuances resulted in a prodigious series of paintings, pastels, monotypes, drawings and eventually wax sculpture. Apart from the portraits it is almost impossible to find a Degas where movement and action are not inherent, yet his method was the exact opposite of the Impressionists. He did not attempt to capture the moment in a quick stroke of the brush – there is nothing impulsive about Degas. Everything is studied, planned and executed in the studio in controlled conditions – "I assure you no art is less spontaneous than mine. What I do is the result of reflection and study of the great masters. Of inspiration, spontaneity, temperament, I know nothing." On another occasion and on a slightly different note he said: "It is all very well to copy what one sees, but it is much better to draw what one remembers. A transformation results in which imagination collaborates with memory. You will reproduce only what is striking, which is to say, only what is necessary. That way, your memories and your fantasies are liberated from the tyranny of nature."

Degas approached his involvement with

This is what the contemporary critic Gustave Geffroy thought of Degas' female subjects. It underlines the profound difference between Degas and Manet, who had presented the female nude and the semi-dressed *Nana* as provocations to accepted notions of art. Similarly Degas' late nudes bear only a passing

DEGAS
Nude Combing Her Hair
pastel/monotype
c.1877–79. 21.5 × 16 cm
*ABOVE It is indeed paradoxical
that the admirer of Ingres' pure
and idealized figures could
produce such pictures.*

DEGAS
Miss La La at the Cirque Fernando
oil on canvas
1879. 117 × 77.5 cm
*LEFT The cirque Fernando was
located in Montmartre and later
became the Medrano circus. As
for Miss La La, she was renowned
for the strength of her teeth.*

the Impressionists from the point of view of a Realist because he considered himself to be one and saw the first Impressionist exhibition in the rue des Capucines as an opportunity to promote what he called "a Salon of Realists." It should be noted that the terms Realism and Naturalism were confused and interchangeable at the time. Realists-Naturalists could also be Impressionists as far as the critics of the day were concerned; the term Impressionism subsumed a great deal that was deemed to be new or revolutionary. Thus Degas and Manet, by virtue of their age and status, were wrongly thought to be leaders of the Impressionist movement, when these titles have been awarded to Monet and Pissarro. It is clear that Degas had no interest in the *plein-airisme* being explored by Monet, Pissarro, Renoir, Sisley, and Morisot in the 1870s; his subjects were exclusively Parisian, from racehorses to prostitutes. Moreover, he was experimenting with new techniques and revitalizing neglected media such as pastel, gouache, and even distemper (used for painting scenery) in an attempt to transcend what were now appearing to be the limitations of oil paint.

DEGAS
Dancer Massaging Her Ankles
pastel on paper
1882. 48 × 61 cm
Dancers were originally working-class girls chaperoned by ambitious mothers who also had a say in the choice of their daughters' "benefactors", wealthy men visiting the Opera backstage to choose pretty young girls for their pleasure.

Abandoning oils meant he could paint rapidly on a paper support which could be infinitely extended by sticking separate pieces of paper together as required. In another vein he was experimenting with alternatives to the traditional gilt frames. Having revolutionized the framing of subjects within the composition, he now addressed himself to the immediate environment of the picture, even including the décor and lighting of the exhibition room itself.

Degas' interest in modern life embraced not only those who lived it but also the technological innovations of his day, from a new electric method of drypoint etching to Eadweard Muybridge's extraordinary photographic discoveries about the nature of human and animal locomotion. Degas himself was a keen photographer. Manet and the Impressionists had all been influenced to varying degrees by the new window on the world photography offered, but Degas, the scientific Realist, absorbed Muybridge's discoveries with particular relish.

In 1872 Muybridge, an Englishman working for the U.S. government, had begun to experiment with a photographic process which captured the movement of a horse in motion in order to discover whether all four hoofs left the ground simultaneously during

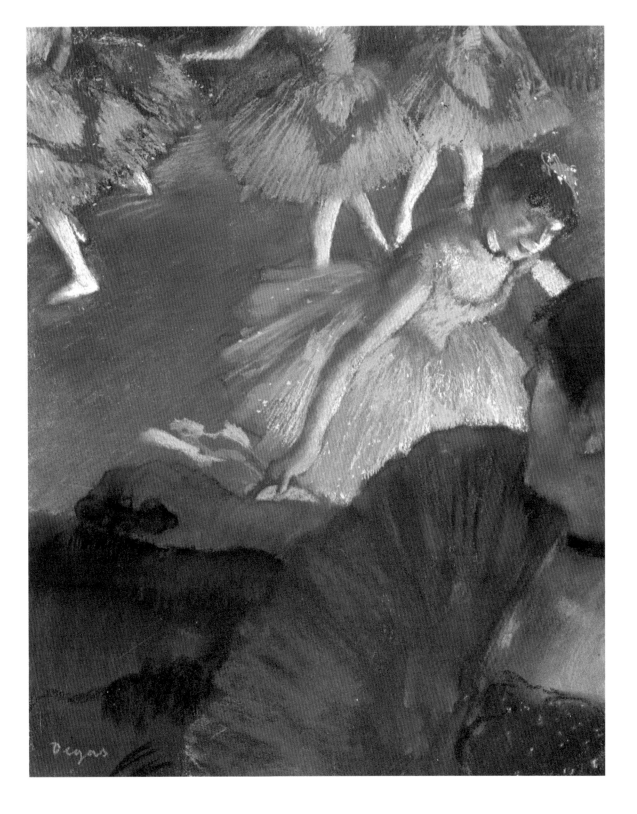

DEGAS
Ballerina and Lady with a Fan
pastel on paper
1885. 66 × 51 cm
*Left This is a good example of
Degas' sophisticated compositions:
the woman in the foreground with
her fan is in the shadow while the
dancer is brightly lit. In the
background, as in a framed
photograph, fragmentary dancers
rendered in subdued tones do not
distract from the star.*

DEGAS
Woman Drying Her Foot
pastel on buff paper
c.1885–86. 54.5 × 52.5 cm
*LEFT Degas painted numerous
bathing scenes, and asked his
models to adopt a great variety of
poses. Of drawing, he said
"Drawing is not form, it is the
sensation one has of it." And:
"Drawing is not what one sees but
what one can make others see."*

DEGAS
Jockeys
oil on paper
c.1886–90. 26 × 36 cm
*OPPOSITE Race horses are a
subject to which Degas frequently
returned throughout his career.
They are usually depicted just
before or after the race itself,
allowing for a variety of
movement. Degas was an intense
observer and had a well trained
visual memory which enabled him
to produce all these works in his
studio, using notes made at the
scene of the action.*

the trot, canter, and gallop. With the financial assistance of Leland Stanford, the Governor of California, Muybridge eventually succeeded, between 1877 and 1878, in using a battery of cameras and trip wires to expose frames at one thousandth of a second of a moving horse thus settling the argument once and for all. The first news of Muybridge's experiments had reached Paris as early as 1874 but until the publication of Muybridge's *Animal Locomotion* in 1887, the punctilious Degas was still drawing his horses' gait in the received manner, which is to say incorrectly. Degas set about studying and making pastel copies of Muybridge's photographs and after 1887 his horses all show the influence of the new information, including a series of wax sculptures of horses jumping and rearing.

DEGAS
And His Housekeeper Zöe Closier
photographic self-portrait
1898–1900.
*Degas had used photography for
his work since 1865.*

In his personal life Degas was a confirmed bachelor but a devoted friend to those who could conquer the barrier of prickliness he erected around himself. His relationship to the Impressionists was marked by an energetic involvement in their cause, even though he himself was uninterested in *plein-airisme* as such. Like Renoir, he was profoundly anti-Semitic and sided vociferously with the anti-Dreyfusards, even though he worked closely with Pissarro and his childhood friend, the novelist and dramatist, Ludovic Halévy. In his last years his eyesight, which had troubled him all his life, began to fail. "Since my eyesight has diminished further my twilight has become more and more lonely and more and more sombre. Only the taste for art and the desire to succeed keep me going," he wrote in the last years of the century. He kept going until his death on 27th September 1917, turning increasingly to sculpture to express himself and producing, ironically, in his last years, his most impressionistic and colourful works in pastel.

DEGAS
Three Russian Dancers
pastel on paper
c.1910. 62 × 67 cm
*Degas produced a series of about
seventeen Russian dancers, of
which this is probably a later
example. Some of the others are
more colourful.*

T HE NAMES OF Claude Monet and Impressionism are nearly synonymous. It was, after all, one of his paintings that gave the movement its title, and he was the most consistent, the most prolific and the most uncompromising of his generation in the struggle to capture the transitory effect – the attempt to depict the totality of the motif before him. There was never enough of anything for him: enough of the right quality of light, enough money, enough time, enough appreciation. To be a friend of Monet in the early days meant a drain on one's financial and emotional resources, as the kindly Bazille discovered. However, in the last few decades of worldwide success and lionization, the once impecunious painter of "tongue-lickings" was fetching thousands of dollars for a painting of a grain-stack, and he made sure that he was not undercut, juggling dealers to get the right price.

LIFE AND WORKS: CLAUDE MONET (1840–1926)

. . . the more I go on, the more I see that a lot of work has to be done
in order to render what I seek: "instantaneity", above all the enveloppe,
the same light spreading everywhere, and more than ever
I am disgusted by easy things that come without effort . . .

LETTER FROM MONET TO GUSTAVE GEFFROY, 21ST JULY 1890

Claude Oscar Monet, the youngest of two sons, was born on 14th November 1840 in Paris. Five years later Adolphe Monet took his family to live in Le Hâvre, a seaport on the Normandy coast, where he joined the busy firm of wholesalers and ship's chandlers run by his relations, the Lecadres. At an early age Claude showed an aptitude for drawing and when he was old enough to attend the Collège du Hâvre he began to study under the eye of Charles Ochard who himself had studied under the great Neo-Classicist, and painter-advocate to Emperor Napoleon I, Jacques-Louis David.

BOUDIN
Honfleur, the Port, Stormy Weather
oil on wood
c.1852–55. 26 × 37.5 cm
This painting does not have the light touch more familiar in Boudin's other work, but it has a simplicity of style and a sense of light characteristic of this artist, who rarely ventured far from the sea.

"I more or less lived the life of a vaga-bond," said Monet in 1900 recalling his early years. "By nature I was undisciplined; never, even as a child, would I submit to rules. It was at home that I learned the little I know. School seemed like a prison and I could never bear to stay there, even for four hours a day, especially when the sunshine beckoned and the sea was smooth." By the age of fifteen Monet was by his own account known all over Le Hâvre as a caricaturist, a pastime he had developed by drawing caricatures of his teachers "in the most irreverent fashion." However the more serious side of his talent was encouraged by his aunt, Mme Lecadre, an amateur painter who took Claude's artistic development to heart, especially after the

death of his mother in 1857. Monet's devo-tion to art worsened his relationship with his father who wanted Claude to stay at school and take his baccalaureate. Mme Lecadre was acquainted with the painter Armand Gautier and together they persuaded the reluctant Adolphe Monet to let his son pursue a career in art. Thus the young Monet got his own way and skipped the examination, leaving school with no qualifications save an abund-ance of energy and an uncompromising belief in himself.

Monet's talents needed to be channelled in the right direction, however; he could not be expected to progress in the art world without formal training of some sort, although this was much against his nature. An early turning

MONET
View of Rouelles
oil on canvas
1858. 46 × 65 cm
OPPOSITE Believed to be the first of Monet's landscapes. We find in this corner of Normandy some of the themes which would later dominate Monet's work: water, poplars and a good deal of sky. Boudin had introduced him to open-air painting about two years previously.

JONGKIND
Fire on the Pont Neuf, Paris
oil on canvas
1853. 27.5 × 40.7 cm
*Jongkind and Boudin were
Monet's real masters and the
younger painter was not in the
least shaken when both were
rejected by the Salon.*

point came when Gravier, the frame-maker, in whose shop Monet often displayed his drawings, introduced him to the local landscapist Eugène Boudin. Monet had been avoiding this meeting – he thought Boudin's landscapes were "horrible, used as I was to the false and arbitrary colour and fantastic arrangements of the painters then in vogue" – but Boudin eventually persuaded Monet to accompany him on a landscape expedition. It was a revelation: "I understood," said Monet, "I had seen what painting could be, simply by the example of this painter working with such independence at the art he loved. My destiny as a painter was decided."

Having failed to obtain a grant to study art in Paris from the municipal authorities in Le Hâvre, Monet gathered up his savings – income from the caricatures – and went to Paris in the spring of 1859 armed with letters of introduction from Boudin to several artists including Troyon and Gautier. Troyon thought Monet showed promise and advised him to enrol at Thomas Couture's atelier (where Edouard Manet had studied). Monet dismissed this idea out of hand, even though Couture was known to be one of the more enlightened masters in Paris at the time, and returned to Le Hâvre. He was back in Paris again the next winter drawing the models at the free Académie Suisse, where his first encounter with Pissarro took place.

In 1861 Monet was called up for military service (which normally lasted seven years).

MONET
Still Life with Bottles
oil on canvas
1859. 41 × 60 cm
Still lifes and nude studies were very much part of an artist's training and Monet, who rarely depicted this kind of subject, shows that he could already produce solid if not exceptional studies. A short while later, Troyon encouraged him to practise drawing.

MONET
Route de Chailly, Fontainebleau
oil on canvas
1864. 98 × 129 cm
Chailly was a village near Barbizon, dear to the landscapists of the previous generation such as Corot, Courbet, and Daubigny. Monet wrote to Bazille about one of his Fontainebleau landscapes, saying that it might remind people of Corot, but insisted that it was not a deliberate attempt to copy the style of the older artist.

MONET
Farmyard in Normandy
oil on canvas
1864. 65 × 81.5 cm
Above In the summer of 1864,
Monet travelled with Bazille
down the Seine to Normandy,
where they rented cheap lodgings
and worked on landscapes before
joining Jongkind and Boudin
at Honfleur.

MONET
Luncheon on the Grass
oil on canvas
1865–66 (fragments).
150 × 42 cm; 248 × 217 cm
Right and opposite
Spurred by Manet's recent and
infamous Luncheon on the
Grass, *Monet decided to paint his*
own version of the subject, which
he did as a plainly contemporary
scene, using his friends as models,
including his girlfriend Camille.
We see the concern of the artist for
clothes, but mainly for light,
which falls from behind the
figures and is rendered in bold
patches. Monet said later that
this picture marked the
beginnings of his experiment with
the principle of the division of
colours, working at effects of light
and colour which ran counter to
accepted conventions.

Young men had to submit their names and be selected by chance. Families with the means, however, could buy their sons out of the lottery. Adolphe offered to do this if Monet would renounce art and join the family business. Instead, Monet defiantly enlisted. He joined the Chasseurs d'Afrique in the French colony of Algeria (where he was deeply impressed by the qualities of light and space), but was home within a year suffering from typhoid. It was then that he met his first "true master . . . the final education of my eye," Johan Jongkind, a Dutch land- and seascapist who was to prove a seminal influence.

Mme Lecadre, who was convinced of Monet's potential, offered to buy him out of the army and a deal was struck with Adolphe whereby Monet would go to Paris with an allowance to study art on the condition that he joined a recognized atelier and undertook formal tuition. Monet agreed and chose Charles Gleyre's atelier. Gleyre was noted for his interest in landscape and had trained many students for the Prix de Paysage Historique. He also charged only for models and equipment, not his teaching, which was an added incentive to Monet, whose father thought him irresponsible with money and was keeping him under tight financial reins.

Thus it was in 1862 that he began his studies at Gleyre's atelier and met Renoir, Bazille, and Sisley and within months was leading them off on landscape painting expeditions to the Fontainebleau Forest and the countryside around Paris. By 1863 French art was in turmoil; Edouard Manet had outraged visitors to the Salon des Refusés with his *Luncheon on the Grass* (*Déjeuner sur l'herbe*). Unknown and unnoticed Monet was forging ahead with his own programme of energetic self-improvement, having rejected Gleyre's teaching. When Gleyre was forced to retire in 1864 Monet was twenty-four and at liberty to pursue his career as he saw fit, though still at the mercy of his father on whom he relied greatly for financial support. Bazille began to help out with money, companionship and by sharing a studio with him between 1865 and 1866, in the rue Furstenberg. Bazille's untimely death in the Franco-Prussian War was a grave blow to Monet.

By the Salon of 1865 Monet had enjoyed some limited success and gained a few commissions. That year the Salon accepted and exhibited two of his landscapes to a mixed reception. One critic thought him "a young Realist who promises much," another compared his work to a child's scrawl. Despite the critics, the artist's intense engagement with the effects of light and colour was clearly emerging as Monet's focus: he was still under the influence of Boudin, Jongkind, Manet, and even Courbet, although his work showed no sign of turning into overt Realism. Monet's experiments with large-scale figure paintings at this time are the beginning of the end of his interest in people as a subject for painting. His own *Luncheon on the Grass* which was never completed was to have been a major integration of light effects and figures in a total composition which would, as Forge says, "monumentalize the language of a *plein-air* sketch."

It was an audacious attempt doomed perhaps to failure. Monet had neither the time, the studio space nor the money to devote himself to its completion. In 1865 he had injured his leg and was laid up for some time, unable to work on the painting. Bazille, who had abandoned his medical studies to become a painter, made good use of his medical skills and rigged up a contraption

which dripped water onto Monet's leg to ease the pain. A touching portrait by Bazille shows an irritated Monet lying in bed at the Cheval-Blanc Inn in Chailly where he had spent the summer working on the ambitious picture, impatient for Bazille to come and model. Bazille's *Monet after His Accident* (*Monet après son accident*) is also an eloquent testimony to the devotion of Bazille to his awkward friend.

203

Monet was in increasing trouble with his father and Aunt Lecadre. He had a girlfriend, Camille-Léonie Doncieux, who had posed for several figures in *Luncheon on the Grass* and a new large-scale picture, which was ultimately rejected by the Salon, *Women in the Garden* (*Femmes dans un jardin*). The lovers fell foul of their respective parents. In 1867, Monet was being chased by creditors, Camille was pregnant and the 800 francs Monet had made from the Salon of 1866 had long since run out. Aunt Lecadre, in league with Adolphe Monet, forced Claude to retreat to Sainte-Adresse on the Normandy coast. In his absence Monet's son, Jean, was born that July in Paris. We know from a letter Monet sent to Bazille in May 1867 that Camille herself was

"ill, bedridden and penniless" and that he did not know what to do, except remind his friend he owed him fifty francs by the first of the month. Bazille had come to Monet's rescue by buying *Women in the Garden* for 2,500 francs to be paid in monthly instalments. In June he was asking Bazille for 100 or 150 francs; by August he was writing a pitiful letter to Bazille saying how much it pained him to think of his child's mother having nothing to eat. The letter ends on a desperate demand from Monet – "Really, Bazille," he says, "there are things that can't be put off until tomorrow. This is one of them and I'm waiting."

The enforced sojourn at Sainte-Adresse enabled Monet to produce several beach scenes

MONET
Terrace at Sainte-Adresse
oil on canvas
1866–67. 98 × 129 cm
In 1866 Monet was forced to leave Camille and go to his aunt's summer house at Sainte-Adresse, where he painted this view from a first floor window. His aunt is barely seen under her parasol and his father sits on the right. His cousin Jeanne-Marguerite stands with a friend by the trellis. Monet has left most of the sea empty to suggest depth, leaving a variety of ships to furnish the horizon.

which showed an increasing maturity of vision. Sadly the whole episode contributed to more disaster. In the autumn Monet was suffering from eye-strain caused by the brilliant sunlight at Sainte-Adresse and was obliged to stop painting during that season. The next year, despite selling a full-length (and very sober) portrait of Camille called *Woman in the Green Dress* (*Femme en vert*) to the editor of *L'Artiste*, Arsène Houssaye, as well as a commission for a portrait of Mme Gaudibert, the wife of a Le Hâvre notable, Monet had his paintings seized by creditors at an exhibition in Le Hâvre. The strain on his relationship with Camille, who had a new baby to look after, must have been severe. The bad times rapidly alternated with the good. In June 1868 Monet, Camille, and Jean had been thrown out of a country inn; Monet had attempted suicide and said so to Bazille in a letter. Whether the hardy Normand was capable of suicide is obscure – his liberal use of bathos in all his begging letters to Bazille is obvious. By December Monet was ecstatic; he wrote to Bazille from Etretat on the Normandy coast where he and his family were installed in a little cottage thanks to the patronage of M. Gaudibert, saying how happy he was surrounded by his family and able to work in peace. He adds with reference to his

MONET
Zaandam
oil on canvas
1871. 40 × 72 cm
Above Leaving London, Monet went to The Netherlands, where he painted a series of landscapes in Zaandam and other sites. Holland was a natural choice for an artist so fond of water.

work: "The further I get the more I realize that no one ever dares give frank expression to what they feel."

In the summer of 1869 this is exactly what Monet began to do in earnest when, working in the company of Renoir at La Grenouillère on the Seine, he produced what are the first truly Impressionist paintings. Monet called them "rotten sketches" but signed them nonetheless. They were indeed sketches for a finished work which is now lost (but survives in a rather indistinct photograph) and which appears to show the existing Grenouillère pictures are not dissimilar to the completed version. At this point in the history of Impressionism in general, the distinction

between sketch and completion was beginning to lose its importance. Monet was now using paint with increasing confidence in swift, bold brushstrokes, painting wet-in-wet in places to create fluid and subtle mixtures of colour. This technique was developed in the work produced the next summer in Trouville on the Normandy coast, and reached new heights during his exile in London of 1870–71 and his subsequent trip to Holland.

Monet had just married Camille when he had to flee to London to avoid being called up to fight the Prussians. Although his time in London was fraught with difficulties – "I endured much poverty," he recalled in 1900 – it meant he was in the company of Pissarro,

MONET
Bathers at La Grenouillère
oil on canvas
1869. 73 × 92 cm
Right La Grenouillère was so popular that even the Imperial couple once stopped to visit it. Set on a small island on the Seine, it consisted of two barges moored under trees and roofed with awnings. Gangplanks linked the barges to a tiny artificial islet nicknamed the "camembert". The series of paintings of La Grenouillère marks a turning point in Impressionism, although Monet thought that he had only produced "rotten sketches".

MONET
Beach at Trouville
oil on canvas
1870. 52 × 59 cm
LEFT The Hôtel des Roches Noires was one subject which he treated several times. As the railway had made the Normandy coast easy to reach, elegant vacationers needed hotels such as this one, which had 150 rooms as well as entertainment rooms. The Monets were not, however, in this financial league and they stayed in a modest hotel in a back street.

MONET
The Thames below Westminster
oil on canvas
1871. 47 × 72.5 cm
LEFT During the war Pissarro busied himself in the area south of the Thames where his mother lived. Monet stayed in town, painting views of the parks but mainly the Thames, to which he often returned in later years, especially in the winter. He was fascinated by the effect of light and fog unique to London and said that London would be ugly without it. While he was there, he tried to exhibit at the annual show of the Royal Academy, but was rejected.

MONET
Poppy Field
oil on canvas
1873. 50 × 65 cm
RIGHT ABOVE This is almost certainly Camille and Jean walking in the tall grass of a field not far away from their home. Argenteuil and the surrounding localities were undergoing dramatic changes since the railway made them so accessible from Paris. This is the archetypal Impressionist painting – atmospheric, sketchy, lively, and full of light.

MONET
The Bridge at Argenteuil
oil on canvas
1874. 60 × 81 cm
RIGHT Argenteuil had much to offer a painter like Monet: open country, a garden full of flowers, the Seine with its pleasure boats. The new bridge, rebuilt after the war, and the train, were modern elements which interested the Impressionists, in contrast to the Barbizon landscapists of the previous generation.

MONET
Train in the Snow
oil on canvas
1875.
OPPOSITE BELOW Monet's house was opposite the station at Argenteuil, and he pictured it several times. This is one of many snow scenes, a subject he never tired of depicting, even if he had to endure the most appalling conditions.

Daubigny, and the dealer Paul Durand-Ruel, all exiles from the war. The all-important business relationship he struck up there with Durand-Ruel was to last the rest of his life despite many ups and downs. London itself – its mercurial climate, prodigious mists and fog, its river, parks and buildings – provided a new set of atmospheric problems for Monet to solve. He was to rediscover the vagaries of English weather to his delight and horror when he returned to London over thirty years later.

In 1871, after the war and the Commune, Monet returned to France and set up home with his family in Argenteuil on the Seine near Paris. There they remained in occasionally frugal stability for seven years. Settled in the growing but as yet rural town of Argenteuil, but near enough to Paris to make possible frequent trips there on the railway, Monet could now concentrate on transferring to the canvas the *enveloppe* which his unique vision disclosed. The subjects that now fell within his view ranged from Argenteuil and Paris streets, to the river and the railway, as well as his house and the surrounding countryside. Working out of doors whenever possible, Monet began the system which was to serve him until his death of having several canvases on the go at once, always ready to capture some fleeting atmospheric effect. He began to

MONET
The Tuileries Gardens
oil on canvas
c.1876. 53 × 72 cm
LEFT The arrangement of the Tuileries gardens, which had been burnt down during the Commune, had been much altered, and Monet, "borrowing" a window from his friend the collector Victor Chocquet, was able to paint four pictures showing the ponds and the symmetrical design. Pictures of new Parisian vistas were likely to sell, a consideration Monet could not ignore, but they also provided a diversion from country and garden scenes.

MONET
Gare St Lazare
oil on canvas
1877. 75.5 × 104 cm
Another view of the station,
with the Pont de l'Europe in
the distance.

produce more varied views of the same subject as seen in different weather conditions. These culminate in his last Paris pictures – the series of Gare St Lazare paintings which treat the station, its massive structure and swirling clouds of steam as intricate webs of colour, truly urban landscapes.

It is perhaps fitting that it was a picture by Monet, *Impression, Sunrise*, which gave the Impressionists their name, for during the 1870s he forged tirelessly ahead and came to exert a powerful influence on his fellow artists. Edouard Manet's summer season at Argenteuil alongside Monet resulted in Manet's decisive shift towards the Impressionist style of swiftly applied bright pigment. Renoir and Pissarro were also visitors to Argenteuil. For a relatively brief period Monet was at the heart of the Impressionist enterprise,

contributing to the Impressionist exhibitions, joining in the discussions at the Café Guerbois in Paris, borrowing money from an increasing circle of friends – including Manet and Zola. The substantial amounts he was now earning were spent on, amongst other things, servants for the large house at Argenteuil. Monet also made important contacts with patrons such as Hoschedé and Chocquet.

In the end circumstances and the solitary, ambitious nature of Monet's personal endeavour drew him further away from the other Impressionists. The fall of his patron Hoschedé, a decline in Monet's modest fortunes, Camille's second pregnancy and, soon after, her worsening illness, led to the two families living together in a new home in Vétheuil, further along the Seine from Argenteuil. Eventually Ernest Hoschedé left the Monet-Hoschedé household, and, after the death of Camille in 1879, Monet, Jean, Camille's new baby Michel, Alice Hoschedé and her six children were left to carry on with life together as best they could.

The turmoil in his personal life, the real threat of poverty with a family of nine to support, and the withering of Monet's links to the other Impressionists, formed an inauspicious start to the 1880s. He had been too poor and depressed by the time of the fourth Impressionist exhibition in 1879 to want to exhibit, however, and the good Caillebotte, who had rented the studio where Monet had finished the Gare St Lazare pictures, had himself collected twenty-nine works from Monet and sent them in for him. The next year Monet absented himself from the fifth Impressionist show. To the extreme disgust of Pissarro and Degas, Monet decided instead to submit to the Salon for the first time in many years.

TURNER
Tours, Sunset on the River Loire
watercolour on blue paper
c.1832. 13.5 × 19 cm
*LEFT During his stay in London,
Monet naturally went to visit the
National Gallery, where a set of
watercolours by Turner was on
show. It has been established that
this particular work was probably
on show in 1870–71. This
watercolour of a French river, not
particularly typical of Turner's
style, is startlingly impressionistic,
some forty years before the first
Impressionist exhibition was held
in Paris. If Monet did indeed see
it, it would certainly have
found its way into the
artist's subconscious.*

MONET
Sunset at Lavacourt
oil on canvas
1880. 101.5 × 150 cm
*ABOVE This picture forms
a sequel to the famous*
Impression, Sunrise.

MONET
The Artist's Garden at Vétheuil
oil on canvas
1881. 150 × 120 cm
RIGHT Here, we see the same blue and white jars first seen in the garden at Argenteuil, but we do not see the road between the garden and the house, a topographical oddity also present in Giverny, nor do we see the Seine behind the painter, at the bottom of the garden.

MONET
Cliff Walk, Pourville
oil on canvas
1882. 65 × 81 cm
BELOW Monet frequently went to the same coastline of Normandy to paint, usually alone. Monet stayed nearly six months in the area, experimenting in depicting the changing light with increasing accuracy. He had started to use boxes specially made for him, capable of holding freshly painted canvases.

Monet's relationship to Durand–Ruel now took on a new importance. Durand–Ruel had found him reasonably bankable in a time of economic depression and Monet was the first of the Impressionists to have a one-man show at the dealer's gallery in 1883. During the 1880s Monet at last began to make a comfortable income from his work and in 1883 he was able to move to Giverny, his last home. But his dedication to expanding his vision was untrammelled.

The search for new inspiration now took him on a series of extended travels in search of problematical landscapes. He went first to the Normandy coast, usually leaving Alice and the children behind, and then to more distant climes – the south of France, northern Italy and Norway. The intrepid artist often found himself battling with the elements. A letter to Alice from Etretat in 1885 recounts how he was working at the Manneporte, a spectacular rock formation off the northwestern coast and the subject for several paintings, when he failed to observe a huge wave which smashed him against the cliff and dragged him down in its undertow: "My first thought was that I was done for . . . My boots stockings and coat were soaked through . . . the palette . . . had hit me in the face and my beard was covered in blue and yellow, etc . . . the worst thing was that I lost my painting which soon disintegrated along with the easel."

For an artist such as Monet who had developed an incredible sensitivity towards colour in a northern French landscape, which is subdued at the best of times and in the winter mournfully so, one might well imagine what the intense Mediterranean sun and landscape could unleash in his mind. The bright blues of the sea and sky were at first, he said, "appalling" and "beyond me": in the end of course he mastered them. During the 1880s Monet's palette was finally liberated from any lingering attachment to naturalistic colour; the *Rocks at Belle-Île* (*Rochers à Belle-Île*), and the *Poppy Fields at Giverny* (*Champs de pivots à Giverny*) are worked and re-worked (in the studio) with thick, startlingly livid pigment. They go beyond the mere *impression* of colour values and have now become a mode of *defining* the complex emotional relationship of the artist to the scene in terms of colour.

In 1892 Ernest Hoschedé died, enabling Monet and Alice to marry. The artist had now cut down on his travels and began to devote himself once again to the landscape around his home. Continually searching for a way to paint the elusive moment, the "fugitive effect," as he put it, Monet had embarked on a multi-canvas series of subjects, the first of which, the *Meules* or *Grain Stacks* (not "hay-stacks", they are stacks of wheat or oats), was begun in the mid-1880s. When the series was due to be exhibited at Durand-Ruel's gallery in 1891 Pissarro was moved to complain to his son Lucien: "All people want at the moment is Monets, apparently he can't paint enough to meet the demand. The worst thing is that they all want grain stacks at sunset! Always the same story, everything he does goes to America at prices of four, five, and six thousand francs."

The series of *Meules* was thus a stunning success, both financially and artistically. The concept of a group of pictures on one subject, which had been seen as a whole, reflected Monet's method – to work on several canvases at once, waiting for the light to change to the correct quality for a particular picture. Moreover, the series now represented a record, in a disturbing totality, not only of the

MONET
Morning, Etretat
oil on canvas
1883. 63 × 81 cm
ABOVE Monet spent part of the summers between 1883 and 1886 at Etretat, painting the various uniquely arched cliffs.

MONET
Grain Stacks, Sunset
oil on canvas
1891. 65 × 100 cm
LEFT The Neo-Impressionists found Monet's works "old hat" by now, because he was merely evolving rather than radically changing direction.

MONET
The Cathedral, Bright Sun
oil on canvas
c.1894. 107 × 73 cm
ABOVE

MONET
Rouen Cathedral
oil on canvas
1894. 100 × 65 cm
RIGHT

MONET
Rouen Cathedral, Albany Tower
oil on canvas
c.1894. 106 × 74 cm
FAR RIGHT

it in various states – is a major consequence of Monet's series paintings. The *Poplars* series of 1891, the Rouen Cathedral series of 1894, and the *Mornings on the Seine* of 1896–97 continue this serial preoccupation. In the late 1890s and early 1900s Monet went on his last travels to London (where he had painted over 100 views of the Thames by 1904) and his last expedition to Venice in 1908.

As Monet's work was now selling for substantial amounts he could afford to realize his dream of creating a large flower and water garden, achieved by buying a plot adjacent to the house, diverting the stream which ran through the land and forming a water-lily pond with a Japanese bridge over it. It was in this garden that he spent the last decades of his life. Over the years the garden expanded into a wonderland of flowers of all varieties.

subject under varying conditions, but Monet's response to it over time. Speaking of the *Meules* series, which he saw in 1895, the painter Wassily Kandinsky said: "Painting took on a fabulous strength and splendour, and at the same time, unconsciously, the object was discredited as an indispensable element of the picture." True enough, contemporary viewers were initially perplexed by the need to see the whole through its parts. The "discredited object" – in other words making the object abstract by repeating

MONET
The Cathedral, Sunlight
oil on canvas
1894. 107 × 73 cm
ABOVE

MONET
The Cathedral Fog
oil on canvas
1894. 106 × 72.5 cm
*LEFT Monet started his series on
the cathedral of Rouen in the late
winter of 1892–93 and the
following year, set himself up in
the window of a shop from where
he could follow the changing light
on the medieval façade.*

MONET
Poplars on the Epte
oil on canvas
1891. 92.5 × 73.5 cm
ABOVE Monet was particularly fond of this quick study, perhaps because it is both a bold and stylized picture, in which the effect is achieved with far less nuances than in most of his other pictures.

MONET
Poplars
oil on canvas
1891. 101 × 66 cm
RIGHT The series of poplars followed immediately after the grainstacks, and was shown at Durand-Ruel in 1892. By then, Monet's eyesight was deteriorating.

MONET
The Japanese Bridge at Giverny
oil on canvas
1893. 97 × 117 cm
Monet had a Japanese-style bridge built over a pond he created by diverting a tributary of the local river Epte. He had already undertaken a great deal of gardening, but no water lilies are growing in the pond, although he had intended to grow them even before he was authorized to divert the course of the river. Monet depicted this pond tirelessly until his death in 1926.

"What I need most of all are flowers, always, always," he said. His artistic attention now turned to the waterscape offered by the lily pond. A prodigious series of *Nymphéas*, or *Water Lilies*, now followed, taking Monet into new realms of vision. As he told Geffroy in 1908: "These landscapes of water and reflections have become an obsession. It's quite beyond my powers at this age, but I need to succeed in expressing what I feel." The consequence of this obsession was the *Nymphéas, paysages d'eau* (*Water Lilies, Waterscapes*) a series of forty-eight canvases exhibited at Durand-Ruel's in 1909. This later became a monumental concept for a huge *décoration* to be donated to the State and installed in a public building in Paris. The plan, encouraged by the politician Georges Clemenceau, was audacious and at times it seemed as though it would never happen. In 1911 Alice Monet had died and to add to his grief his son, Jean, died in 1914. Cared for by his step-daughter Blanche Hoschedé-Monet and with the support of Clemenceau, the seventy-four-year-old artist was able to persevere with the project for the massive *décorations*.

To realize the *décorations* Monet proposed the building of a new studio specially to house the work in progress. As World War I raged around him, Monet supervised the construction of the studio and worked on the *Nymphéas* in the old studio. He had developed

MONET
Nymphéas (*Detail*)
oil on canvas
undated. 132 × 84 cm
*Monet painted hundreds of
pictures of this pond or parts of it.*

operation in 1923 eventually restored enough of his sight for Monet, now eighty-three and dying of cancer caused by habitual cigarette smoking, to near completion of the *décorations*. The immense work was designed to be housed in a circular or oval room and to this end the Orangerie near the Louvre was designated to house it, but not without political and personal complications on a huge scale.

Monet died on 5th December 1926, a month after his eighty-sixth birthday, with Clemenceau at his side. He had lived just long enough to see the completion of the *décorations*, his troublesome masterpiece of a gift to the French nation. As Gustave Geffroy said of the lily pond, the inspiration for his last great works:

> There he found, as it were, the last word on things, if things had a first and last word. He discovered and demonstrated that everything is everywhere, and that after running round the world worshipping the light that brightens it, he knew that this light came to be reflected in all its splendour and mystery in the magical hollow surrounded by the foliage of willow and bamboo, by flowering irises and rose bushes through the mirror of water from which burst strange flowers which seem even more silent and hermetic than all the others.

cataracts which made it increasingly difficult for him to discern colour, yet he carried on remorselessly. When the new studio was finished in 1916 he began what was almost a decade of unremitting work on the *décorations*. His failing eyesight meant he was frequently uncertain of what he was doing and, in despair, he destroyed several canvases. An

Monet was famed throughout the world and his work fetched enormous prices; his persistence and stubborn devotion to his art had made his fortune. He had also outlived two wives, a son, the Second Republic, the Second Empire and all of his contemporaries including Pissarro, Degas, and Renoir.

Six months before his death he wrote: " . . . in the end the only merit I have is to

MONET
An Alley at Giverny
oil on canvas
1902. 79 × 90 cm
*Above The garden at Giverny
is vast and arranged in
several parts.*

MONET
Alley in Giverny
oil on canvas
c.1920. 89 × 100 cm
*Left Monet's bad eyesight cannot
entirely explain the semi-abstract
style he had now reached. It often
happens that ageing artists lose
their stamina and produce works
which do not compare favourably
to their earlier ones. With Monet,
this was not the case.*

have painted directly from nature before the most fugitive effects, and it still upsets me that I was responsible for the name given to a group, most of whom had nothing Impressionist about them . . . "

A series of paintings of the Japanese bridge and the garden at Giverny are among Monet's last works apart from the *décorations*. The last canvases are covered by violent, feverish brushstrokes with an inferno of colour; the last challenges to sunlight of one of the first great Impressionists.

renoir

GEORGE MOORE, AN ENGLISH WRITER who was reasonably close to the Impressionists during the Batignolles days, thought Pierre-Auguste Renoir possessed a certain "vulgarity", a feeling expressed, though not of course explicitly, by Renoir himself, whose eventual fame sat uneasily on the head of a self-confessed artisan. Although his ambivalent social position gave him much to be nervous about, Renoir was existentially nervy, a source of perpetual motion who would whistle incessantly whilst painting and fall into utter moroseness and depression when idle.

As an iconoclast of his own work, his dissatisfaction with the extraordinary surface effects of his "high Impressionist" period culminated in a search for classical simplicity in line and volume which lead him back to the work of Raphael, and sideways to the experiments of Cézanne. In the end he found his métier in the female figure. Even when his eyesight and rheumatic hands began to fail him, he branched out into sculpture, using an assistant, as well as tapestry design and ceramics – he had after all begun his career as a porcelain-painter.

LIFE AND WORKS: PIERRE-AUGUSTE RENOIR (1841–1919)

Artists do exist. But one doesn't know where to find them. An artist can do nothing if the person who asks him to produce work is blind. It is the eye of the sensualist that I wish to open.

PIERRE-AUGUSTE RENOIR

RENOIR
Bazille at Work
oil on canvas
1867. 105 × 73.5 cm
BELOW Renoir has produced an honest and forthright portrait of his close friend. The rendering is fluent but the artist has not yet found the style to which he owes his fame.

Pierre-Auguste Renoir's father Léonard "Raynouard", as the land register of the time called him, was a tailor from Limoges who had moved to Paris in 1844 with his family. Renoir's mother, Marguerite was a dressmaker and Pierre-Auguste, born on 25th February 1841, was the sixth of seven children, two of whom died in infancy. At the age of fourteen Renoir was apprenticed in the traditional way to M. Levy, a porcelain-painter. To improve his skills he also studied drawing at a free school and when Levy's firm could no longer compete with the machine-produced porcelain-ware taking over the market and closed down in 1858, Renoir then painted fans for his brother, Henri, copying the work of Watteau, Lancret, Boucher, and Fragonard, and blinds for a M. Gilbert until he entered Charles Gleyre's atelier in 1861. A year later he met Monet, Bazille, and Sisley there. His capacity for self-improvement was formidable, and in 1862 he won a place at the Ecole des Beaux-Arts where he studied as a pupil of Gleyre's until 1864. He had also gained permission to copy in the Louvre and the Cabinet d'Estampes. In later years, when he and his friends were famous, Renoir was the only one to recognize the efforts of the good Charles Gleyre: "It was under Gleyre that I learnt my trade as a painter," he said, and in the 1880s he was to return to the techniques Gleyre had taught him. At the time, however, his relationship with Gleyre had its humorous moments. On one occasion Gleyre inspected some of Renoir's work and wryly advised him that painting shouldn't be done for one's own amusement, to which the plucky Renoir replied "If it didn't amuse me I wouldn't paint."

Renoir's career at the Ecole des Beaux-Arts

was hardly spectacular; on one occasion he came fourth with an honourable mention in the perspective drawing examination, but generally his results were undistinguished. Not so his formative relationship with the other Gleyre students. In 1862 he was already accompanying them on landscape painting expeditions to the Fontainebleau Forest. "When I was young," he said nostalgically many years later, "I used to go to Fontainebleau with Sisley, with just my paint-box and the shirt on my back. We would wander round until we found a village, and sometimes come back a week later when we had run out of money." Monet, Bazille and Sisley had soon become important allies. They were all from the prosperous middle class, though Renoir, from the skilled working class, an *ouvrier de la peinture* as he called himself, had to earn a living by undertaking decorative work. As the art historian John House observes in his study of "Renoir's Worlds", when Bazille, comfortably supported by his parents, shared his studio with his friends, Monet played the role of a bohemian who had rejected parental authority, whereas Renoir simply had to seek the cheapest way he could find to live. Renoir strove to become a *bourgeois* through his art and his friends. His first successful submission to the Salon in 1865 was a portrait of Sisley's wealthy father, and the greater part of his career was to depend on patronage by and portraiture for the bourgeoisie. Yet the question of class troubled him throughout his life; his later affair with and marriage to a laundress, Aline Charigot, was kept secret from his friends – Renoir was terrified that they might think of her as a lowly peasant.

By nature Renoir was a restless soul and in this respect he was later to be compared to

RUBENS
An Allegory of Fruitfulness (*DETAIL*)
ABOVE These were women after Renoir's own heart, miles away from the cold and polished beauties praised by the Salon.

RENOIR
Lise
oil on canvas
1867. 181.5 × 113 cm
LEFT Painted in 1867, the portrait of the artist's mistress was exhibited at the Salon the following year.

Watteau, one of his early influences. He was also highly impressionable. Unsympathetic analyses of his work held up the considerable influence of his contemporaries, firstly Monet and later Cézanne, as proof that he was ambivalent and confused as to his own identity as an artist. To a certain extent this is true, but his talent was both convincing and original, chiefly in his portrayal of the modern life of Paris for which he is most admired.

In 1868 Renoir and Bazille moved into rooms with a studio in the Batignolles quarter of Paris. As a member of the group of future

Impressionists who had gravitated towards the Batignolles and the Café Guerbois where Edouard Manet held court, Renoir was now becoming involved in the struggle for recognition. Following the Salon's rejection of his painting *Diana the Huntress* (*Diane chasseresse*) in 1867, he had signed a petition calling for another Salon des Refusés and was soon to be a prominent member of the *Société anonyme* which launched the first Impressionist show. In 1868, he received considerable acclaim at the Salon for his painting *Lise with a Parasol* (*Lise au parasol*), which Zola thought "a successful exploration of the modern". The critic Duret had bought a previous *Lise*, also known as *The Gypsy Girl* (*La Gitane*), and Renoir's name was increasingly to be heard mentioned in connection with the avant-garde whilst his style remained subtly tailored

to the Salon. Lise Tréhot, the subject of *Lise* and many more paintings to come, was the sister of Clémence Tréhot, the mistress of Jules Le Coeur, a painter and close friend of Renoir and Sisley. In 1865 Le Coeur had bought a house at Marlotte in the Fontainebleau Forest where Renoir, Sisley, and the Tréhot sisters would frequently spend the summer months. Nearby was the famous Cabaret de la mère Anthony, a country inn frequented by artists, writers, and bohemians of every hue. The Cabaret is the subject of an early picture which Renoir remembered with great pleasure. "It is not that I find the picture itself particularly exciting, but it does remind me of good old Mother Anthony and her inn at Marlotte. That was a real village inn!"

During the late 1860s Renoir's style was at a crossroads. The rapidly executed *Skaters in*

RENOIR
La Grenouillère
oil on canvas
1869. 65 × 93 cm
RIGHT Here we see people standing on the gangplank between the bank and the "camembert" from which they could watch the bathers. Renoir's brushstrokes are lighter and lack Monet's bravura handling.

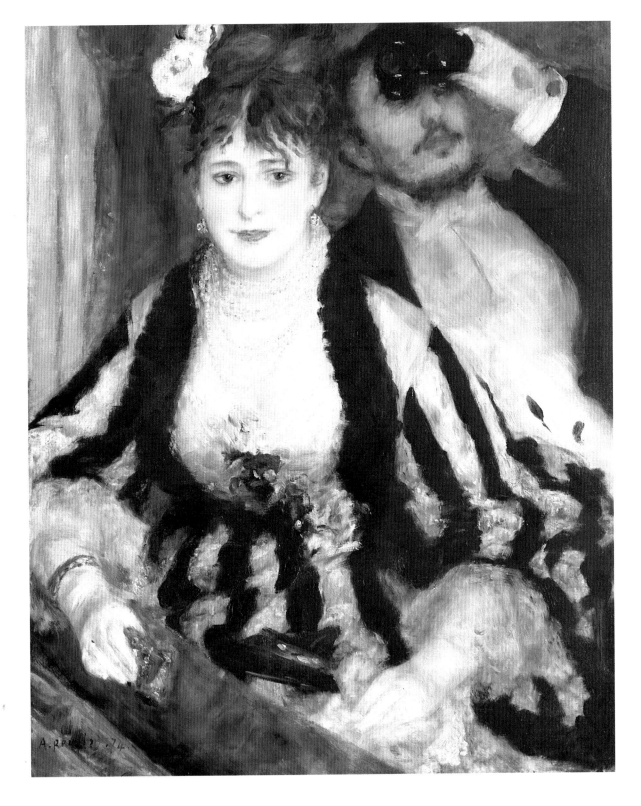

RENOIR
La Loge
oil on canvas
1874. 80 × 64 cm
This now famous picture passed unnoticed at the first Impressionist exhibition, as did the artist's other works, although it was the first Impressionist treatment of this subject. It has since been acknowledged as a masterpiece. A work of charm and candour, the mismatching of the sitters to the setting adds to the painting's appeal. The woman was the model Nini Lopez, who does not have the allure of a high society woman. The man was Renoir's brother, Edmond; willing accomplice in many of the artist's works.

RENOIR
Victor Chocquet
oil on canvas
c.1876. 46 × 36 cm
*ABOVE Chocquet, a modest civil
servant with a small private
income, was a compulsive
collector of paintings.*

RENOIR
The Gust of Wind
oil on canvas
c.1872. 52 × 82.5 cm
*RIGHT ABOVE Renoir has
abandoned his emulation of
Monet's boldness, as in the
Grenouillère pictures, and is now
attempting to capture the effect of
a windy day and the movements of
the clouds with a light brush.*

the Bois de Boulogne (*Patineurs au Bois de Boulogne*) of 1868 showing the marked influence of Monet, contrasts with the sobriety of the touching double portrait of Sisley and his wife-to-be, *The Engaged Couple* (*Les Fiancés*) of the same year. In 1869 Renoir spent the summer living with his parents in Louveciennes. Nearly every day he travelled the few miles up the river to Bougival where Monet was living and together they went to paint at the popular bathing establishment known as La Grenouillère (The Froggery) on the Île-de-Croissy in the Seine. To many minds this is where Impressionism was born. The two artists worked side by side at the same views with practically the same palette and brushstrokes. A comparison of the results of that summer shows that Renoir had tried to apply

a great deal of Monet's approach. The short, rapid brushstrokes and high-keyed colours employed by Monet are echoed by Renoir, but in a more uncertain fashion. Renoir's approach to the subject concentrates more on the crowd of figures in the scene.

With the outbreak of the Franco-Prussian war in July 1870, Renoir joined the Tenth Cavalry Regiment and was posted to Libourne in the Bordeaux region. There he succumbed to a severe attack of dysentery and was rescued by his uncle who took him to the town of Bordeaux to recuperate. By the end of February 1871 he was back with his regiment and his record states that he "conducted himself well for the duration of the war." By the time in April when he had been demobilized and returned to Paris, the

RENOIR
The Path in the Grass
oil on canvas
c.1875. 60 × 74 cm
The composition of this painting is reminiscent of the Poppy Field *painted by Monet two years previously; though Monet's work includes a greater depth of sky and his horizon is firmly marked*

by a row of trees. Here, the path is clearly the axis of the picture, balanced by the vertical tree off centre. The vegetation is detailed in Renoir's own fluttering style.

RENOIR
Ball at the Moulin de la Galette
oil on canvas
1876. 131 × 175 cm
*In order to paint this composition,
Renoir called on some patient
friends. The three men on the
right are Pierre Franc-Lamy and
Norbert Goenette, both painters,
and the writer Georges Rivière.
On the bench are two sisters,*

*Estelle and Jeanne, the latter was
Renoir's new model, who also
posed for* The Swing. *The
dancer in pink is Margot
(Marguerite Legrand) with the
Cuban painter Solarès. The girls
were all from the working classes
and the men were younger friends
of the artist.*

RENOIR
The First Outing
oil on canvas
c.1876–77. 65 × 49.5 cm
*ABOVE Two years after La
Loge, the atmosphere of this
picture is very different. The girl
is a young and unsophisticated
figure. It has been recently
discovered that Renoir had
originally painted a male figure
in profile, which occupied most of
the space now taken by the distant
boxes, and that the blue garment
left of centre was part of this
man's jacket.*

RENOIR
Under the Arbour, Moulin
de la Galette
oil on canvas
1876. 81 × 65 cm
*It is a sunny Sunday, the
characters are all younger than
the artist, and life has no more
weight on this leisurely afternoon
than it has in the works of the
eighteenth-century artists.*

Commune was in power and the city was under siege. Nothing could stop him painting though, and he obtained a pass from the Prefect of Police and was able to leave Paris on painting expeditions and to visit his parents in Louveciennes.

Between 1871 and 1874 Renoir continued his close association with Monet, visiting him at Argenteuil during the summers, as well as becoming more intimately involved in the fledgling *Société anonyme*; he now had a studio in Montmartre in the rue Saint-Georges where the *Société anonyme* often met in 1873 to plan its first exhibition. His style was beginning to mature; his view of the *Pont Neuf* of 1872, though the choice of the subject was influenced by Monet, presents a highly original use of colour and contrasts strongly

with a rather dour view of a similar subject, the *Pont des Arts*, done in 1867. Renoir's brother Edmond, a journalist, had an interesting anecdote about how the *Pont Neuf* was painted. The two brothers would take up residence at a little café and for ten centimes each they could sit with two coffees for hours. Whilst Auguste painted, Edmond scribbled, occasionally venturing onto the bridge to engage passers-by in conversation so that Auguste could sketch them *in situ*. In another vein the *Morning Ride in the Bois de Boulogne* (*L'Allée cavaliére au Bois de Boulogne*) of 1873, an enormous canvas eight and a half by seven and a half feet, is an attempt by Renoir to paint a large-scale work with the Salon in mind. Despite this ambition, it was rejected and appeared at the Salon des Refusés.

RENOIR
The Seine at Asnières (The Skiff)
oil on canvas
c.1879. 71 × 92 cm
Victor Chocquet bought this painting, one of a series of boating scenes which Renoir painted between 1879 and 1880. Renoir succeeded in rendering the flickering of light dancing on the river, using small brushstrokes to depict the water. In the background a train advances from behind a hedge. This is the archetypal rainbow palette.

RENOIR
Madame Charpentier and Her
Children
oil on canvas
1878. 154 × 190 cm
*In 1876, Renoir had the good
fortune to meet the Charpentiers,
a wealthy and influential couple.
Marguerite commissioned her
own portrait and, using her*
*connections, made sure that it was
prominently displayed at the
Salon. However, this did not
spare the work from criticism,
some of which could be applied to
much of Renoir's work: a gifted
colourist but lacking in
draughtsmanship.*

RENOIR
Venice, Piazza S. Marco
oil on canvas
1881. 64 × 81 cm
*ABOVE This lively picture is
unfinished and Renoir's dealer,
Durand-Ruel, declined to
purchase it although it has
glowing qualities and the
rendering of the basilica itself is
complete. The ultimate purpose of
this trip was to study the works of
the Italian old masters at a time
when he was seeking to improve
his technique.*

RENOIR
The Umbrellas
oil on canvas
c.1885. 180.5 × 115 cm
*RIGHT Many artists begin with a
tighter style which becomes
somewhat looser as they gain
experience and self-confidence.
The opposite was true in Renoir's
case: he felt he had reached a
dead-end and his observation of
the neat contours and finish of
painters such as Raphael
prompted him to work with more
discipline and care.*

When the accounts for the first exhibition of the *Société anonyme* were drawn up after the disastrous exhibition of 1874 each member of the society owed 184 francs 50 centimes; few paintings had been sold, although Renoir had managed to avoid most of the hysterical criticism aimed at colleagues such as Monet, Pissarro, and Degas. One of the pictures Renoir exhibited, *La Loge*, the first of several paintings on this theme and now considered an icon of Impressionism, was later bought by Père Martin, a rather dubious small-time dealer, for the sum of 425 francs. This was not an insubstantial amount for an impecunious artist – in any case Renoir owed it in back rent – but a Salon picture by Meissonier, for example, could fetch 40,000 francs. In

December the *Société* terminated, with Renoir as the chairman. The next year, resourceful as ever, he had the idea of a joint auction with Monet, Sisley, and Morisot to be held at the Hôtel Drouot. The newly named Impressionists were by now so infamous that there were demonstrations when the paintings went on show in March. Renoir sold twenty works for an average of 112 francs, with some going for as little as 50 francs. Thankfully Renoir's precarious position was now helped by the fortunate arrival on the scene of the collector Victor Chocquet who commissioned several portraits of his family which kept the artist financially afloat.

In 1875 Renoir had rented for a hundred francs a month the dilapidated outbuildings of

RENOIR
Luncheon of the Boating Party
oil on canvas
1880–81. 130 × 173 cm
On the left, holding a small dog, is Aline Charigot, Renoir's future companion and wife. Alphonse Fournaise, son of the establishment's owner, stands next to her. The girl leaning on the balustrade is a model. The man wearing a top hat is Charles Ephrussi, a wealthy writer and collector. Angèle, another model, is seated, drinking. The painter Lhote leans forward to talk to the actress Jeanne Samary, and the painter Caillebotte, another close friend of Renoir's, wearing a singlet and a straw hat, is seated in the foreground. This was the last of Renoir's crowd scenes, and one of his most popular works ever.

RENOIR
Dance in the Country
oil on canvas
1882–83. 180 × 90 cm
*OPPOSITE LEFT Renoir painted
three nearly life-size dancing
couples between 1882 and 1883.
The differences are quite marked
between the relaxed and happy
Aline in* Dance in the Country,
*who was putting on weight, and
the more composed, elegant couple
of* Dance in the City, *for which
the young model Maria
Clémentine (later known as the
painter Suzanne Valadon) was
the model. Renoir's old friend
Lhote, who had posed for several
other pictures, is the partner in
both panels.*

RENOIR
Dance in the City
oil on canvas
1882–83. 180 × 90 cm
OPPOSITE RIGHT

RENOIR
Landscape at Guernsey
oil on canvas
1883. 46 × 56 cm
*LEFT Renoir and his family spent
a month on the Channel Island of
Guernsey in the late summer of
1883, where he painted around
fifteen pictures, many of them
intended as sketches to be used for
studio compositions later on.*

an old folly with a garden in the rue Cortot as a studio. The next summer his friends Pierre Lamey, Frédéric Cordey, and Georges Rivière often joined him in outings to a popular haunt, the Moulin de la Galette – a dance hall and café beneath one of the last remaining windmills of Montmartre. According to Georges Rivière, in the mornings he and the others would help Renoir carry his canvas and easel round the corner to the dance hall where the artist spent the summer painting a large scene of the crowds there now known as the *Ball at the Moulin de la Galette* – one of several masterpieces he was to produce that summer. Although he certainly worked on it *in situ*, posing his friends and acquaintances, including Rivière, it was prepared with sketches and finished in the studio in the rue Cortot. Nevertheless, it is Renoir's first large-scale figure painting to deploy the swift technique he had been perfecting since the summer of 1869 at La Grenouillère with Monet. The dappled sunlight is a particular feature of this period, as is the abandoned use of colour in the shadows. The painting was shown at the third Impressionist group exhibition the next year when a critic under the pseudonymous name of Flor O'Squarr said of Renoir's painting:

The painter had caught perfectly the raucous and slightly bohemian atmosphere of this open-air dance hall, perhaps the last of its kind in Paris . . . The harsh sunlight is filtered through the greenery, sets the blonde hair and pink cheeks of the girls aglow and makes their ribbons sparkle. The joyful light fills every corner of the canvas and even the shadows reflect it. The whole painting shimmers like a rainbow and makes one think of the dainty Chinese princess described by Heinrich Heine: her greatest pleasure in life was to tear up satin and silk with her polished jade-like nails and watch the shreds of yellow, blue, and pink drift away in the breeze like so many butterflies.

RENOIR
Aline Charigot
oil on canvas
c.1885. 65 × 54 cm
ABOVE The rendering of this portrait, which Renoir kept all his life, evokes the diagonals of Cézanne.

RENOIR
Maternity
sketch in red chalk
1885.
Opposite right Renoir made a number of sketches and three paintings of Aline with their first son, Pierre. The artist, who already complained of being old when he was forty, and who was forty-four at the time of his son's birth, was very moved by the birth of his children.

RENOIR
The Apple Seller
oil on canvas
c.1890. 66 × 54 cm
In this rustic scene, Aline poses with a young girl and probably her son, Pierre, seated to the right. This is the most elaborate of three pictures Renoir painted on the same theme.

RENOIR
Berthe Morisot and Her Daughter,
Julie Manet
pastel on paper
1894. 59 × 45 cm
*In his later years, Renoir had
become close to Berthe Morisot
and Degas. Distressed by the death
in 1892 of her husband Eugène
Manet, Morisot had aged rapidly.
She is seen here with her fifteen-
year old daughter, Julie, who fills
most of the space and attracts the
eye, perhaps subconsciously
because Renoir was essentially a
painter of youth, though the
balance between the two sitters is
somewhat restored in the
oil portrait.*

This summer also produced the equally famous *The Swing* (*La Balançoire*), thought to have been painted in the garden at the rue Cortot. A young woman from the neighbourhood, Jeanne, posed on the swing (and is also present in *The Ball*). The same dappled light is more intensely expressed here and imbues the picture with that insouciant charm of which only Renoir (who had of course once copied Watteau for a living) was capable. Zola was so taken with the painting that he used it in his novel *Une Page d'amour* of 1878, where the heroine is "standing on the very edge of the swing and holding the ropes, with her arms outstretched . . . she was wearing a grey dress decorated with mauve bows . . . That day the sunlight was like light-coloured dust in the pale sky . . . "

Towards the end of the 1870s Renoir began to be less involved with the Impressionists as a group. After the third Impressionist exhibition in 1877 he forsook the group and began to concentrate on the Salon as an outlet for his work. His new patrons the Charpentiers were now beginning to commission portraits as well as decorations for their town house in Paris, and Renoir scored a relative success at the Salon of 1879 with the *Portrait of Madame Charpentier and her Children*. Marcel Proust includes a long description of the painting in *Le Temps retrouvé* (*Time Regained*) and likens it to "Titian at his best". The most favourable reviews concentrated on Renoir's use of colour, which was by now quite brilliant. The steady development of what became known as his rainbow palette can be seen in perhaps its most scintillating and impressionistic form in *Boating on the Seine* (*Canotage sur la Seine*), (also known as *The Skiff*, or *The Seine at Asnières*, though it was probably painted at Chatou), produced around the same time as the Charpentier portrait. The painting shows an almost textbook application of Chevreul's principles of simultaneous colour contrast. Renoir uses only seven pigments and white, applying them to the canvas in bold, practically unmixed patches to convey an impression of sheer luminosity.

It is ironic and typical of Renoir's nature that at a time he was producing veritable icons of Impressionist art he was also beginning to have serious doubts about his own ability. The financial need to paint an increasing number of society portraits no doubt aggravated the strain on his own artistic judgment of himself. To make matters worse, in 1880 he and Monet had fallen out with Degas, who they suspected was highjacking the Impressionist exhibitions and populating them with his protegés. A trip to Algiers, his first abroad, in the spring of 1881 reassured

RENOIR
Landscape
oil on canvas
c.1895. 46 × 33 cm
*Above Renoir was
deliberately trying to adapt
Cézanne's diagonal brushstrokes
to his own style and to adapt his
colour harmony. This is an
atypical work, more vigorous
than his usual pictures.*

RENOIR
Girls at the Piano
oil on canvas
1892. 116 × 90 cm
*Left Renoir, at last an
established artist, was asked by the
French government to provide a
substantial painting for the
national collection, for which he
was to be paid 4,000 francs.*

him of the direction he was taking as an Impressionist and he was soon back in France at Chatou and Bougival painting masterpieces such as *Luncheon of the Boating Party* (*Le Déjeuner des canoteurs*) with rekindled vigour. But by October he had left for Italy, writing to Mme Charpentier: "I have suddenly become a traveller and I am in a fever to see the Raphaels . . . "

Renoir had gone to Algeria in the Romantic footsteps of Delacroix, but he now approached Italy seeking the formal classicism of Raphael, which he was to find in the great decorations at the Villa Farnesina. He was also profoundly influenced by what he called "the grandeur and simplicity" of the ancient Pompeian wall paintings in Naples. It was some time, however, before these new influences could reconcile themselves in his work: " . . . it's all a mess. I'm still making a mess and I'm forty years old," he wrote to Durand-Ruel from Italy in November 1881.

Renoir returned to France in January 1882

RENOIR
Bather, (Eurydice)
oil on canvas
1895–1900. 116 × 89 cm
*FAR LEFT This nude is not any
nude, it is Venus in the nude.
Here, four tiny figures in the
background provide a pretext for
the title. Renoir had by then
completely returned to his "soft"
style, which he attempted to
control only when he was painting
commissioned portraits.*

RENOIR
Gabrielle and Jean
oil on canvas
1895–96. 65 × 54 cm
*LEFT The Renoirs' second son,
Jean, was born in September
1894, shortly after Gabrielle, a
distant relative of Aline's, came to
live with them as a housekeeper.
She stayed more than twenty years
with the family and became a
frequent model for Renoir.*

RENOIR
The Artist's House at Essoyes
oil on canvas
1906. 31 × 40 cm
*RIGHT Renoir's late style became
increasingly loose, which is partly
explained by his failing eyesight
and the crippling arthritis which
in the end confined him to
a wheelchair.*

RENOIR
Claude Renoir Playing
oil on canvas
1905. 46 × 55 cm
*RIGHT BELOW Renoir liked to
portray children, particularly his
own, and his style is well suited to
their tender features.*

RENOIR
Portrait of Durand-Ruel
oil on canvas
1910. 65 × 54 cm
Above Surprisingly, Renoir did not paint his longtime dealer and friend before 1910.

RENOIR
Self-portrait
oil on canvas
1910. 42 × 33 cm
Right In this honest work, the artist has depicted himself at the age of sixty-nine.

dealer Durand-Ruel were mystified by the new linear style and said so, but Renoir persisted in his experiments with a series of *Bathers*, culminating in the monumental *Bathers* (*Baigneuses*) of 1887. His interest in the female form had also taken a new turn in 1885 when his mistress, Aline Charigot, bore his first son Pierre, prompting the artist to produce the Raphael-inspired *Maternity*, developing the simplified theme of the *Bathers*.

Renoir's "*manière aigre*" ("sour period") as he called it, came to an end in the late 1880s. After a trip to Spain in 1892 he drew new inspiration from Velazquez. The work of the eighteenth-century French painters Watteau and Fragonard which he had copied onto fans in his youth also came to influence him and he rediscovered the delicate virtues of Corot whose work was now much in demand by collectors. The insistence on line gradually softened but his humanistic concern with the figure remained overwhelmingly important.

In 1902 Renoir and Aline moved to the south of France where the warm climate eased the severe arthritis which was making it difficult for him to paint. He could now "only paint broadly" as he put it, and the nerve in his right eye was partially atrophied. Undaunted by his illness he embarked on a series of sculptures echoing the nude figure paintings, though he had to use the hands of an assistant to model them.

Aline died in 1915 of a heart attack caused by overweight; she was a compulsive eater. Renoir died on 3rd December 1919 and was buried next to her in Essoyes.

In 1900 he had been made a Knight of the Légion d'Honneur and in the last year of his life, he became a Commander of the Légion d'Honneur, a triumphant honour for a humble "*ouvrier de la peinture*".

and joined Cézanne at L'Estaque in the south of France where the two went on landscape expeditions and Renoir caught pneumonia. He had also caught something of Cézanne's vision of the hidden structure of planes and lines in nature. The confluence and confusion of the diverse influences at work on Renoir can be seen in *The Umbrellas* (*Les Parapluies*), which shows him struggling to reconcile a linear style with Impressionist brushwork. More importantly, in the mid-1880s there is a new concentration on the female nude as a vehicle for expressing light, colour and form. He told Berthe Morisot that, "the nude seemed to be one of the most essential forms of art." Renoir's fellow Impressionists and the

RENOIR
The Bathers
oil on canvas
c.1918–19. 110 × 160 cm

With this work, the ailing painter was determined to make a final statement, showing nude women in a landscape, two of his favourite subjects. Crippled by illness, he had the easel set up in such a manner that he could reach any part of this large canvas. Pain sometimes interrupted his work. His son, Jean, stated that his father "considered it as a final achievement. He thought he had summed up in it the research of his whole life", though to many people the painting is more often seen as the final work of a weakening artist. Georges Duthuit probably echoed the modern public's feeling when he wrote that "Renoir's late work was short of imagination, and deprived of any dramatic sense . . . so that one finds something slack and overblown."

F ROM COMFORTABLE BEGINNINGS as the son of a successful English businessman in Paris, Alfred Sisley's story is one of tragic decline and late success. After the crash of his father's firm in the Franco-Prussian War, Sisley and his family were reduced to a state of penury which persisted almost to the end of his life when cancer of the throat killed him at the age of sixty.

Part of Sisley's lack of wordly success is undoubtedly due to the subdued and comparatively unspectacular nature of the landscapes which were his almost exclusive preoccupation. Had he been interested in the colourful effects of dazzling sunlight or violent seascapes he may have enjoyed more attention than the belated admiration of a small number of collectors and connoisseurs. Yet his work is dramatic and powerful in its own way and his snowscapes, especially, convey something of the unremitting sadness which plagued him.

ALFRED SISLEY
By Renoir
1874
ABOVE

SISLEY
The Road from Mantes to
Choisy-le-Roi
oil on canvas
1872. 46 × 55 cm
OPPOSITE

The light of glory will never shine on his work in his lifetime.

GUSTAVE GEFFROY ON SISLEY, 1894

RENOIR
Sisley and His Wife
oil on canvas
1868. 106 × 74 cm
*ABOVE Although this picture is
usually accepted as being the
Sisley couple, it is possible that
Renoir used his mistress Lise
Tréhot since he wrote to Bazille
that, "I put Lise and Sisley on
show at Charpentier and shall try
to get a hundred francs out
of him".*

SISLEY
St Martin Canal, Paris
oil on canvas
1870. 50 × 65 cm
*RIGHT Sisley, like most of his
Impressionist friends, was
interested in depicting water and
sky, the two elements which best
suited their stylistic research, and
amongst the most difficult
to render.*

Alfred Sisley was born in Paris on 30th October 1839 to affluent English parents. His father, William, ran a business exporting artificial flowers to South America and his mother, Felicia, was well known as a society lady interested in the arts and music. At the age of eighteen Alfred was sent to London to prepare for a career in business, but his four years there were not solely devoted to the commodities market; he spent a great deal of his time in the art galleries and museums dreaming of being an artist. The works of Constable and Turner attracted him especially, and it was in landscape that he was to make his name.

In 1862 Sisley returned to Paris from a trip and persuaded his parents to consent to his pursuing a career as an artist and in October he joined Gleyre's atelier. By December he was enjoying a dinner party given by Bazille

SISLEY
The Bridge at Argenteuil
oil on canvas
1872. 39 × 60 cm
ABOVE *Argenteuil is closely associated with Monet, who lived there and made well over 175 pictures of the area.*

at which the other guests included Monet and Renoir. By the next Easter the budding Impressionists had all left Gleyre's, and Sisley and his friends were to be found on the edge of the Fontainebleau Forest at Chailly painting landscapes *en plein-air*. And this is what Sisley was to concentrate on for the rest of his life, combining the English tradition of landscape painting with the new techniques evolving amongst the young Impressionists.

By 1866 Sisley was exhibiting two works at his first Salon. He had been working in close contact with Monet, but unlike Renoir, who was to incorporate much of Monet's technique into his early work, Sisley had already developed a more subdued palette, which in many ways suited his calm and reserved temperament. Shortly after the 1866 Salon he married a young Parisienne, Marie Lescouezec, who was to bear him two children, Pierre and Jeanne. Two years later, when the Sisleys were living in the rue de la Paix in the Batignolles, Renoir painted a large-scale double portrait of them which conveys something of the gentleness of Sisley and his devotion to his wife. In the late 1860s Sisley was increasingly part of the Batignolles Group meeting in the Café Guerbois, and like Bazille he was essentially a man of leisure, painting when and as he liked and under no pressure to achieve financial success with his work. Nevertheless he was to be a founding

SISLEY
The Road at Louveciennes, Winter
oil on canvas
1874. 38 × 46.5 cm
*As with Pissarro and Monet,
Sisley liked to paint snowy
landscapes, and indeed his style
at the time was close to that of
Pissarro and Guillaumin, plain
and simple compared with most of
Monet's works.*

SISLEY
The Aquaduct at Marly
oil on canvas
1874. 54 × 81 cm
*RIGHT The castle was destroyed,
but the aquaduct which brought
the water for the basins and
fountains of the castle was
restored by Napoleon III in 1858.*

member of the *Société anonyme* in 1873, by which time his life had taken a drastically different course.

The Franco-Prussian War of 1870–71 proved to be the downfall of William Sisley and inaugurated a long period of struggle for his son, Alfred, and his young family. Sisley's father had been taken ill and his business had crumbled; when he died in 1871 the family was ruined and Sisley was now forced to paint for a living. Fortunately Monet and Pissarro, who had met the sympathetic dealer Durand-Ruel in London during the war, introduced him to Sisley in 1872 and he was assured of a moderate number of sales, but not enough to regain his previous leisured lifestyle. Sisley's post-war output increased exponentially as he painted the landscapes around his home in Louveciennes.

When the first Impressionist exhibition opened in 1874 Sisley was represented by five paintings. Perhaps fittingly, for Sisley did not court scandal, they were overshadowed by the "tongue-lickings" of Monet and the other "scandalous" paintings. Monet's influence was in fact discernible in Sisley's work; he was beginning to use brighter pigment in the broken patches which characterized the work of Monet, Renoir, and Pissarro during the 1870s and early 1880s. A trip to England in July 1874 produced some of Sisley's most colourful views of the Thames and the regattas at Hampton Court.

Sisley continued to exhibit with the Impressionists in 1876, 1877, and 1882. Between 1874 and 1877 he lived with his family at Marly-le-Roi, and it was here that he produced a series of his finest paintings of the floods which periodically inundated the area. The critic Georges Rivière, writing in the influential, short-lived, Impressionist organ

SISLEY
Regattas at Molesey
oil on canvas
1874. 66 × 91.5 cm
Above During a trip to England, Sisley painted pictures similar to Monet's work at Argenteuil.

SISLEY
The Watering Place, Marly
oil on canvas
1875. 49.5 × 65.5 cm
Left This work was quite understandably quickly executed in the cold weather, and retouched at home later on.

SISLEY
The Road to Versailles
oil on canvas
1875. 47 × 38 cm
Right This road, linking Marly to Versailles since the seventeenth century, was a favourite theme for Pissarro, Renoir, and Sisley.

l'Impressionniste, said of Sisley: "In all his [canvases] one discovers the same taste, the same finesse, the same tranquillity . . . " The effects of light reflected by water under a dull grey sky and the melancholy aspects of the snowscape characterize Sisley's own depressed state of mind at this time. He was in permanent financial crisis, alleviated only by Durand-Ruel and the patrons that the prospering Renoir had cultivated, the wealthy Charpentiers, and the *pâtissier* Eugène Murer, who invited Sisley and his wife to his restaurant every Wednesday along with Guillaumin, Renoir and the famous colour merchant Père Tanguy.

By the end of the 1870s Sisley was still as desperate as ever for money. Several arrangements whereby he would be paid in advance for a number of canvases helped him eke out a living, but in 1879 he decided to renounce the Impressionist exhibitions and try his luck with the Salon once again. "I am tired," he wrote to Théodore Duret, "of vegetating as I

SISLEY
The Path of the Old Ferry at By
oil on canvas
1880. 50 × 65 cm
Right Sisley desperately tried to paint commercial pictures but was unsuccessful all his life. Sisley tried to emulate Monet's compositions and even his style, hoping that he, too, might be rewarded for his efforts.

SISLEY
Flood at Port Marly
oil on canvas
1876. 60 × 81 cm
*Left One in a series, this is not
an alarming scene of distressed
people trapped in their homes but
a peaceful and bucolic one in
which the water is seen as a
soothing element in which the
houses are reflected.*

SISLEY
Spring at Veneux
oil on canvas
1880. 73 × 90 cm
*Below Sisley's pictures were not as
strongly individual as those of the
other Impressionist painters.*

have been doing for so long. The moment has come to make a decision. It is true that our exhibitions have served to make us known, and as such they have been very useful, but I think we ought not isolate ourselves much longer. The time is still far off when we can do without the prestige which the Salon offers. Thus I have resolved to submit to the Salon. If I am accepted, and there is still a chance this year, I think I will be able to get things sorted out . . . "

But Sisley was rejected by the Salon and then evicted from the house in Sèvres where the family had been living since 1877. With the help of Charpentier other lodgings were found and throughout the 1880s, when the

SISLEY
Farmyard at St Mammet
oil on canvas
1885. 73 × 93 cm
ABOVE His style is more compact than in his other landscapes of this period but he still uses short strokes to suggest the texture of the ground and of the tiled roof.

SISLEY
Flood at Moret-sur-Loing
oil on canvas
1889. 64.5 × 81 cm
LEFT This is a rather extreme example of Sisley's return to his more spontaneous style, in which the brushstrokes blend to produce the more plain effect of his earlier years.

SISLEY
Landscape with a River
oil on canvas
1881. 54 × 73 cm
OPPOSITE The light, lively brushstrokes in this landscape were not typical of Sisley's style and show his attempt at diversity.

Sisley's lived in the Fontainebleau area, the artist's fortunes slowly began to revive. Never very keen on self-promotion, Sisley had worked quietly in the country. His landscapes were, however, greatly admired by his friends and critics, as well as several dealers; and by the early 1890s he was able to find a growing, if modest market for his work. This now featured series of paintings of the same subject, particularly the church at Moret where the family finally settled. In the mid-1890s, when Monet and Renoir were selling at huge prices, Pissarro in fact complained to his son Lucien: "Doesn't Monet sell at a high

price, and Renoir and Degas too? But Sisley and I are still bringing up the rear of the Impressionists."

In 1897, despite severe rheumatism brought on by long hours painting snowscapes *en plein-air* – some of his most beautiful works – Sisley set out on a tour of southern England and Wales, producing several landscapes; but on his return to Moret another, fatal illness began to take hold of him. He was dying of throat cancer. On 31st December 1898 he wrote to his doctor: "I have given up, my dear Friend, I have lost all my energy; I can barely get into my armchair so they can

SISLEY
Lady's Cove, Langland Bay
oil on canvas
1897. 65 × 81 cm
OPPOSITE Two years before his death Sisley's style had become more hesitant, mixing small brushstrokes with a broader rendering, especially in the sky.

SISLEY
The Loing Canal
oil on canvas
1892. 73 × 93 cm
RIGHT Sisley painted at least ten views of the canal, which was not far from his home at Moret.

SISLEY
The Church at Moret
oil on canvas
1894. 100 × 82 cm
RIGHT BELOW In this picture, one of a series echoing the famous Rouen cathedrals painted by Monet the same year, Sisley has also chosen the medieval façade of his local church to render the effect of light and shade.

make the bed. I can't move my head anymore because of the swelling in my neck, my throat, and around my eyes. I don't think this can go on much longer. However, if you know of someone you can trust and who won't charge me more than 100 or 200 francs, I will see him . . . " A brief remission followed in the new year. However, a week before his death Sisley summoned Claude Monet to take his leave and to entrust his affairs to him. The artist whom Pissarro had called "a great and beautiful painter" died on 29th January 1899 and was buried on a cold grey day in the cemetery at Moret-sur-Loing; the ceremony was attended by a few friends including Monet and Renoir.

Bazille

T HE FRANCO-PRUSSIAN WAR of 1870–71 robbed the young Impressionist movement of the talents of Frédéric Bazille. Bazille's role in the history of Impressionist art rests largely on a very few paintings which were highly regarded by his contemporaries. Without Bazille's generosity and care the early careers of Monet and Renoir, in particular, would have been immeasurably more difficult then they undoubtedly were. Bazille was genuinely pleased to be able to report to his parents in 1867 on moving into a new studio that, "counting Renoir, I am housing two hardworking painters." On the untimely death of the young artist his close friend Edmond Maître said of Bazille that he "was the most gifted, the most lovable in every sense of the word", and none of his contemporaries denied it.

FRÉDÉRIC BAZILLE
Self-portrait
1865
ABOVE

BAZILLE
The Ramparts at Aigues-Mortes
oil on canvas
1867. 46 × 55 cm
OPPOSITE

LIFE AND WORKS: FRÉDÉRIC BAZILLE (1841–1870)

Bazille, unlike Monet, did not seek the trembling visual moment . . . His profound originality was to "live his painting and paint his life."

FRANÇOIS DAULTE

Frédéric Bazille was born in Montpellier on 6th December 1841. He was killed on 28th November 1870 at Beaunes-la-Rolande near Orléans in the last days of the Franco-Prussian war. Renoir remembered him as, "that gentle young knight; so pure in heart; the friend of my youth." His untimely death meant the loss of a promising young artist as well as a severe blow to the friends he had met at Gleyre's atelier in 1862 – Monet and Renoir

– who had relied on him to support them in many hours of need.

Born into a wealthy family of wine-growers from Montpellier, Frédéric Bazille, like Manet and Degas, had the world at his feet. Encouraged in his painting by Alfred Bruyas, the great patron and collector of Courbet's work, Bazille had nevertheless followed his father's wishes and entered the medical academy at Montpellier where he studied for three years. In 1862 he arrived in Paris to continue his medical studies and at the same time enrolled in Gleyre's atelier. Eventually, medicine fell by the wayside and he began to devote himself to being an artist.

Bazille's new friends at Gleyre's were mentioned in his letters home. On one occasion he wrote that Monet was "quite good at landscapes; he has given me advice which has helped me very much." For his part, the wealthy Bazille became a vital source of financial and practical support for Monet and Renoir, who lived precarious existences in the early days. Bazille's generosity was legendary. When Monet injured his leg in 1865 it was Bazille who put his medical studies to good use by rigging up a contraption to ease the pain; when Monet was in trouble Bazille would lend him money and buy his paintings in instalments; when Monet needed a model Bazille would oblige; when Monet and Renoir needed a studio, Bazille would offer his.

Between 1865 and 1866 Bazille shared his Paris studio in the rue Furstenberg with

MONET
Garden in Full Bloom
oil on canvas
c.1866. 65 × 54 cm
Bazille admired Monet's style as early as 1866 when the artist was still so influenced by Corot.

Monet. After the arduous summer of 1865, when Monet was hard at work on his own huge version of *Luncheon on the Grass* (*Déjeuner sur l'herbe*), suffering from a damaged leg, penniless, and demanding that Bazille should drop everything he was doing to pose for him in Chailly, we may well imagine that Bazille's patience and generosity were somewhat stretched. In January the next year, Bazille threw a fancy-dress party in his studio at which he appeared in the uniform of a cavalry officer and Monet typecast himself as a Normandy fisherman. The party was a stunning success, but the other tenants in the building complained so that Bazille and Monet had to move. Bazille took an apartment on his own; the irrepressible Monet had taken his toll. As Bazille wrote to his brother, Marc, in February 1866, shortly after moving to a new address in the rue Godot-de-Mauroy: "I must admit that I won't mind living alone for a little while; sharing with someone has its drawbacks, even if you get on well together."

This isolated spell was very short-lived; Monet and Renoir were soon sharing various studios that Bazille acquired and then left. The penultimate studio, in the rue de la

BAZILLE
The Terrace at Méric
oil on canvas
1867. 55.5 × 91.5 cm
This painting shows Monet's influence, with well defined areas of light and shade.

Condamine, is the setting for a group portrait of some of his friends including Monet, Manet, and Zola. By nature Bazille was sociable and by class a socialite; his friends ranged all the way up the social and artistic scale – from the struggling Monet and Renoir, via Manet and his circle, to the composers Fauré, Saint-Saëns, and Chabrier. His class allowed him entry to the most respectable salons of Paris and he made good use of them, but he was also a frequent participant in the artistic gatherings at the Café Guerbois. It was there that the first ideas for an independent exhibiting society would have been thrashed out, seven years before the *Société anonyme* staged its show in the boulevard des Capucines, by which time Bazille had been dead for four years. In a letter to his parents of 1867, Bazille mentions the idea of renting a large studio where the nascent group would exhibit as many of their pictures as they wished, and not be at the mercy of the Salon. "With these people [Courbet, Corot, Diaz, Daubigny] and Monet, who is stronger than all of them, we are sure to succeed." (In the end the older generation of *plein-airistes* and the Realist Courbet did not participate, and neither, of course, did Bazille.)

The Franco-Prussian War of 1870 interrupted the evenings at the Café Guerbois; the future Impressionists who had met at Gleyre's dispersed – Monet and Pissarro moved to London, Renoir was mobilized to the South, and Bazille joined the Zouaves regiment, soon reaching the rank of second lieutenant. From the start of the war the French armies were in disarray and the Prussians made swift advances. Bazille's regiment spent its time marching up and down the country. He wrote to his parents in October 1870 describing his experiences: "We're a stone's throw

BAZILLE
Self-portrait
oil on canvas
1865. 109 × 72 cm
*Opposite The tall Bazille was
known for his kindness and
generosity towards his friends.
This self portrait, executed three
years after he had started to paint,
is evidence of his early promise.
When Bazille arrived in Paris in
1862, he soon befriended
Cézanne and Zola (both from the
south of France like himself),
Sisley, Guillaumin and in
particular Monet, whom he much
admired.*

BAZILLE
View of a Village (Castelnau)
oil on canvas
1868. 130 × 89 cm
*This painting, exhibited at the
Salon of 1869, is a much
improved version of* The Pink
Dress *of 1864. Elegantly
rendered, the earlier stiffness has
disappeared and the figure of the
girl sitting on a parapet
overlooking the southern village
below is very attractive. In her
comments on the Salon of 1869,
Morisot praised the* View of a
Village *highly.*

from Besançon, wandering about aimlessly from camp to camp . . . the short marches and manoeuvres they make us do tire the men and sap their morale . . . Always this monotonous rain, cold feet. I'm bored and I never thought I'd suffer from that in wartime." Another letter reads; "The grass in the meadows we pass is losing its colour; we are doing as much damage as the Prussians." A month later on 28th November Bazille's company received orders to march on Beaunes-la-Rolande near Orléans. François Daulte, Bazille's biographer, describes the young artist's last moments:

The company halted on the top of ridge overlooking Beaune. It was greeted with a hail of Prussian bullets. The first of the men advancing towards the town fell like flies . . . In the general chaos women and children were escaping from the town and running towards isolated farm buildings which would offer some protection . . . Bazille's turn came and he charged, crying: "Don't shoot! Women and children!" He was hit by two bullets to the arm and chest. He fell, face down in the earth, fifty metres from the château where Corot had painted one of his masterpieces.

BAZILLE
The Family Reunion
Charcoal on paper
1867.
This study highlights Bazille's inferior draughtsmanship in comparison to the skilful sketches of Degas.

Bazille was buried in the snow. Six days later his father came to dig up the body and take it back to Montpellier.

In his brief time, Bazille was at the very heart of the growing Impressionist movement and his prematurely curtailed oeuvre proves that he had considerable talent, especially for the figure, portrait, and serene landscape. His career in the Salon, for example, was not undistinguished. His *Family Reunion*, a frozen and static work, highly

BAZILLE
The Family Reunion
oil on canvas
1867. 152 × 230 cm
Bazille has altered his original composition for the better: the standing woman is now seated; he has given more depth to the picture, which allows him to place the group of three figures near the parapet on the right. The dog has disappeared, and he has filled the foreground with a well-rendered bunch of flowers and a straw hat over a folded umbrella. The figures appear rather formal, as if they are posing for a photograph, though the general atmosphere of genteel bourgeoisie in the light and shadow of a summer day is well evoked.

BAZILLE
The Studio Rue de la Condamine
oil on canvas
1869–70. 98 × 128.5 cm
Above This picture was painted shortly before Bazille was killed during the war of 1870, and it is more interesting as a document than as a work of art, because we see his surroundings and some of his close friends: Zola leans on the railing of the steps, talking to

Renoir, seated below; Manet is looking at the painting on the easel and Monet stands behind him. As for Bazille himself, he is the tall, disproportioned figure standing alongside the easel. Manet painted this, exaggerating his friend's height. Bazille's studio was a welcome refuge for penniless friends such as Renoir and Monet.

BAZILLE
Verlaine as a Troubadour
oil on canvas
1868. 45 × 37.5 cm
Right This is an evocative and thoughtful portrait of the tormented poet and absinthe drinker. Bazille has movingly framed the sitter's pensive looks and sensitive features with the colourful fancy beret.

influenced by photography, enjoyed some success at the Salon of 1868, and when in 1870 his *Toilette* was accepted and hung in a decent position, he wrote to his parents: "I am delighted . . . my picture is very well placed. Everyone can see it and is talking about it . . . Judgements on it have been various; some people have laughed, but I've also received some hyperbolic eulogies, which modesty forbids me to set down in writing." (The Salon in the Palais de l'Industrie was so vast that many pictures were skied high up on the walls – to get one's work hung at eye-level was a great achievement, as Berthe Morisot discovered.)

Bazille's early landscapes are lost, so it is impossible to determine how much Monet did help him, as he wrote, in this respect. Some later views by Bazille of the Aigues-Mortes from varying distances and angles show that he was an accomplished landscapist, but far from the vein of Monet. His view is one of stillness and tranquillity: no "fugitive effects" are captured in Bazille's work. Indeed it is doubtful whether Bazille would have ever developed into the Impressionism of Monet, Pissarro, or Sisley. This, as Daulte believes, is partly because Bazille "is a son of the Midi, of the land where men have always been 'gatherers of form'. The light of southern France does not lend itself to the interpretation of landscape in the manner of Monet, Sisley, or Pissarro. It carves objects up rather than joining them together. It tends towards the expression of planes and contours . . . "

"Bazille," Daulte concludes, "unlike Monet, did not seek the trembling visual moment . . . His drawings, like his sketches and his paintings, follow his life . . . His profound originality was to 'live his painting and paint his life'."

Berthe Morisot

WRITING IN *Le Temps* in 1877, the perceptive critic Paul Mantz called Berthe Morisot, "the one real Impressionist". The work of Monet, Pissarro, Renoir, and Sisley notwithstanding, Berthe Morisot was a major exponent of the popular style of Impressionism, with a uniquely delicate and controlled vision of her environment; an environment, however, bounded by the severest restrictions.

Morisot painted the life in her home, her daughter, her sister Edma and her women friends, attacking her subjects with a vitality and originality which was put down to "feminine charm" by most critics, but appreciated by her contemporaries in the Impressionist movement for what it was. Most histories of Impressionism relegate Morisot, along with Cassatt, to the sidelines as a picturesque adornment to the main body of Impressionist work. Not only did Morisot achieve consistent success at the official Salon, but as a regular contributor to the Impressionists' exhibitions, she was a major figure in the development of the movement.

LIFE AND WORKS: BERTHE MORISOT (1841–1895)

Poor Mme Morisot, the public hardly knows her.

CAMILLE PISSARRO IN A LETTER
TO HIS SON LUCIEN, 1895

Berthe Morisot and her sisters Edma and Yves were born into the wealthy and respectable household of a top civil servant who had retired to the exclusive Parisian suburb of Passy – in the nineteenth century, a rustic suburb at the edge of the bustle of the growing city. Here they were brought up with a host of cultural accomplishments, including the art of conversation, music, and drawing. In a comfortable establishment like the Morisot's, the talents of young women were nurtured for the benefit of their mortal souls, their parents and ultimately their husbands. A modest and respectable *bourgeoise* was expected to be a cultured, but not over-cultured, adornment in a male-dominated

society which valued above all grace, charm, and sociability in its wives and mothers.

The education of Berthe Morisot and her sisters was in this respect quite normal – an English governess, an exclusive school and of course drawing lessons from a respectable professional artist, in this case Joseph-Benoît Guichard – a follower of Ingres and Delacroix. The aim was to engender in the young ladies the skills of an appreciative amateur, not to make them into artists. During the nineteenth century there had been dangerous precedents which the bourgeoisie did not at all costs wish their daughters to emulate. In the field of literature, for example, the prodigious, immensely popular woman novelist

BOUCHER
Pan and Syrinx
oil on canvas
1759. 32.5 × 42 cm
BELOW Boucher was one of the old masters Morisot used to copy in the Louvre around 1858.

COROT
Mur, Côtes du Nord
oil on canvas
c.1855. 33 × 56 cm
RIGHT At about the same time, Morisot met the much older Corot.

COROT
Limay
oil on canvas
1870–72. 41 × 66 cm
ABOVE

MORISOT
View of Paris from the Trocadéro
oil on canvas
1872. 46 × 81.5 cm
*LEFT ABOVE This panorama is
unusual for Morisot. It shows the
continuing influence of Corot.
Morisot opted more and more for
intimate domestic scenes which
were more practical subjects for
her to work on.*

and playwright George Sand had scandalized respectable society both by being a free literary spirit and by proclaiming her freedom to move about society wearing men's clothes. Her novels centred on the right of women to choose their loves, if not their lives, and were profoundly shocking, but also entertaining. When Berthe and Edma began to take more than a moderate interest in their art studies, the vain Guichard lost no time in warning Mme Morisot of her daughters' dangerous inclinations: "Considering the character of your daughters," he is reported by Berthe's brother Tiburce to have said to Mme Morisot, "my teaching will not endow them with minor drawing room accomplishments: they will become painters. Do you realize what this means? In the *haute bourgeois* milieu to which you belong, this will be revolutionary, I might almost add catastrophic. Are you sure that you will not curse the day when art, having gained admission to your home, now so respectable and peaceful, will become the sole arbiter of the fate of your two children?" Perhaps Guichard feared that before long they might be wearing trousers and standing on the Pont Neuf, quite unchaperoned, save for an easel.

Thankfully Mme Morisot trusted in her better judgment and allowed her daughters' talents to flourish. She and her husband were, in any case, friendly with the respectable artistic circles of Paris (to which even the dangerous Manet belonged, thanks to his otherwise impeccable social status). Berthe and Edma soon outstripped what Guichard could teach them and came under the tutelage of his illustrious friend Corot, who began to join the Morisots for dinner on Tuesdays when he was in Paris. In the summer of 1861 the sisters persuaded their parents to decamp to Ville d'Avray to be near Corot and continue their studies. Early on it was clear that, following in the footsteps of Corot who influenced so many of the Impressionists, Berthe was going to be a keen *plein-airiste*,

BAZILLE
Eva Gonzalès
oil on canvas
1870. 191 × 133.5 cm
*ABOVE Eva Gonzalès was
Manet's only pupil, and Berthe
felt quite jealous of someone she
saw as an unwelcome rival.*

MANET
Berthe Morisot
oil on canvas
c.1869. 74 × 56 cm
*RIGHT This is a sketchy picture,
but it has the light touch and the
liveliness of Morisot's brush in
contrast to the darker rendering
of Manet.*

and she was later to become one of the most atmospheric and impressionistic of her contemporaries, having developed a swift, fluid technique using broken patches of bright colour.

By 1864 she had two paintings accepted at the Salon, *On the Banks of the Oise*, and *The Old Path at Auvers*; the next year she was again successful with a landscape and a still life. This success brought her to the attention of admiring critics, although many thought her work a "charming", or "feminine" aberration. During the 1860s Morisot had, in common with her contemporaries, been an assiduous copyist at the Louvre, studying the old masters and developing her drawing technique. Then in 1868 she was introduced by Fantin-Latour to the *infamous* Edouard Manet who took an immediate liking to her artistic talent and her beauty. He included her in *The Balcony* (*Le Balcon*) which he produced in the autumn of 1868, and she reciprocated by giving him her painting *The Harbour at Lorient* which shows Edma sitting on the harbour wall with a parasol.

The fact that Manet painted Morisot's portrait on more than one occasion, but that Morisot never painted his, is of more than passing interest. A respectable woman and a female artist in the higher echelons of society could not receive a lone gentleman, or any sort of man for that matter, in her studio without causing comment. A male artist, on the other hand, was expected to paint the portraits of society women. And by the 1870s they could also pass freely through brothels, low-life cafés, theatre dressing rooms – anywhere indeed they chose in the effort to capture Baudelaire's bustling "Modern Life". Baudelaire, Manet, and Degas were all *flâneurs*, strollers through the life of Paris.

As Griselda Pollock has recently demonstrated in an essay called "Modernity and the Spaces of Femininity", women artists in nineteenth-century Paris could not be the "Painters of Modern Life" (such as Manet and Degas) that Baudelaire sought. The space in which they could move was both literally and symbolically limited to a set of places which were the realm of bourgeois women and which they could safely depict; dining-rooms, drawing-rooms, bedrooms, private gardens, verandas and balconies. Outdoors they could paint scenes in the park and the

DEGAS
Eugène Manet
oil on canvas
1874. 65 × 81 cm
*ABOVE When Manet was
painting Berthe's portrait in
1872, he suggested that she
should marry his brother Eugène,
which she did two years later.*

MORISOT
Madame Edma Pontillon
pastel on paper
1871. 81 × 64.5 cm
*LEFT The young woman is Berthe
Morisot's sister. The portrait
shows Manet's influence on
Berthe Morisot's style with its
sober stillness.*

private box in the theatre, as long as they showed young women chaperoned; a respectable young women could not under any circumstances be seen alone in public. An artist contemporary with Morisot and Cassatt in Paris, Marie Bashkirtseff, described the enormous restrictions placed on her in a diary entry for January 1879:

> What I long for is the freedom of going about alone, of coming and going, of sitting in the seats of the Tuileries, and especially in the Luxembourg, of stopping and looking at the artistic shops, of entering churches and museums, of walking about old streets at night. That's what I long for, and that's the freedom without which one cannot be a real artist. Do you imagine that I derive much benefit from what I see, chaperoned as I am, and when, in order to go to the Louvre, I must wait for my carriage, my lady companion, my family?

These restrictions were being eroded, but not fast enough for Morisot to break free of them, even if she had wanted to, and there is no reason to believe that she did.

The subjects available for Morisot to paint were thus centred around motherhood, child-rearing, domestic labour, female companionship, in short the world of the bourgeois woman with all its rituals – a rich enough field, but one that had hitherto been condemned to the lowly status of genre painting. Until Morisot, Cassatt, and Marie Bracquemond (who, like Cassatt, first showed with the Impressionists in 1879) began to paint scenes from their daily lives in a new way (in their version of Baudelaire's "Painting of Modern Life"), women and children were generally either the subjects of

TISSOT
Holiday
oil on canvas
c.1876. 76 × 99.5 cm
*LEFT In contrast to Morisot and
the other Impressionists, Tissot
depicts scenes with great
precision, in which no detail is
left out.*

MORISOT
Eugène Manet and His daughter
Julie at Bougival
oil on canvas
1881. 73 × 92 cm
*LEFT BELOW Charles Ephrussi
said of Morisot's paintings that
"One step further and it will be
impossible to distinguish or
understand anything at all."*

documentary portraiture or appeared translated into mythic or religious symbols, as Madonnas or cherubs. Though Morisot did not transgress the social and personal norms of the day, she did achieve an evocation of her life, in her own artistic terms, which had not hitherto been possible.

Yet the problem for the critics of her day remained the fact that she was a gifted artist and a woman. The two could not easily be reconciled – there was no tradition (acceptable to men) of women in art, and all the critics and judges were men – and so her paintings were damned with faint praise for their freshness, delicacy, sensitivity, and femininity, and simply damned outright for betraying, as Joris-Karl Huysmans put it, "hysteria". Typically the critic Albert Wolff, arch-enemy of the Impressionists, had trouble coming to terms with Morisot's gender and her obvious talent. In his vitriolic denunciation of the second Impressionist exhibition in 1876 he wrote, "There is also a woman in this group, as there almost always is in any gang; she is called Berthe Morizot [sic], and she makes an interesting spectacle. With her, feminine grace is retained amidst the outpourings of a mind in delirium." Although he dismisses Morisot in two sentences, he centres on a problem in art history and criticism which has persisted to this day.

"Above all else," writes one historian of Impressionism, "she provided a social and inspirational centre for the Impressionists." It is true that Morisot was at the very centre of the Impressionists, a regular contributor to the group's exhibitions, loved and respected by Manet (whose brother Eugène she married), Degas, Renoir, Monet, Pissarro, Whistler, and the poet Mallarmé (who became the guardian of her only child, Julie,

MORISOT
In the Garden, Maurecourt
oil on canvas
1884. 54 × 65 cm
Above Morisot painted several pictures set in the park-like garden.

MORISOT
Copy of Apollo and Latone
after Boucher
oil on canvas
c.1885. 63.5 × 79 cm
Right Towards 1885, Morisot was prompted to make more studies and draw more nudes, following the example of Renoir.

274

MORISOT
Self-portrait
pastel on paper
1885. 46 × 36 cm
*Above In spite of the fluttering
lines, the style of this portrait is
greatly influenced by Manet, who
had died two years previously.*

MORISOT
Young Girl with a Doll
oil on canvas
1886. 97 × 58 cm
*Left This young girl is probably
her daughter, Julie Manet, who
was born in 1878. Morisot liked
to paint and draw children, even
if they were impatient.*

after her death), but she could do no more than play out her predestined role as a society hostess, even if it was as one of the most select group of artistic revolutionaries. She could not join in the discussions in the cafés and, symbolically, she is not in Bazille's or Fantin-Latour's portrait of the Batignolles Group of which she was an important part.

It is only in the last twenty years that a critical debate has arisen which treats her work and that of her female contemporaries as the product of original minds working in a restrictive system, as producers of art, rather than women artists, and this has opened up new ways of seeing Morisot's oeuvre. Griselda Pollock, for example, has delved into the important complexities inherent in the representation of space in Morisot's paintings and the relationship between the bourgeois female figures in them to the world depicted outside the salon and beyond the balcony.

In 1896, on the first anniversary of Morisot's death, Durand-Ruel mounted a retrospective which had Monet, Degas, Renoir, and Mallarmé fighting over where to hang which picture. Each thought they knew best, just as twenty years before that Edouard Manet had known what was best for Morisot's intense painting of her mother and sister. Morisot wrote after the incident: "He cracked a thousand jokes, laughed like a madman, handed me the palette, took it back and finally by five o'clock in the afternoon we had made the prettiest caricature that was ever seen . . . I am left confounded . . . Mother thinks the episode is funny, but I find it agonizing."

In her diary Morisot's daughter, Julie, described the effect of her mother's posthumous retrospective: "Everyone is astonished on entering the room, exclaiming 'I would never have believed she did so much work!' They say that Maman never showed all these drawings, that she hid part of her work. Today it comes as a revelation." Or as Pissarro said, "Poor Mme Morisot, the public hardly knows her."

MORISOT
Lucie Léon at the Piano
oil on canvas
1892. 65 × 80 cm
*The peacock pattern of the
wallpaper is blended in the
background so as not to draw
our attention from the morose-
looking adolescent.*

Mary Cassatt

MARY CASSATT SPENT most of her life in France and together with Whistler and Sargent formed part of the great triumvirate of American expatriates working in Europe. From her earlier paintings we can see that in part Mary Cassatt inhabited a Jamesian world of endless afternoon teas, gentle conversation and hushed admiration in the long halls of the Louvre (where Degas pictured her in an etching), punctuated by the occasional excitement of the theatre. These pictures do indeed offer us a keenly observed insight into the strictures and rituals of a bourgeois gentlewoman in late nineteenth-century Parisian society, but her most impressive work shows us women at work – her sister Lydia at work on her tapestry frame, Lydia crocheting in the garden, a woman bathing her daughter – and these images tell us as much about Cassatt's concern to depict the reality of modern life for women as the eternally poised *Cup of Tea*.

MARY CASSATT
Self-portrait
c.1895
ABOVE

CASSATT
The Boating Party
oil on canvas
1893–94. 95 × 117 cm
OPPOSITE

LIFE AND WORKS: MARY CASSATT (1844–1926)

What drawing! What style!

EDGAR DEGAS ON MARY CASSATT'S
GIRL ARRANGING HER HAIR

Mary Cassatt was born in Allegheny City, Pennsylvania, on 22nd May 1844. When she was ten the family moved to Paris on the advice of doctors who thought Europe would provide a cure for their ailing son, Robbie, the second of two sons. A year later they quit Paris and arrived in Germany where the oldest son, Alexander, continued his engineering studies. Europe was to no avail and Robbie died, so the Cassatts went back to America in 1855. There Mary Cassatt studied art at the Pennsylvania Academy of Fine Arts where the teaching mirrored that of its French counterparts and included the same rigorous drawing exercises from plaster casts that had served would-be artists for generations.

Two years later, despite the profound misgivings of her father, who said he would rather see her dead than an artist, Cassatt returned to Paris and began to study under Gérôme and Chaplin. In 1868 she had her first work *The Mandolin Player* accepted at the Salon, but two years later she was back in Pittsburgh as the Franco-Prussian War, and later the Commune, devastated Paris. In 1872 she continued her European travels, studying the work of Correggio and Parmigianino, as well as printmaking, at the academy in Parma, followed by a tour of Spain, Belgium, and Holland before resettling in Paris. Cassatt's *Portrait of Madame Cortier* shown at the 1874 Salon drew her to the attention of Degas, who conceived a liking for her work. Her own encounter with Degas' work was crucial. She described "seeing for the first time Degas' pastels in the window of a picture-dealer on the boulevard Haussmann. I used to go and flatten my nose against that window and absorb all I could of his art. It changed my life. I saw art then as I wanted to see it." For his part Degas said of her, "Here is someone who feels as I do." In 1877 Cassatt's parents and her sister Lydia, who was to feature as a model in many of her paintings, arrived in Paris to settle there permanently.

MANET
The Reading
oil on canvas
1868. 60.5 × 73.5 cm
Cassatt chose the most traditional artists of the Impressionist group, those who in fact were the least Impressionist in style, to emulate.

DEGAS
Estelle Musson
oil on canvas
1872. 94.5 × 129.5 cm
*ABOVE This is a scene of quiet
domestic simplicity, close to
Cassatt's own style. Here, though,
the bouquet shares the centre of
the composition with the sitter,
who is eclipsed by the brightness of
the flowers.*

CASSATT
Lydia
oil on canvas
c.1878. 81.5 × 65 cm
*LEFT Cassatt found most of her
models from amongst her close
relatives. This is a natural
and relaxed portrait of her
sister, Lydia.*

CASSATT
The Cup of Tea
oil on canvas
1880. 64.5 × 92.5 cm
Lydia Cassatt poses with the tea-cup. This is a rather formal scene which is matched by the artist's highly controlled style.

As a protégée of Degas , Cassatt became a regular contributor to the Impressionist exhibitions. She was represented in the shows of 1879, 1880, 1881, and 1886, but her close alliance with Degas meant her absence from the contentious penultimate exhibition which featured Monet, Renoir, and Sisley, who would not exhibit with Degas or his followers. Despite the influence of Degas, Cassatt's work was as individual as her character; the early period of her work is marked by airy compositions, many on the theme of domestic life reminiscent of Berthe Morisot's paintings. And as we have seen in the case of Morisot, there was little else Cassatt could legitimately paint without breaking the bounds of convention; she was limited in scope, but not in vision, to her immediate surroundings. As her painting of 1878 *Young Girl in a Blue Armchair* shows, Cassatt had made the subject of children comfortably her own, and although Degas is believed to have worked on the painting, particularly the background, the painting evokes the strange perspective that children have on the world to great effect. The distortions of space in the foreground and the plunging perspective to the back of the room with its huge, solid armchairs show Cassatt applying her classical training to an intensely personal vision of the world, seen simultaneously from the point of view of a child and an adult.

One of Cassatt's most famous paintings, shown at the fifth Impressionist exhibition in 1880, is *The Cup of Tea*. This, and a work such as Morisot's *The Artist's Mother and Sister* provide a powerful insight into the commonplace, immensely dull, but powerful rituals of the bourgeois woman at the time. The sense of time passing with excruciating languor is as tangible as the oppressive atmosphere of the rooms in which it passes.

In the 1880s Cassatt began to move away from a style which was never as loose and impressionistic as Berthe Morisot's, cleaving as it did more to the example of Degas and Manet, and became strongly influenced by Japanese art, particularly in her own attempts at the problematic process of colour print-making, in which she managed to reconcile line and colour with unrivalled results.

Although she joined the Impressionist group at a point when it was beginning to splinter, Cassatt was highly respected by all sides and did much to foster a sense of common purpose, working for example with Pissarro and Degas between 1879 and 1880 on the ill-fated journal of prints *Le Jour et la nuit*.

SARGENT
Study of Madame Gautrau
oil on canvas
c.1884. 206.5 × 108 cm
*Above Sargent, like Cassatt a
celebrated American expatriate,
was forced to leave Paris for
London after Mme Gautrau
denounced the finished portrait
that he developed from this study.*

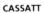

CASSATT
The Loge
oil on canvas
1882. 80 × 64 cm
*Right In this composition,
another work on the theme of the
theatre box which was treated by
Renoir, Degas, and Gonzales
among others, Cassatt depicts two
very dispassionate girls who seem
to be waiting for a break in
the pose.*

On a commercial level, Cassatt was instrumental in introducing Impressionist art into America through her brother, Alexander, and by advising the important collectors Louisine and Henry Osborne Havemeyer. Mary Cassatt was a childhood friend of the suffragette Louisine and it is in no small way thanks to her that from the 1880s onwards substantial amounts of money were available to back the Impressionists in France and endow the United States with a formidable collection of French Impressionist art, in the form of the Havemeyer Collection in the New York Metropolitan Museum.

In 1892, the year she bought her country mansion, Château Beaufresne, Cassatt was commissioned by the Chicagoan Mrs Berthe Honoré Palmer to produce a mural on the theme of "The Modern Woman" for the Women's Building of the World Columbian Exhibition in Chicago. Cassatt's influence in America – although she only returned there twice, in 1898 and 1908 – was now becoming considerable via important patrons such as the Havemeyers and her contacts with the increasing numbers of young American artists coming to study in Paris. Unfortunately the design for "The Modern Woman" has been lost, but photographs show it to be a major work, edging towards a new assertion of the dignity of women's labour and Cassatt's own important status in the world of art.

Although she was effectively a French citizen for the remainder of her life – she was awarded the *Légion d'Honneur* in 1904 – Cassatt maintained that she was "first and last an American". In her last years, suffering from the onset of blindness, increasingly out of touch with the world and bereft of her friends the Impressionists, she became what one visitor to Beaufresne,

Forbes Watson, described as, "lonely, unreasonable, and vituperative, still a burning force and a dominant personality, capable of a violent burst of profanity in one breath and, with the next, of launching into a plea to save the coming generation of American art students from turning into café loafers in Paris." She died on 14th June 1926, the same year as Monet, bitter and alone.

CASSATT
Mrs Cassatt Reading
oil on canvas
c.1883. 101.5 × 81.5 cm
Cassatt expresses well the unaffected atmosphere of the home, and the nuances are rendered with great sensitivity.

INDEX

ACKNOWLEDGEMENTS

Amsterdam, Rijksmuseum: p. 10. Baltimore, Walters Art Gallery: pp. 28 top, 60, 168 right. Berlin, National Gallery: pp. 168 left. Boston, Museum of Fine Arts: pp. 46 top, 109 bottom, 155, 176 left, 178, 214 right, 282. Cambridge, Fitzwilliam Museum: pp. 226 right. Cambridge, Mass., Fogg Museum of Art: pp. 205 right, 226 left. Cardiff, National Museum of Wales: p. 164 top. Chicago Art Institute: pp. 11, 17, 32 top, 41 top, 45 bottom, 54 bottom, 55, 79, 90 left, 100 right, 110 left, 118 right, 130, 145, 149, 161 bottom, 188, 212 bottom, 213 bottom, 245, 257, 260, 275 right. Cincinnati Museum of Art: pp. 24 bottom, 259. Cleveland Museum of Art: pp. 15, 64, 237. Cologne, Wallraf-Richartz Museum: p. 246 top. Copenhagen, Ny Carlsberg Glyptotek: p. 151. Dallas, Museum of Fine Art: pp. 265. Dijon, musée des Beaux-Arts: p. 150 left. Edinburgh, National Gallery of Scotland: p. 142. Egham, Royal Holloway College: p. 25/Bridgeman Art Library. Essen, Folkwang Museum: p. 223 left/Bridgeman Art Library. Florence, Uffizi: p. 70/Visual Arts Library. Fort Worth, Kimbell Museum of Art: pp. 110 right, 169 top right. Genova, Palazzo Rosso: p. 68 right/Visual Arts Library. Glasgow, Burrell Collection: pp. 113, 185 top. Hamburg, Kunsthalle: p. 165 right/Bridgeman Art Library. Hartford, Wadsworth Atheneum: p. 207 top. Kansas City, Nelson-Atkins Museum of Art: p. 103 bottom. Leningrad, Hermitage: pp. 108 right/Edimedia, 146 right. Lisbon, Gulbenkian Foundation: p. 13. London, Christie's: pp. 37, 46 bottom, 56, 57 top, 119 bottom, 129, 199, 200, 239 right, 241 top, 252, 275 left. London, Courtauld Institute Gallery: pp. 171 top, 225. London, courtesy of the Noortman Gallery: pp. 8, 198. London, National Gallery: pp. 22, 24 top, 29 right, 36, 87, 96 top, 98 right, 100 left, 127, 131, 139, 147, 154 bottom, 167 left, 175, 187 left, 206 bottom, 207 bottom, 210, 229 right, 230, 232 right, 249 bottom, 268 left, 270 left, 272 bottom. London, Tate Gallery: pp. 97 right, 186, 211 bottom, 216 left, 250 bottom, 273 top, 284 left. London, Victoria & Albert Museum: pp. 21 bottom, 69, 153 bottom. Los Angeles County Museum of Art: pp. 66, 205 left, 269 right. Lugano, Thyssen-Bornemisza Collection: p. 189 left. Lyon, musée des Beaux-Arts: p. 183 right. Madrid, Prado: p. 77 bottom/Visual Arts Library. Mannheim Kunsthalle: p. 77 top/Giraudon. Minneapolis Museum of Art: p. 232 left. Montargis, musée Girodet: p. 40/Giraudon. Montpellier, musée Fabre: pp. 256/ Giraudon, 260/Giraudon, 261/Giraudon, 272 top. Moscow, Pushkin Museum: pp. 72/Edimedia, 229 left. Munich, Neuepinakothek: p. 121 bottom. Nancy, musée des Beaux-Arts: p. 170 top. New York, Frick Collection: pp. 28 bottom, 158 top. New York, Metropolitan Museum of Art: pp. 14, 43 top, 48, 50, 74 left/Edimedia, 84 bottom, 96 bottom, 163, 164 bottom, 204, 231, 279. New York, Museum of Modern Art: p. 121 top. Oberlin Museum of Art: p. 78 left. Omaha, Joslyn Museum of Art: p. 143. Oslo, Nationalmuseum: pp. 78 right. Oxford, Ashmolean Museum: pp. 23. Paris, Bibliothèque Nationale: pp. 40/Visual Arts Library, 59 right/Visual Arts Library, 63/Visual Arts Library, 76 left/Visual Arts Library. Paris, Louvre: pp. 21 top, 27/Giraudon/Bridgeman Art Library, 41 bottom/Edimedia, 44 right, 49/Edimedia, 57 bottom/Edimedia, 61 right, 67 top, 67 bottom, 111 right, 141/Giraudon, 283 right. Paris, musée Carnavalet: p. 90/Visual Arts Library. Paris, musée d'Art Moderne de la Ville: p. 38/Edimedia. Paris, musée d'Orsay: pp. 12, 34/Giraudon, 35, 39/Giraudon, 42, 43 bottom, 44 left/Edimedia, 51, 58, 59 left/Giraudon, 61 left, 62, 65 top, 65 bottom, 71, 73, 81, 82 right, 86, 91, 99/Edimedia, 102 right/Giraudon, 104 bottom, 107 top, 107 bottom, 108 left, 111 left/Visual Arts Library, 112, 114 top, 114 bottom, 125, 128, 132, 133, 136 right, 136 left, 137, 138 top, 138 bottom, 140 left, 144, 150 right, 156 bottom, 157, 159/Giraudon, 160 bottom, 166 bottom, 169 top left, 173, 179, 181 left/Giraudon, 182, 183 left, 184 right, 189 right, 192, 197, 202 left, 202 right, 203, 206 top, 208 top, 208 bottom, 214 left, 222, 227, 228, 234, 239 left, 240 right, 241 bottom, 242 left, 243, 246 bottom, 247, 249 top, 250 top, 251 top, 253 right, 254 top, 258, 262/Giraudon, 263/Edimedia, 264/Giraudon, 271 left/Giraudon, 280. Paris, musée Marmottan: pp. 92, 104 top, 109 top, 209 top, 209 bottom, 214 centre, 276. Paris, musée Picasso: pp. 184 left, 240 left. Paris, Petit-Palais: pp. 32 bottom, 118 left, 212 top, 238, 254 bottom. Passadena, Norton Simon Foundation: pp. 80 left, 190. Pau, musée des Beaux-Arts: p. 180/Giraudon. Philadelphia Museum of Art: pp. 33, 98 left, 103 top, 154 top, 160 top, 181 right, 191, 236 left, 268 right, 283 left. Private collections: pp. 18, 26, 30, 31 top, bottom, right, 47/Bridgeman Art Library, 53, 54, top, 75, 76 right, 80 right, 82 left, 85, 88, 93 top, 94, 105, 106, 116, 117/Giraudon, 119 top, 120, 124, 134, 135, 140 right, 148, 156 top, 165 left, 169 bottom, 170 bottom, 171 bottom, 172, 176 right, 177, 185 bottom, 187 right, 193, 194, 196, 201 top, 201 bottom, 213 top, 215 left, 216 right, 217, 218, 219 left, 219 right, 220, 223 right, 242 right, 244, 248 top, 251 bottom, 253 left, 255, 266/Giraudon, 271 right, 273 bottom/Giraudon, 274 bottom, 277, 281, 285. Providence, Rhode Island School of Design Art Gallery: pp. 89, 270 right/Giraudon. Santa Barbara Museum of Art: p. 269 left. Stockholm, Nationalmuseum: pp. 84 top, 195. Strasbourg, musée d'Art Moderne: p. 236 right. The Hague, Gemeentemuseum: p. 74 right. Toledo Museum of Art: pp. 102 left, 146 left, 248 bottom, 274 top. Tournai, musée des Beaux-Arts: pp. 97 left, 115/Edimedia. Washington, National Gallery of Art: pp. 45 top, 83, 93 bottom, 101, 153 top, 158 bottom, 166 top, 212 top, 279/Edimedia, 284 right. Washington, Phillips Collection: pp. 152 bottom, 174, 233. Williamstown, Clark Institute of Art: pp. 13, 215 right, 221, 235. Winterthur, Oscar Reinhart Foundation: p. 224. Yale University Art Gallery: p. 152 top.